River Odyssey

In Search of the Long-toothed Platypus

LEE SALVEMINI

Cover illustration by George Cooper.

RIVER ODYSSEY

The song of the river ends not at her banks,
but in the hearts of those who have loved her.

Buffalo Joe

At the base of the Australia's Snowy Mountains in a river reminiscent of a creek, the 2500 kilometre journey to reach the river mouth by kayak begins. Within minutes, a slimy twig is all that comes between the 52 day journey and a swift bolt to oblivion.

Ride along with Lucky Lee to discover the ancient river's beauty and treachery, and the omnipresent voices of those past. Join in the moments of dark and light, joy and despair, interaction with nature and a salmagundi of characters along the river. Relax on the magnificent glassy water during wind-less days where you can hear the animals on the banks speaking about you. Then brace as you dodge obstacles as they race upon you: river snags, rock islands, rushing channels, perilous lakes, labyrinths of misleading anabranches, monster wave-producing paddle steamers, storms and rain, falling trees, and locks and weirs. But most of all, expect the unexpected.

Discover unique aspects of river life with quirky philosophical musings and honest appraisals of the condition of the troubled Murray-Darling river system. A light river history assists understanding Australia's premier river and its importance to pre- and post-colonial settlement. Included for the aspiring kayaker, details of essential food and equipment are included in the appendices.

And then just as the lazy old river loses its mojo and you relax into the lambswool seat cover of the kayak, the final two days declare the climax of reaching for the river mouth will be as thrilling as the first.

To Ali and Bobby

I am not who you think I am, but I am trying

Contents

Prologue   xiii

INTRODUCTION   1

PART I
THE HEADWATER TO MILDURA

1   Biggara to Indi Bridge   4

2   Lake Hume Resort   15

3   Lake Hume Resort to cow field outside Albury   18

4   Cow field outside Albury to Howlong   23

5   Howlong to Corowa/Wahgunyah   29

6   Corowa/Wahgunyah to Swan Cove   37

7   The Food Plan   44

8   Swan Cove to Little Bruce Bend   47

9   Little Bruce Bend to Tarn Pirr Vineyard Bend   55

10 Tarn Pirr Bend to Top End Beach   60

11 Top End Beach to Kings Landing   66

12 Kings Landing to War Creek   70

13 War Creek to Barmah   77

14 Barmah to Echuca/Moama   85

15 Echuca/Moama to Wills 1   91

16 Wills 1 to Norris Bend   98

17 Norris Bend to Sandbar Bend   103

18 Sandbar Bend to Barham Mill Bend   110

19 Barham Mill Bend to Lucky Lee's Beach   115

20 Lucky Lee's Beach to Funnel Bend Cove   122

21 Funnel Bend Cove to Beveridge Island   127

22 Beveridge Island to Wood Wood   134

23 Wood Wood to Gundagai Bend   142

24 Gundagai Bend to The Wreck of Little Ruby   151

25 Wreck of Little Ruby to Silver Beach   158

26 Silver Beach to Yungera Island   166

27 Yungera Island to Robinvale/Euston   172

28 Robinvale/Euston to Happy Valley   178

29 Happy Valley to Retail Bend   185

30 Retail Bend to Big Tree Bend   189

31 Big Tree Bend to Bonnie Doone   196

32 Bonnie Doone to Mildura   203

PART II
MILDURA TO THE MURRAY MOUTH

33 Mildura to Horseshoe Bend   224

34 Horseshoe Bend to Jackson's Reach   228

35   Jackson's Reach to Lock 9   233

36   Lock 9 to Bluey Bend   239

37   Bluey Bend to Lake Victoria Station   245

38   Lake Victoria Station to Customs House   252

39   Customs House to Murtho Forest   259

40   Murtho Forest to Renmark   265

41   Renmark to Lyrup   271

42   Lyrup to Proud's Sandbar   275

43   Proud's Sandbar to Cobdogla   280

44   Cobdogla to Maize Island   286

45   Maize Island to Hogwash Bend   292

46   Hogwash Bend to Brenda Park   297

47   Brenda Park to Blanchetown   303

48   Blanchetown to Kroehns Landing   309

49   Kroehns Landing to Younghusband   314

50   Younghusband to Mypolonga Flat   318

51   Mypolonga Flat to Wellington   324

52   Wellington to the Murray Mouth   329

53   Afterword   341

Appendix A   344

Appendix B   345

Appendix C   346

Appendix D   347

Appendix E 348

Appendix F 349

Appendix G 350

Acknowledgements 351

The Platypus 352

About The Author 355

Prologue

'There is a fine line between danger and excitement. As I set out on my quest to paddle the length of the Murray an element of apprehension lingered like a dark cloud over the excitement. I told myself this was normal, just pre-game nerves which would settle once the journey into the unknown began. Surely everyone knows this feeling and as one person will confidently walk a tightrope another will fear walking out at night. Fifteen minutes into the journey, as I lay with my head underwater unable to reach up for air, time stood still and, whereas another might have revisited their life to date, my mind drifted serenely towards futile plans and the consequences of naivety.'

I was 28 years of age when the idea of paddling the entire length of the River Murray moved beyond the threshold of an idea to an absolute in my life's plan. I had completed an epic six-day ultra-triathlon that consisted of cycling 371 kilometres over two days, paddling 96 kilometres down the Murray for the next two, and running 105 kilometres to the finish line during the final two days. But it was the paddling leg of the endurance race—the thrill of the moving water, the spirit of the river, and a living world so removed from my own—that tapped into a deep-rooted yearning, unrelenting in its call. Strong, ancient, powerful, and yet fragile, ever-changing, and friendly, the river had heard my promise on that day to return for a longer embrace.

On a cold and damp winter's evening, thirty-three years later, the River Odyssey came in like a flash. That same night, I imagined floating down the river in silence and absorbing the scenes, relishing a brief primitive existence that I had been yearning for over the years. Would the trip be as magical as I had pictured? Was it going to be hard slog? What if it did not live up to my expectations? What if *I* did not live up to my expectations? The journey's initial purpose was to accomplish an exciting and ambitious feat, but after spending four years at university as a mature age student—a very mature aged student—watching the outdoors from behind the books, it needed to be more than that. The world had changed, I had changed. Now it was about fulfilling a deep and aching desire to live and breathe and know the river. I did not know it then but no matter what had happened over the last three decades, the Murray had always been with me.

It did not take long to achieve a rhythm between the kayak and the flow of the river. My return proved thrilling and effortless. Both kayaks and paddles had improved enormously since my early gung-ho 20s, as had my meticulousness in planning. The biggest concern was how I could sit for up to 10 hours per day on a hard seat for the 50 days expected to complete the journey. During this time, I hoped to savour the freedom of its banks, appreciate the birdsong around me, and meet the people who live along the river, from farmers to fisher folk, paddle steamer captains to houseboat skippers, and tourists to local residents. I wanted to stand with those who have a unique bond with the river through working, visiting, or living on its shoreline.

Adventures are never without challenges and adaptations. I was compelled to examine options, make difficult decisions, and face my choices head-on. It was not about completing the distance; it was about being out there and fulfilling a promise I had made to myself and the river all those years ago. As the planning progressed, the logistics for what and how many of the 'essentials' grew disproportionately. I examined river conditions, adopted a dependable food plan, and stocked gear for camping and cooking. Despite notions of comfort over practicality, a list of equipment that eventually became essential follows in the appendices.

Never once did I question whether this was the right time. Because time was not waiting for this man.

Nevertheless, something kept surfacing in the back of my mind telling me there was danger ahead on this nice gentle river, the sort that could be fatal.

Before putting in, I rang my children to tell them I loved them.

Lee Salvemini

INTRODUCTION

The River Murray, given its western name in 1824 after the British Secretary of State for War and the Colonies, Sir George Murray, is Australia's longest river. Beginning in the Southern Alps near Australia's highest mountain, Mount Kosciusko, it travels through New South Wales and Victoria before it empties into the sea near my home at Goolwa, South Australia. It is the third-longest navigable river in the world and reported to be the world's fifteenth longest river. Both claims are open for debate depending on the source of information. In either case, paddling the entirety of the river is a damn long way. Whether the journey is Australia's version of Everest is open to conjecture, but few would argue it is indeed a monumental challenge. Seasonal variations, fast-flowing channels, river obstacles, river height, and poisonous snakes and spiders are all factors that can be planned for. But, as the wilds of nature rub their hands with glee, determined to test a traveller's humour and resolve, all certainties are off the table.

Traversing the Murray can be broken into three sections: The Upper Murray—from its headwater to the Hume dam near Albury/Wodonga; the Central Murray which finishes downriver at Wentworth and includes the riverfront towns of Yarrawonga, Cobram, and Echuca; and the Lower Murray that covers the final distance to the river's mouth at Goolwa. Like most of the English language, to confuse locals and tourists alike, it is named Murray River until it reaches the South Australian border where it changes to River Murray.

Throughout its length, the river's flow is arrested by sixteen weirs, principally for irrigation, effectively partitioning the river into a series of lakes. A series of locks are in place at all but two of the weirs to allow river craft to travel the river via a water-controlled chamber. With gates at either end that slowly empty or fill to adjust travellers to a higher water level upstream or lower-level downstream they cater for paddle steamers to kayaks—and may the two never meet.

PART I

The Headwater To Mildura

Chapter 1

Biggara to Indi Bridge

Day 1

Tuesday, April 2

Blue sky, perfect conditions 24°C

It is a 10½ hour drive east of the Murray mouth from where my brother Dave and I travelled to the joint river towns of Albury/Wodonga. I anticipated it would take only 50 days to paddle back.

Dave and I arrived at good friends Jim and Linda's home in Wodonga with a car full of essentials and a kayak strapped to the roof. Apart from providing a venue for pre-odyssey round table discussion and entertainment, their roomy garage offered a safe, dry warehouse where I could pack and stack the necessary food and equipment essentials. Most items could be squeezed into the kayak's supply hatches.

The Seabird Expeditioner kayak has a 6'8" foot carbon hull with fibreglass top and a load capacity of 145kg. Considering my weight of 86kg, the maximum load for essentials was 59kg.

I reasoned that these specifications erred on the conservative side. After all, I would be travelling along a gentle river, not white-water rapids, so what could possibly go wrong?

With all in readiness, Dave and I attempted to carry the kayak out to car. We soon discovered the difference between a well-packed weighty kayak and a packed 'tight as a sardine' extremely heavy kayak. It took all four of us to hoist the kayak onto the custom-made roof racks.

Before leaving, Linda, a keen Tarot Card reader, took a moment to draw a card from her 78 card deck to predict the future of the expedition.

'Hmm, the death card is not as bad as it seems,' she said.

I had no thoughts beyond the obvious.

'It means you'll be faced with challenges and some serious,' she continued. 'But...'

Keen to grasp at straws I hoped the *'but'* would be more promising.

'But with resourcefulness, which you have in abundance, Lee....' Then, after a moment of hesitation. 'Yes, with calculated application, everything will work out fine.'

Oh, joy. Dave and I glanced wide-eyed at each other. A death card that claims all will be okay. Comforting? Just.

Linda, fondling the card, stood back smiling at my good fortune.

Outside of Wodonga, Dave drove past the barren remnants of a water deprived Lake Hume before getting us safely to Corryong where a café guaranteed the best cooked farm fresh eggs and smoky bacon. Two hours further upriver at Biggara Bridge, and still with a full stomach and a promised guarantee fulfilled, my dream to escape the circus I had begun to call modern life was fast becoming reality.

A day earlier, Dave and I had driven to the Biggara bridge on a reconnaissance mission. It rests at the bottom of Mt Kosciusko where the cool bite in the air confirmed our entry into Snowy Mountain's country. The cool bite would be over-come by my body heat when paddling. The water level in the river sat around one metre and the unassuming flat bridge was as serene a place to start paddling as any.

After a last minute repack, I and my marginally lighter kayak slid into a smooth clear river. Wide at this point, around seven metres, the river was energetic but the flow manageable.

Despite my protests, Dave insisted on waiting seven kilo-metres downstream at the Indi bridge to ensure all was well, before driving back to Adelaide. With the pace of the flow added to my paddling speed, I would see him in 45 minutes. All available river reports, of which there were scarcely any, suggested care-free travel. So, with a wave goodbye and a couple of snapshots, I paddled off as innocent and wide-eyed as Bambi entering the woods.

Living within ten kilometres of the Murray mouth, I revelled in the romantic notion of 'paddling home'. To mark the occa-sion, I brought a top hat for a lark: an interesting spectacle while rambling along the old ancient lifeblood of southern Australia. However, conservatism is the eternal adversary of old age, so with a heavy heart I renounced my distinctly cul-tured lid for the regular unfashionable peak hat with attached sun protection flaps. Gliding along the river was most pleasant and I was feeling quite cocky singing to the cows that towered above me as they shat on the banks before walking across in front of me.

A thousand kilometres downriver the water is murky but here the pebbles of many colours sparkled through the clear water. From water level, glimpses of green grassy flats appeared between swaying branches of weeping willows and river gums that lined the one metre high banks. As I dreamily dipped my paddle blades into the water, pulling with gentle strokes to complement the flow, I peered into the perforated holes in the banks. From under cloudless skies, I imagined sleepy round wombat faces resting on their short, crossed legs while calling out to their joeys deeper in each burrow, 'Hey kids, there's another crazy half body paddling down the river.'

After 15 minutes of peaceful cruising the water level began to drop dramatically. Shallow sections exposed large outcroppings of rocks, and smooth river stones collided with each other only inches below the surface. With the kayak scraping the riverbed and taking a bit of a battering my only choice was to direct it through the two metre wide channels on the outside bends. The flow in these bends could best be described as 'rushing'. The first couple of bends presented an awkward challenge as I steered the heavy kayak with rudder and paddle and, while exciting, the unceasing bends along this section forewarned of a difficult task ahead should they continue.

The outside bends featured—keeping in mind, not all features are necessarily pleasant—a multitude of exposed tree roots that reached from the top of the bank to anchor well below the riverbed. Known as strainers, the exposed roots are caused by the soil erosion of the constant fast flow and are both fixed and unforgiving.

I thought back to the warnings I had received concerning strainers. They were to be avoided at all costs lest they trap the kayak, and paddler, in their inescapable and undemocratic web of roots.

While negotiating the third bend the current's ferocity took control. Despite my best efforts, and gritted teeth, the kayak rocketed directly into a strainer. In the split second it took for the nose to lodge itself in the root system, I tipped underwater. I fell not in the direction of the bank where I could hold myself upright, but toward the inside of the channel where the flow is at its most intense. From underwater I confidently pulled the kayak skirt free and, using the standard exit procedure, hoisted myself from the cockpit. Instead of the desired smooth exit, my left leg below the knee became caught in the cockpit. The current had forced my body backwards, parallel with the kayak. I was now stuck underwater at a descending 45 degree angle. Try as I might, I could not release my lower leg. The current was too fierce and all efforts to free myself by pulling forward was useless. The angle at which I was being held underwater did not allow me to reach up for air.

The immediacy of the danger struck quickly. All escape efforts proved futile, and my thoughts began to wander to the inevitability of my final resting place, the shortness of my quest, and the premonition of danger I had suspected before leaving. The serenity of drowning began to flood gently into my consciousness.

The will to survive must have taken over. After a number of attempts I contorted my body unnaturally upwards where in desperation my lips extended a centimetre above the bubbling water. I managed a breath. How the rushing current did not fill my mouth with water is a mystery. It was only a gulp of air and a millisecond, but it bought some time. Once again, I was under the water, unable to invent a solution and desperate for more air. My leg would not budge and once again my protruded lips sought the surface.

With no hope of releasing my leg and no sign of help, I resigned myself to this bend in the river being my final resting place. Even though I wished for a miracle from the river—my joyful river—I knew the current was not going to diminish for me.

After four or five attempts to free my leg, going underwater one breath at a time, I twisted further upwards. A twig no thicker than my little finger extended from one of the main roots of my host tree. Over the back of the kayak and at full stretch, my fingertips squeezed hold of it. Covered in slimy moss, I held the twig gently, and in those precious moments devised a plan: any plan. *There is no-one to call out to; my trip is so short; I will be found eventually as a body protruding from a kayak with arms flailing in the current; the family and people I will leave behind will look upon me as both foolish and a failure; and it's physically impossible to hold on long enough for anyone to come to my rescue.*

Desperate thoughts crowded my mind, all orderly and in full uninterrupted technicolour. But I did not want my children to read about their father's demise in tomorrow's headline. I went down again and with an almighty shove managed to move my foot two centimetres. Again, I came up for air. My fingers searched for the twig. The slimmest, slimiest shimmer of hope. Going back under, movement became easier and with a mighty determination my foot rotated bit by bit until my leg came free. The current picked me up and washed me quickly downstream. My PFD (life jacket) lifted my torso above the water line where, most importantly, I could breathe.

My cheque cashed, my resignation tendered, either way, I had dodged a bullet; remarkably, luckily. My time had just not come today. Washed down through a channel to a reach, the river widened and slowed offering me an opportunity to climb up onto the bank. I ran the 50 metres back to the scene of a now unfulfilled headline.

My kayak remained stuck fast in the roots. It was full of water and not budging. With adrenalin surging through my veins —or wherever it surges—I climbed up on the tree roots and clambered towards the kayak. With my back pinned against the roots, I pushed my feet against the kayak until its rear began to swing around. In a flurry of action, it broke free and still upside down, I leaped on it. Bucking and rearing, it bolted around the bend before heading into the reach, quieting down enough that I could lead it over to the shallows. We both sat. No blood, no broken bones, no time to rest.

By some miracle of osmosis, the water-tight storage hatches were now filled to the brim with water. I reaffixed the water-proof covers and began emptying the water from the cockpit with my trusty hand pump. With Dave waiting downstream, I could deal with the small details later. One side of my life jacket had ended up under my arm, and the paddle by some other miracle had remained attached with what I had considered was a flimsy paddle leash.

I wasted no time. I was in control and decisions were coming fast. No time to dwell, I leaped back into the cockpit and paddled. The river continued along with reaches of 50 metres interrupted by similar fast-flowing channels on the bends. At times, ankle-deep water barely covered the exposed rocks and pebbles of the riverbed. As each bend approached, I established a technique of leaping from the kayak, taking hold of the tie down rope, and directing the kayak through the channel (or over the shallow rocks) while stumbling over rocks varying in size from tennis balls to footballs. If my foot or leg had become lodged between the rocks, a similar fate to my earlier predicament awaited, but along I plodded in my naïve and inexperienced way.

Further downriver an old river red gum tree had toppled from the bank and blocked the entire river. The banks were lined with these ancient trees which can live 500 to 1000 years. I stopped to consider my options. CPR was out of the question for this calamity. Deliberating, not procrastinating, I lunched on a Growling Dog protein bar. Held fast to the deck of the kayak with zip ties, the five-piece kayak trolley had remained attached and intact. The solution was to remove and assemble the trolley then portage up and around the bank. Still lost in the river was my peak hat, sunglasses, and my foam seat cushion, all of which I cared as much for at this stage as cats and Nicholas Cage movies.

Once loaded on the trolley it was clear the kayak had taken on more water weight in the storage hatches than I had anticipated. Although the bank was angled agreeably for pulling the kayak up, the added weight combined with the rocks, scrub and tree branches on the bank presented an almost insurmountable challenge. Exhausted and downcast, my pleasant day of sun and song was not going to plan. Grunts escaped involuntarily, and veins reached just short of popping as I drew on all reserves. But this was my moment. My journey. And dig in I must.

After disassembling the trolley and re-attaching it with more zip ties, I put back into the water only to face the same shit, different tree, on three more occasions. Time was now spent jumping into the cockpit, leaping from the cockpit, walking, slipping, and scampering over another rocky bottom while negotiating another channel of intense flow at every bend. At least half the time was spent leading and guiding the kayak with the rope. Many thoughts had been rushing through my mind but the at the forefront was that I could not keep Dave waiting.

A human emerged from the bank. Had it been hours? The farmer happily revealed that the Indi bridge was only five minutes downriver. But what is five minutes to a farmer—by car, by tractor, walking? As it turned out it was five minutes by paddling, or more descriptively, leaping, leading, and directing.

It turned out that the bridge, a somewhat exaggerated description, was little more than a road across the river. There was just enough room for a kayak to slip underneath. But to me, it was the best bridge I had ever seen! Tired, emotional, and wondering if I had bitten off more than I could chew, I let out a blustery laugh of joy so removed from any other noise I had expelled during the day. I pulled the battered ol' girl up onto the sandy bank.

Climbing onto flat, safe ground I surveyed the surrounds from the bridge. Dave was nowhere in sight. The horrifying reality that he had headed home, as I had earlier insisted, hit me. My shoulders slumped down to my hips. Four and a half hours had passed since he waved me off from the bridge instead of the predicted 45 minutes.

Phone reception was intermittent. Dave had texted me to ask if all was okay and my reply 'difficult but alive' may or may not have got through. Had he read it as 'okay and having fun' and headed off back to Adelaide? I stood gazing out at the clear blue sky absorbing what had taken place during the first part of my odyssey. The narrow river below flowed on to where the next part of my journey would take place. This is how a river works. All I could see before me was more of the same. It was 3pm and a lifetime from Biggara. I resigned myself to getting back in water and continue to a suitable campsite. Scanning the banks, movement caught my eye. One hundred metres downriver Dave stood with a group of campers, beer in hand, in a camp park. I did not have to hear Dave to know his infectious good cheer would have bought him that beer and more. The sight of him brought on about 50 different emotions—some I did not even know I had. 'Oh bliss!' being one of them.

I raced back to the kayak and floated it down to the small landing. Dave, relieved that I had finally shown, slapped me on the back while he helped me to unload all my soaked food and clothes, and the seven varieties of fish that had hitched a ride. It was clear the river was not navigable at this water level for my style of kayak. The only option would be to put in further downstream. With the kayak now in slightly less than show-room condition, we loaded it onto the car and drove away. The campers, now a beer or two short, had informed Dave the river had dropped nearly three feet in the last couple of days. Getting this information beforehand would have been helpful. As the water level drops, according to fellow paddlers on the River Murray Expeditioners social media page, paddling is far more dangerous than high water paddling conditions due to the formation of channels concentrating the mass of water into such a small space.

Dave had waited anxiously at the campground realising early on that my delay most likely indicated trouble. He wandered upriver numerous times to a point where we could not miss one another only to return to the bridge, powerless and defeated each time. His calm now provided much needed relief and I was beyond grateful that he assumed control. Normally one with a quick wit and a ready laugh, he sat stone-faced as I remarked 'I nearly died back there'.

We headed to the resort at Lake Hume for a reassessment. More than once along the drive heavy sighs left my body until, after a short while, tension-breaking shaky laughter erupted from both of us. Refreshment was essential so we stopped at the very closest pub, the Corryong Hotel Motel. In the carpark, pain quickly replaced adrenalin and I could barely walk.

'Can't come in here, mate,' said the barman behind the empty front bar.

'What's the problem?' Dave jumped in first. 'We only wanna beer.'

'Can't enter without shoes,' he replied.

And that's fair enough—I would not want to step on a piece of glass caught in the carpet and injure myself. Not willing to forgo a tipple to ease my nerves, I hobbled back to the car and rummaged through the kayak to find my sandals. The saturated neoprene paddle boots were creating a puddle in the back of the car.

Back at the Lake Hume Resort, I tried to recreate the bodily contortion needed when surfacing for air. My throbbing body parts confirmed it a movement only gifted to yoga disciples. Walking without assistance was difficult despite strong pain relief. Further inspection of the kayak confirmed the poor thing had taken a pounding. As well as my aching knee, hip, and torso it needed urgent repair work.

Reflecting on the day, the choice to begin in that section of the river was not without research and consideration. The old scouting rule of, 'never leaving where you say you'll be', was never more pertinent. Even though Dave was concerned for my safety, he stuck to the code, knowing that if he had gone in search, he may have missed me as I paddled around another side of the many islands that temporarily separated the river. If Dave had not been at the bridge, I would have had no choice but to continue downstream in shallow water in my injured condition. I did not want to think about that.

How strong are we really, and what is the correlation between inner strength and outer strength? Can we ever know exactly how strong we are physically or mentally until circumstances demand an answer?

Dave and I booked a room, ate dinner in the resort restaurant and enjoyed a couple of well-earned drinks. And, as good fortune would have it, it was half-price pizza night. Lucky Lee!

Even with the day safely over, sleep did not come easily.

Chapter 2

Lake Hume Resort

Days 2 & 3

Wednesday and Thursday, April 3 and 4

Sunny skies, cool clear evenings, 24°C

There was no possibility continuing in my injured state, so I spent the next two days recovering at Lake Hume Resort. Although a little tired, at the discounted rate of $110 per night—and because sleeping in my small tent was not within the first 50 things on my 'to do' list—there were no complaints. In the adjoining caravan park, with expansive views overlooking the Hume Dam, a café offered tasty muffins but with consistently terrible coffee it was also relegated down the list.

By Thursday night, with the aid of painkillers, I could walk relatively freely. The show must go on. Dave had remained with me and had taken control of the kayak repairs. Following the advice of an old-timer in Albury he repaired the deep scrapes in the kayak's carbon hull with Five-minute Araldite and replaced the broken rear carry strap with seat belt webbing. His enthusiastic assistant was a small brown kelpie pup that would squeeze its head into the cockpit every time Dave's head went in. Most likely an engineer in a past life, the pup was more interested in licking Dave's ear than offering sage advice. Laughter is a great remedy for pain. What a godsend my brother is.

My downtime presented the opportunity to reassess the trip essentials. I took a spartan approach and removed half the food that instantly reduced the weight by ten kilograms. Spare clothes, camp kettle, jaffle iron, camp oven, small motorcycle, kitchen sink, all gone. As a hiker I am used to packing a modest rucksack but with all that spare space in the kayak, I confess to getting carried away. In my defence, the drawback of travelling solo is that I had to carry much of what could have been shared between two kayaks. Still on the heavy side, I reasoned the flow of the river would compensate for the kayak's excess weight.

The Hume's capacity was down to 19 per cent exposing huge areas of dry land where remnants of dead gum trees stood defiant against the orchestrators of the man-made lake. Upstream the Mitta Mitta River, which should act as a feeder for the lake by way of a weir, did not have enough water left to fulfil its role. When full, the 20 square kilometre Lake Hume holds six times the water of Sydney Harbour but surveying it now, it held only enough to trace the route of the old river. At the time of white settlement, the upper section from this point was named the River Hume with the River Murray leading downstream. It was not until Captain Charles Sturt's 1830 river odyssey that the combined sections amalgamated into the River Murray. I expected, even with a battered kayak, to outpace Sturt's 77 day journey.

Over the two rest days, I had time to daydream about chancing upon an elusive platypus that saves appearances for the lucky few who had never heard of politics or rap music. Gifted a bill like a duck and a tail resembling a beach bat, it was high on my 'to see' list. The Aussie native is the size of a small dog, has a fur-covered body, and is supported by stumpy legs finished off with webbed feet. This fanciful combination is matched, to my knowledge, by only one other Australian native, the pelican. Designed by the creator during his or her surrealist phase, neither enjoy success eating ice-cream from a cone.

Dave from the Mitta Mitta Canoe Club in Albury came through with some appreciated information confirming that travel would be much safer and comfortable downriver, although he came up short on platypus hangouts. The river prognosis was welcome news.

Confidence began to return as my memory faded and I visualised myself as a 'hard as nails' John Wayne aquatic type. To my knowledge Wayne never ventured into a lake other than on a horse and I doubt they ever made a kayak big enough for him anyway. The truth is, I did experience a couple of emotional moments when speaking with friends during these two days. During mid-conversation, I would lose it when recounting the hopelessness of the 'what might have been' moment. John 'Duke' Wayne had also been known to cry. But usually for the poor horse that had to bear his huge frame.

Meanwhile, Linda, my Tarot Card reader friend, learned of my *calculated application* escape on social media. 'Good news,' she wrote. 'It's blue skies and calm water from here on.'

For the optimist, I am now one day ahead of schedule and on Thursday found a five dollar note on the ground. Lucky Lee!

Chapter 3

Lake Hume Resort to cow field outside Albury

Day 4

Friday, April 5

Sunny, breathless conditions 24°C

A pup yapped around daybreak. It did not interrupt my sleep; only the formulation of a dreamed itinerary I had been working on for the previous two or three hours. I was champing at the bit to get the odyssey back underway. For the next hour I fidgeted with ropes and straps, newly acquired dry packs and maps, and pup chasing and pats. Eventually that little person that sits on my right shoulder gave my ear a flick and whispered, 'Come on! Get on with it.'

The Hume weir does not have an internal river transportation lock so with the kayak packed and nestled securely on the trolley, I held on tight and rolled 500 metres down a steep embankment towards a little beach. From there a rough dirt track guided me around the weir so I could launch down-stream. The pain from rolling the first few hundred metres was disagreeable but hobbling through the scrub to reach the water level another 50 metres below was like being stabbed with a knife. Painkillers were only mildly effective and by the groans coming from the kayak as it bounced over the rough ground it could have done with some as well.

I stopped to reign in the kayak and tighten the trolley straps. At my feet, half buried in the rubble, was a sparkling metallic object: a 50 cent piece! As I bent down there was another, then another, and another. After rummaging around, I had found a total of five dollars in 50 cent coins! I tucked them into my day hatch for something special. The road to the Murray is paved with 50 cent pieces—Lucky Lee!

On a small bank of sand, with the trolley again strapped to the top of the kayak I surveyed the sweep of land and river. An involuntary deep breath focussed my attention. What fur-ther surprises did my joyful river have in store? The banks were intact, though some of the trees had fallen, their roots unable to hold in the soft soil. I was nervous, pondering the fine line between bravery and recklessness. As I tentatively put the kayak into the river, a riot of kookaburras set about raucous laughing. Not yet understanding kookaburra speak, I did not know whether they were laughing at my apprehension or wishing me well.

Settled back into the cockpit, I gazed across forty metres of welcoming, smooth river and slid in. Behind me, the water was releasing from the Hume weir through the hydro valves. As it crashed, a massive eruption sent mist into the air. Above, a cloudless blue sky and not a breath of wind to trouble the leaves of the river gums. The odyssey recommenced.

I punted through the day with good flow. The hand-drawn mud map I had taken to avoid taking a wrong turn proved un-necessary. Navigation was obvious when sticking to the wider stretches with the stronger flow. What the map did not show was the beauty of river red gums and willows glistening in the early morning sun nor the potential homesites of platypuses. Dead trees littered the river, some stretching halfway across the water while on the banks strainers called like fair-stall hucksters, beckoning me to come closer and try my luck. Whirlpools and eddies in the narrower parts swung the nose of the kayak around while I stared at trees that spun in the opposite direction. I soon became attuned to the river's idiosyncrasies, paddling on under my John 'Duke' Wayne persona.

The river was serving up a real dose of Australian wilderness. I could almost feel the pulsating beat of a heart vibrating from below. Yes, the river is a living entity—ever growing, ever changing, ever willing to throw in a surprise. Richard Bangs, sometimes called the father of modern adventure travel, got it right when he said,

'Wild rivers are earth's renegades, defying gravity, dancing to their own tunes, resisting the authority of humans, always chipping away, and eventually always winning.'

Coarse gravel bars appeared just below the surface in the middle of the river and small trees, resolute, holding firm against periods of higher raging waters, grew randomly and isolated on the stony islands now exposed at this low river level. Numerous flooded trees and stumps projected upwards out of the water while others hid just beneath the surface. I managed to avert any more white-knuckle rides by giving them a wide berth, avoiding a collision, a tipped kayak, or more deep scratches in the gel coat. Before long I was easily detecting their bubbling tell-tale V-shaped wakes resulting from the current until...wait on...the wakes were headed upstream toward me. As they got within a couple of metres of the kayak, what looked like exposed tree stumps were heads as large as my fist rising out of the water. The faces of freshwater turtles smiled at me as we passed, and I was thankful they have not the teeth or temperament of crocodiles.

For this trip I had been so focused on finding platypuses that I had underestimated how much I would appreciate seeing all types of wildlife. Already I had seen and heard so many birds that I could not put a name to them all. Maybe that was because they were all trying to talk at once.

Within a kilometre on the New South Wales bank, a large blue sign—approximately two foot by one foot—was nailed to the thick trunk of a river red gum. The number 2220 in large white print indicated the remaining distance to the Murray mouth. More than 2000 kilometres was a long way, but I was in no hurry. The actual plan for the odyssey had already changed a few times. Wanting to paddle from the 'Source to Sea' had been a technical impossibility as the source is only a trickle of water, a baby, barely a crawl, barely a dribble. Then all at once it would learn to walk and run. The Murray's rapids rush down the Snowy Mountains like a child desperate to run but with limited control until it lands safely on flat ground. That flat ground is at Biggara, where I began.

At 2pm I reached Albury and took a tea break at a shallow spot where, in the days of yore when children listened to their parents and tattoos were only worn by pirates, people used to cross the entire river by foot. Spreading across the shallow riverbed, scores of long strap-like leaves streamed through the water like windswept ribbons. Growing where it finds clear water and adequate light, this plant—Triglochin—is an indication of a healthy river system and provides dense cover for who knows how many aquatic residents.

Paddling on through the afternoon, I passed many spots on the Victorian side of the river that would have made ideal campsites. The New South Wales side is owned by the farmers down to the riverbank and they are partial to fencing their property as close to the bank as possible. On the Victorian side, a crown land easement of approximately 30-50 metres from the water's edge—which can extend further inland where there is a significant wetland, swamps, or conservation areas—helps the riverbanks to maintain their natural state. The easements also create an ideal habitat for fisher folk, campers, and lone kayak paddlers.

At 5pm, I set camp on a green field shared by a small herd of cows. Experience told me that cows will go about their business and leave me to mine but as they came closer to silently watch me erect the tent, I suspected they had more sinister notions behind those hormone-dilated big black eyes. I was outnumbered—ten to one—and admit being wary of a chaotic *cat and mouse* revenge strike at midnight. I pinned a 'vegan inside' sign to the front of my tent.

Considering the threat now dissolved, I began my familiar routine eating two pieces of dried mango, setting a fire to boil up an instant soup followed by dinner of rice, couscous or pasta accompanied with onion, potato, and carrot, spiced with chilli and cumin. From a three-legged folding stool on farmland that blushed beneath a ruby sunset I overlooked a glassed-out river lacking even one ripple. The evening retreated to darkness and neither I or a mosquito disturbed each other's company.

As the moon rose, and the small herd of inquisitive cows wandered through my peaceful campsite, the weariness of a big day of paddling washed over me. I crawled into the tent and apart from the hip with its lingering pain, all else was okay. As my head hit the pillow a troupe of river critters howled at the moon accompanied by the sound of fish splashing in the moonlight. That lawless space where consciousness drifts to dreams came quickly. Spinning trees... turtles like crocodiles... commando cows... *zzzz.*

Distance 2224 – 2179 45 kilometres
Easy day to get in the groove

Chapter 4

Cow field outside Albury to Howlong

Day 5

Saturday, April 6

Rain spots early to blue sky, occasional light breeze 28°C

'*Love thy neighbour—and if he is tall, debonair and devastating, it will be that much easier,*' said Mae West. My neighbours were tall and potentially devastating, yet when I awoke to the nudge of a cow's broad nose during the night the best response I could muster was—play dead. I did not need any jealous bulls taking matters into their own hooves. The herbivorous variety of cattle have grazed from the banks of the Murray River since Sturt's arrival in the 1830s. Many ancient river red gums have been ring-barked and left, presumably to make way for all-terrain cows that do not have any trouble scaling the river's banks. With the disturbing notion that my allure extended to cows, sleep came and went throughout the night. The inflatable mattress that had become a deflatable mattress did not help.

The light rain that fell during the night continued into the morning's pack up but not enough to dampen my spirits. Although waking at 8.30am was later than an adventurer should aspire to, after a dangerous and disrupted night, the sleep-in was welcome.

I gave time to reorganising and balancing my gear. The fore section of the kayak held the medical kit, sleeping gear, and a couple of dry bags of food. The aft had the repair and emergency equipment (that I hoped never to have to use again), cooking and kitchen utensils, more food, and clothing. The mid-section held the daily needs, flares, an EPIRB and other miscellaneous essentials. Attached on top of the deck was the trolley that broke down into five pieces as well as the solar panel and battery pack to keep my phone charged. Behind the seat in the cockpit was a full water bladder which I did not envisage using while the quality of the river water remained clean. With the kayak better balanced, I slipped into the water at 10am. Waving my bovine friends *adieu*, I paddled off. They did not wave back.

Apart from fallen trees that had left roots and branches cluttering the river above and below the surface the morning's water and weather conditions made for easy paddling and improved as the day went on. The river had become more predictable with nothing to push my limits or panic my thoughts. Happily working away stroke after stroke, the problematic currents and channels of Day 1 were fading back upriver with every stroke.

At each river bend, shallow rock beds reached out across the river. I paddled wide to avoid further scars to the hull of my floating palindrome. This was not so easy or necessary evidently for tinnies—those indestructible aluminium dinghies—often seen getting dragged from one of the many rock beds. River fisher folk need endless patience in more ways than one.

'G'day, mate,' I called while gliding past the beached tinnie. 'Need a hand?'

'No problem, mate,' came the slow reply. 'Gives us somethin' to do.'

I paddled on feeling like I had the better deal. Silently meandering around banks with the element of surprise that motorised boats rarely have, I often passed a bird or beast going about their business quite unaware of my presence.

Campers lined the Victorian side's riverbanks—in tents, swags, and caravans. Swing ropes hung from many of the trees, their interesting array of heights and lengths evidence of the changeable river levels for the duration of one's life. I was so lucky to have this peaceful poignant reminder of what river life was like in the past. Which brings me to mention the '56 flood. 'Whatever you do, do not forget the '56 flood,' cry river folk everywhere. Kids, meanwhile, oblivious to the 'Big Wet' swing into the river twisting and piking with all manner of impressive acrobatics and bellyflops completely unaware of the rapid flow, destruction, and debris their elders witnessed.

Right now, there was nothing—absolutely nothing—as pleasant as paddling along a river in 28°C sunshine while whistling my favourite river-song. Huckleberry Finn, eat your heart out. Which does not mean to literally 'eat your heart out', a bizarre phrase that originated from around 1200 BC. It just means I was having a better day than Huckleberry.

My routine was to stop twice during the day for breaks; one at around 11.30am and the latter about 2.30pm. During my first break of the day, I would devour a Growling Dog protein bar designed to provide carbohydrates and loaded with protein. For the second break, I would feast on six Vita-wheat biscuits with peanut butter or Vegemite (a spread that kick-starts your day and tastes like Australia). Apart from taking a little time to stretch my legs, I was generally back into the water within 15 minutes.

My 2.30 break came and went without much fanfare. At that time of a warm afternoon, the local fauna had its siesta time, but I still had plenty of work to do. 'Work' can sound such a pejorative term yet, as Mark Twain said, 'find a job you enjoy doing, and you'll never have to work a day in your life.' I'm not a fan of the idiom 'work/life balance.' To me, work is a crucial part of life and should not be separated. I prefer work/social balance... there was a lot of time to contemplate life out on the river.

Along a section of two metre high embankments, a cow mooed in my direction. It had come down to the water to drink and was now stuck up to its knees in the mud. She did not appear distressed and might just as well have been saying, 'Hello Lee, the water's nice today,' but I vowed to phone the owner as soon as I stopped. I hoped the sound of a nearby quad bike was patrolling the area and would free her.

The afternoon progressed in a haze of paddling in which I passed half a dozen fisher folk trying their luck from tinnies tied to overhanging branches. All reported little success, which I suspect was the guise of a cagey fox to conceal secret fishing spots that had served them well over the years, and possibly handed down through generations. Too bad I was carrying a GPS and could log all potential sites for when I paddled the river next time. Along this leg of the river, all the fisher folk had been very respectful, slowing down to reduce wakes that unsettled the kayak.

The sun started to appear below the peak of my cap, the vibrant scent of gums dulled, and nature itself softened. The pace around me also slowed and the domesticated comforts at the caravan park with a shower and a pub meal became option one. Knowing my destination was close, I pushed on shortly passing under the John Conway Bourke Bridge and into How-long. It then required pushing up against the current in the Black Swan Anabranch that led to an off-the-beat park where town folk clearly do not value a river view as visitors might. The negligible current suddenly had my attention.

Howlong derives its name from the gathering of Brolgas, a native Australian bird known for its dancing, and appropriately I was led a merry dance on the search for the elusive caravan park which, like the Brolgas, remained hidden.

With the park, shower, and pub cuisine now off, I sought an alternative site and pushed into a low sandy bank around 5.30pm and set camp. Daylight saving in May afforded me plenty of light to set up. The first step of the daily ritual, though, was to enjoy two pieces of dried mango as a reward for the day's effort followed by a moment to stop, breathe, and absorb the sights and sounds. Most items now on-board the kayak were daily essentials, so it ended up all but empty after setting camp. Once everything has been laid out, the next step is to gather wood and make a fire to boil the billy for soup. While the billy boils, I erect the tent, lay out the sleeping gear and change into my dry nightwear.

By some miracle my Vodafone (Telstra is the preferred carrier in this region) worked long enough for me to say, 'There is a cow stuck in the mud.' Vodafone did not allow me enough signal to say much more nor enough signal to contact a small group of family and friends who had requested progress reports so that I can at least be traced to an area, broad as it may be, where the search for my yabby eaten body could commence. This obligation would have been amusing had my memory of past events not been so crystal clear. The harder I tried not to think about my unfortunate incident, the more it insisted on sloshing around in my mind. The image was as clear as the water upriver. A shiver washed over me.

Because I was working so hard during the days, a protein dinner every third night was essential. So, tonight necessitated pasta mixed with the standards of onion, carrot, and chilli, and a sachet of tuna in a rudimentary sauce that elevated it to edible standard. The river water was so clear and fresh that I happily used it for cooking and drinking.

I sat back on my three-legged stool to enjoy a quiet dinner when a crackle of corellas started harmonising in the trees above. Surely, a more succinct collective name for these tone-deaf buggers is a blackboard scratch of corellas. I had not seen a great deal of wildlife during the day—the cows (which do not really count), lots of crows and corellas, and as luck would have it one turtle that dragged its smiley face and stumpy, padded heels past me. The turtle reminded me of a post by a friend of mine, Peter Phillips, who reported turtle sightings as rare (Lucky Lee), but a good indication that river conditions were returning to normal following the 2016-17 floods. Neither Peter nor I were around during the '56 flood but I can imagine it might have a while longer for the turtles to return. Thinking of turtles with their leathery skin, I gazed down at my own weather-beaten hands to scrutinise the blisters that had formed on my fingers where the fingerless gloves ended. Without methylated spirits, my age-old remedy for blisters, I considered using the Shellite stove fuel but settled instead on rubbing in the jojoba oil that I had brought along to keep *my* complexion young and beautiful.

Before turning in for the night, I listened out for any approaching cows. Not a sound.

During a restless night, I was startled awake by the growling and gnashing of teeth ravaging my food rations. I opened the flap of the tent. Through bleary eyes a long-toothed platypus was waddling off with my food bag between its teeth. All this clean country air must have been doing something to my head …

Distance 2179 – 2127 48 kilometres
Very easy day with good flow

Chapter 5

Howlong to Corowa/ Wahgunyah

Day 6
Sunday, April 7
Perfect weather
conditions 24°C

Come dawn there was not a breath of wind to disturb me or the gum trees. A lone kookaburra decided the morning was too good to miss and made a sleep-in out of the question. Clear as the morning air it started with a low, hiccupping chuckle, before throwing his head back in raucous *koo-koo-koo-koo-koo-kaa-kaa-kaas*. Within seconds the tribe on the opposite bank had joined in and soon the surrounding bush was ringing with laughter.

Feeling well-rested after a sound night's sleep, it was not long before my blade entering the water was the only thing that created a disturbance on the surface. While some paddlers might not think much of paddling on dead flat water, I found that paddling on any type of water holds plenty of excitement:

like this morning. I had anticipated travelling downstream past the modest grassy Howlong town embankment and harbour of last evening but in some weird directional mystery I missed it altogether. How could I have reached a blue kilometre sign without passing it? To have gone any other way I would have had to paddle against the current. Whenever faced with a quandary, I often turn to the minds of great thinkers such as Macedonian aphorist, Ljupka Cvetanova who was inspired to write, 'A blink of an eye is what separates you from reality.' Had she been paddling here at Howlong?

On the topic of mysteries, my food bags and rations had all remained intact. However, the unsolved flat mattress dilemma inspired my own moments of deep contemplation while lost in the 'blink' yesterday. Given that it deflates within five minutes and given that I am bushed after a day's paddling. What if I just blew it up as I hit the sack? Last night, it worked a treat. I was out like a light before the hard ground had me tossing and turning.

River lesson #126: Fresh country air works best when *contained* in an inflatable mattress.

Still early morning, I had not seen any turtles but there were plenty of trees and logs in the river that demanded my attention. Back as far as 1853, self-interest, safety of navigation and, short sightedly for aesthetics, snags began to be removed from the river. Today's regulations state that fallen trees and limbs must remain where they fall. Re-snagging, where dozens of snags of various shapes have been placed along the river, has been ongoing since 2002. The purpose is to restore habitat, maintain the health of the river and its occupants, and return the river to as near as possible to its natural environmental state. Of course, it could be argued that water flow, or more precisely, the management of water flow through numerous weirs would impact the river's natural state, but that's an argument for another day. Today the river is too peaceful. The Murray is like that.

It is we humans who disrupt the river's peacefulness. For instance, New South Wales property owners enjoy rights across the river to the Victorian banks and guard that territory with unceasing passion. This has led to a range of unusual rules such as forcing any person fishing in the river to hold a New South Wales fishing license even if they are fishing from the bank on the Victorian side. The river police cruise the river obligated to issue infringement notices to any fisher folk who cannot produce a valid license. Very complicated.

During the morning I had passed only a couple of tinnies, some with fisher folk who desperately hung onto line and rod while others sat forlorn with lines that dangled unattended. With water traffic so sparse, it made for something completely different when a water police officer came shooting up the river on a jet ski. He paused 50 metres in front of me. Had I been following the water safety rules? I veered to the right. The stern-faced officer stared at me. I took a deep breath, feeling guilty for something I had not yet done. Then, as if I had suddenly passed rule 7b, section III, pt. 4 the officer gave me a nod, fired-up the jet ski, and continued— I imagine disappointed—upriver. I looked over my shoulder to see his ticket book flapping from his back pocket. 'Phew,' I called to the magpie comically strutting along the opposite bank while watching. 'I am glad he didn't notice I was speeding in a 4 knot zone.'

During my morning break, I checked my paddle to inspect the degrees at which the angle of the blades was set. Feathering a kayak paddle simply means adjusting the ferrule on the shaft, so that the blades are at an angle to each other rather than straight. I had the degrees set correctly... for a left-handed paddler... which I am not! How had I made such a rookie mistake? Yes, paddling had been more awkward than during my training runs at Encounter Lakes. The two-piece paddle shaft allows for three different degree settings for both left and right-handed paddlers. Was I so nervous when leaving Hume, that I had set it at the wrong angle? Or was it set wrong when I got into trouble on Day 1? I looked down at my blistered hands wrapped in tape. How to Prevent Blisters When Kayaking? Adopt the correct paddling technique and proper grip, which now at the more comfortable right-handed angle of 30 degrees should alleviate the problem.

For my second break of the day, I slid into a sandy beach, stripped down and dived into the clear water. Time was on my side to wash and enjoy a swim in a very hospitable water temperature. The strong flow throughout the day was helping me to fulfil my daily goal of 50 kilometres and allowed me time to lay back in the sun and enjoy this pretty part of the river. I closed my eyes, tilted my head back and dreamed of... nothing other than exactly where I was, 'a sun-kissed wonderland full of striking natural landscapes and winding waterways.[1]'

I pushed back out into the water and leisurely paddled through a lovely stand of old river red gums feeling rather blessed to be a tourist in the company of this grand old river.

Almost 50 kilometres had passed when the riverbanks closed in on each other and through the trees appeared the town of Corowa. The river approach to the town—where Australia's federation was signed—was under the Federation Bridge, a new bridge opened in 2005 to relieve the joint towns of Corowa and Wahgunyah of heavy vehicles. Three kilometres downriver I passed under the John Foord Bridge, built in 1892 which replaced the less convenient Foord's punt. It is used these days for local traffic and remains the only iron lattice bridge on the Murray.

It was Nobel laureate TS Eliot who noted in his cycle of poems *Four Quartets* that, once bridged, rivers are 'almost forgotten by the dwellers in the cities'. Nowhere did he say that rivers would be forgotten by dwellers of houseboats, and it appeared I had paddled into the realm of the Murray River houseboat.

Shortly beyond, on the Victorian side of the river, in the twin town of Wahgunyah, was a gravelled area allocated for campers and caravanners as part of the Free Camp scheme. Sprouting up all around the country for small towns that either do not have a caravan park or cannot support the growing number of travellers, the camps are often decked out with water, cooking facilities and restrooms. The benefit of facilities in these towns is that it provides an economic boost to businesses that would otherwise survive on a modest clientele. I pulled up to the manicured grass park adjoining the Free Camp.

The dual-town-name is a River Murray phenomenon not unlike the Rio Grande River between Texas and Mexico where towns are separated by name and legislation on both sides of the border. In this case, New South Wales is on the northern border with the state of Victoria to the south. This cumbersome arrangement originated when Australia's states were governed independently before federation joined them together in 1901. The border separating these states stretches for some 2000 kilometres until the river reaches South Australia. Also, not unlike the Texas/Mexico border, many would prefer a wall built between them—in this case, from residents both north and south. Aside from the friendly rivalry, the national and state laws have created a unique set of regulatory conditions when stepping from one side of the river to the other. Thank goodness both states agree to the same time changes during daylight savings unlike the obstinate state of Queensland on New South Wales' northern border which refuses to acknowledge the modern conveniences of the time alteration. Queenslanders sit smugly knowing their sheets will not fade prematurely in the extra daylight and their chickens can rise and sleep without complication; the rest of the country is used to Queenslanders' odd ways and simply smile at their eccentricities.

After setting up the tent I pulled out my waterproof Nikon camera to take a snapshot of the spectacular riverbank scenery. The camera was holding water perfectly, giving the rear screen the appearance of a lava lamp. My mobile phone, which was enclosed securely in its waterproof zip-lock was now my only camera.

Screams of delight signalled that a fella with his partner and two children were enjoying their river getaway. Not out of screaming distance but just out of snoring range. Unaware how secure the area was, I asked him if he would keep an eye on my kayak while I ventured to town. In my moment of hunger and thirst, and I was very thirsty, I had to trust someone. A fellow camper is usually the best bet.

Up the grassy bank I trudged, onwards through the park, followed by a couple of hundred metres along the road. My thirst was building. Finally, I reached the front door of the pub and learned forward to read the notice: 'Closed Sundays'. Honestly, what sort of pub in country Victoria closes on a Sunday? 'This would not have happened in John Foord's day,' I grumbled. By the 1870s, Wahgunyah had seven hotels and was the busiest Murray port upstream of Echuca.

I peered in submission across the bridge into the Corowa township, my throat dry, then limped the 700 metres into New South Wales. All was quiet on this Sunday evening but that did not stop me from enjoying a couple of ciders and a *mice* Thai Green Curry. Mice is not a typo. Let's just say that a carnivorous long toothed platypus would have loved to crunch that curry down!

Satiated, I limped back to my campsite. Despite painkillers, and a stomach sloshing with rodents and cider, I was still suffering from substantial hip pain. I try not to take drugs, but when I capitulate my drug of choice is paracetamol, which Dave had bought for me after learning I had not included them with my original 'essentials'. So far paracetamol had enabled me to paddle without too much discomfort, but the pain quickly re-emerged when I was out of the kayak walking about. Dave had also bought me a stronger painkiller, but its whereabouts had escaped me.

Aah! The absent drugs must be with my missing rigger's glove. Usually, my attention to detail is deliberately militaristic with all my equipment. I make certain that everything that comes out of the kayak is grouped closely in either the tent or cooking areas. It is all then checked when re-packing into its rightful place in the kayak. Not able to admit that I could be responsible for the loss, the obvious answer was the cows of a few nights ago that were over curious around my campsite. Could they have been searching for drugs and gloves? I conjured up images of a black and white suspect of bovine origin wearing a glove and a permanent silly grin. All this on only a couple of ciders!

In the fading light back at my tent, I waved to my neighbouring security guards. They gave me an enthusiastic wave back. I was conscious that my limp gave the appearance of me staggering from the pub back across the bridge, through the town and along the road to my tent, and kayak.

Returning to the task at hand, that of being an adventurer, I checked my solar phone charger battery. With day-long sunshine from dawn to dusk it should have been charged. A potential problem loomed. I could live with my camera being out of action, but the prospect of broken charger brought home how vulnerable I had been without outside contact. I gave myself a metaphorical slap. When had I become a pampered city boy instead of Lee 'Duke' Salvemini, the river adventurer?

The moon shone bright, and I had a sudden desire for cheese. Crawling into my little green cocoon of a tent, sleep

drifted in well before the clock struck one under the words of
Speedy Gonzales...

'You better come home, Speedy Gonzales
Away from tannery row
Stop all a-your a-drinkin
With that floozy named Flo'.

Distance 2127 – 2079 48 kilometres
Easy, a most enjoyable day

---

[1] *'a sun-kissed wonderland full of striking natural landscapes and winding waterways', https://www.visitvictoria.com/
regions/the-murray/see-and-do/8-reasons-to-visit-the-murray*

Chapter 6

Corowa/Wahgunyah to Swan Cove

Today, April 8, is exactly 206 days before Magic Day; a day that celebrates amateur and professional magicians who harness the mystical powers of nature. Harry Houdini, often regarded as the sentimental father of magic and an expert in escaping from tight situations, died performing a trick that went wrong at 1.26pm on October 31, 1926: Magic Day. Because the number 206 has a connection to faith, guidance, and relationships, I had no reason to believe that this day would not be both magical and spiritual.

I woke to the happy laugh of a kookaburra but with daylight savings now ended, I did not know whether it was early or late. I packed up quickly—only 90 minutes instead of my normal hour and a half—and wandered over to chat with my faux security fella in the other tent. He and his family had enjoyed their short swimming and fishing break and were ready to begin a new family chapter. They too were packing up, ready to leave. It turned out that the one hour bus trip to their new home in Albury would cover what it had taken me two days to paddle.

As we talked, I took a wider angled look noticing no car, but a shopping trolley full of the family's possessions. The children raced towards a bus that honked from the road above the park. I dropped my head when I thought about how easy it is to pass judgement and how succinct is the saying, 'Judging a person doesn't define who they are, it defines who you are'. He was excited and committed to forging a life for he and his family—the same as all of us—and if not for the grace of good parents, teachers, or some sound advice, we might all face more challenging prospects. And even with that good grace it might just simply come down to luck. Our world needs more benevolent mentorship on a scale to make a significant difference. Why do so many seek an audience only with those of equal social status or above?

As evidence to my ruminations, he described how last night a local city guardian approached the family aggressively demanding they move along. And yet not 20 metres away both I and the caravaners enjoy free camping with the blessing of the town.

While I prepared to leave a ranger came over for a chat.

'The river's dropped another 30 centimetres over the last week,' he said.

The rev of the bus's engine sounded as it accelerated away.

'Best wishes, see you again,' he said.

Into the water I slid. It was glass—and spoiler—it stayed glass all day. For non-boaties, 'glass' refers to the water at surface level being perfectly flat and without a ripple. This only happens in breathless wind conditions. It was the weirdest sensation paddling in mirror-like water. The sense of sight temporarily reduced all other senses to peripheral.

As the river widened, houseboats appeared for the first time and along the Victorian bank to which they were moored non-native thirsty willow trees grew in abundance. The willows were originally planted in the 1800s to delineate the river proper for navigation by river vessels during times of flood. Their presence is no longer appreciated, and they are gradually being removed from some sections of the river. Native reeds, bulrushes, blackberry, and pampas grass also sprung from both banks. Ever-changing, the river narrowed again reintroducing the tide-worn mossy stumps that rose indiscriminately from the water. Helpfully, to alert rivercraft, many of the mid-river snags had white-painted milk containers tied to them. Houseboating will have lost its charm for the time being.

An hour downriver, I found myself diverted into a backwater only 10-15 metres wide. Fallen trees covered three-quarters of the river's width. I slowed almost to a stop at times before advancing through the snaggle puzzles that resembled well-designed computer games. Navigating bend after tight bend, the current reduced to walking pace and when the river narrowed to a creek-like width I resigned myself to having slipped inadvertently into a secluded backwater. Morning break beckoned, so I slid onto a sandy beach to recharge and reassess.

What sort of hocus-pocus was this? Three caravans sat on the beach above me, and when turning back to the river, a blue 2058 sign hung on a tree trunk opposite. It was hard to comprehend this was one and the same river that I had been paddling along not half an hour ago. I sat to digest this phenomenon as well as my protein bar. Curiosity and good manners got the better of a retirement-aged lady who ambled down through the sand from her caravan.

'You must be melting out there,' she joked. 'Would you like something to wet your whistle?'

My hydration bladder contained tepid water from the Wahgunyah Park tap that resembled a flavour somewhere between cow hooves and what a Brolga would eat. I drank it, but I did not like it.

'Forever in your debt,' I replied without hesitation.

'I've got loads of fruit and vegetables if you'd like 'em,' she continued insistently. 'Goin' to shop in town tomorrow so you're welcome to 'em.'

I declined the offer with genuine thanks and much shyness, explaining I had plenty on board.

Across river, not 15 metres away, the lady's elderly husband fussed about in a tinnie while he instructed their six year old grandson on the finer points of fishing. Barked orders blasted across the river suggesting the elderly man was a little deaf. The boy reacted enthusiastically although a touch nervously. To some, this gruff behaviour smacks of irritability or impatience but it is more likely an ingrained habit from times when men were raised tough, and feelings of love and nurturing often considered unmanly. 'Leave that to the women,' the men would say—when out of earshot. But generosity of spirit and big-heartedness cannot be concealed behind words. I smiled when turning back to the old woman, although a touch nervously.

Back in the water and into the groove, meditation fused into contemplation as I paddled along in the twin world glass river. I peered through the reflection on the water's surface and imagined a whole other world below. I had no fresh fruit and vegetables onboard and questioned why I could not accept such a generous offer. It stems back to a childhood in simpler times when strong parental influence made me believe that people only offered kindness out of duty, regardless of personal circumstances. How many times I had held my breath and waited for my father's nod of approval before I could accept a biscuit. Was this just my experience or the etiquette of an era? Do children today face similar mind games? While contemplating an unlikely shift in my own paradigm pathways, I paddled past a fully grown pig. Introduced species of animals —rabbits, foxes, goats, pigs, and cats—are not uncommon in the Australian outback, growing disproportionately in numbers and negatively affecting the biodiversity in regions such as the Murray. But this was a large PINK pig. I called out to. It froze perfectly still, holding its gaze in another direction like a child hiding, convinced it would not be seen if it continued to hold its stare. I was not fooled by its attempt at coyness.

Oh, pig! He has killed... and he will kill again.

Bend after bend, not a breath of wind and I often peered deep into the mirrored world below the water's surface. I love magic. The unexpected, the illusion, the drama; it is real, but I know it is not real. Back into reality, I took up conversation with two black swans paddling in the same direction and slightly in front of me. Native to Australia and prolific along her waterways, this was our first encounter on this trip. As I closed the gap, they took flight, landing a short way ahead. The swans were relaxed and unflustered by my presence. As I slowly gained on them, they took flight again exposing their white under-feathers. Again, they landed a short distance ahead turning their red beaks to me before continuing.

Each time I became uncertain as to the direction of the river proper, among the many narrow anabranches that shot out both left and right, I accepted these grand marshals were, after a fashion, guiding me. This continued for nearly three hours when, after meeting two more black swans on the river, the original pair rose and flew back over my head. The new pair did not follow the same rules and shortly disappeared from view.

Thirty minutes later a series of wrong turns ended my progress in a blocked backwater. Left with no choice but to retrace my steps, I was not confident I would recognise the twists and turns back. Dusk was creeping in. From nowhere two swans appeared at the end of the cul-de-sac, honking for my attention. I spun the kayak around and paddled closer. Together, they led me to a wall of reeds where I spied a slender opening, barely wide enough for the kayak to squeeze through. With thick reeds surrounding me, the passage was barely discernible yet an unequivocal feeling of trust compelled me forward. I continued carefully through five foot high reeds that completely enveloped me. I pushed further in, unable to turn back, the slender opening closing further. Then, as if I had imagined the whole episode, I emerged into clear water. From the tree trunk in front of me, hung a blue kilometre sign. I was back on the Murray.

Now with no time to spare I powered up again but when the greenery on the banks began to melt to grey it was clear I would not make my planned destination of Bundalong (a small town with a generous population of retired fisher folk). Search as I might, there were no beaches or suitable banks for a camp pull-in. With my energy tested and daylight on the decline, I rounded a bend and sat stunned. Over 30 swans sat occupying a cove. Directing me still? And then, as if by magic, I pushed through a thick cover of weed to discover a tranquil little campsite.

Blue fairy wrens danced along the bank as I set camp. With the fire burning and a mug of soup cooling, I had a quick swim to freshen up, rinsing my clothes at the same time. With two pieces of mango in one hand and my phone in the other, I walked around to the cove to take a picture of my guides. They had all gone. Back in time, swans were considered so imaginary they were only spoken of in a figure of speech—like flying pigs. But today's connection was so real.

The late day quickly became a late-night dinner. Sitting before the fire on my three-legged foldaway stool (which I did not expect to last the duration of the trip) I remembered lessons from my father, a fisherman on the open sea, who gauged the moon as an old-fashioned predictor for the next day's weather conditions. Following a stunning pink sunset, a sliver of a new moon was reflected on the calm still river. Until now, the moon's horizontal smile had brought fine weather. But this new sliver was vertical.

As I laid on my flat mattress, a mopoke finally settled for the night. The sound of heavy flops in the water confirmed their owner as the notorious carp that tease fisher folk by stealing their bait and breaking their lines.

I dozed off with blue signs parading under my heavy eyelids. I am continually drawn to them and yet do not want to look. Every sign means the trip is being shortened yet still they bring me a joyful sensation. My guilty pleasure? Yes, they are my chocolate.

Distance 2079 – 2024 55 kilometres
Magic day of paddling

Chapter 7

The Food Plan

This is a good time to explain the food plan. I don't like to use the word 'diet' because of the connotation that it is about eating less. The food plan is based around the experience from many treks and hikes when it is necessary to be prudent with weight in the backpack while still being able to satisfy the relationship between energy and hunger. The kayak has a larger capacity than a backpack, but this is offset by the need to carry extra quantities should there be no option to replenish provisions.

Eating three meals a day just won't cut it when expending large amounts of energy throughout a day. The body is a good indicator when sustenance is necessary and if you pay close attention you can feel the time when energy levels diminish. To counter this, I consume modest amounts every two and a half hours, providing the perfect excuse to take a break and recharge. I generally take between 15 and 30 minutes to enjoy the views and digest my snack.

As with other elements of this adventure, the attention to detail and the regimented quality and quantity keep me feeling good and, dare I say, looking good. One could, and many have, nevertheless described my food plan as Spartan and my attention to detail as anal.

My gourmet meals consist of the following:

Breakfast – While the billy is boiling for a coffee, I measure seven dessert spoons of muesli with five prunes which I consume with water. Coffee is taken black and without sugar. This alleviates the need to carry both sugar and milk.

10.30 am – A Musashi Growling Dog protein bar. This contains carbohydrates for energy, protein to support muscles from breakdown, and Creatine for added energy. While this is my preferred bar, depending on supply options I will use other similar protein and carbohydrate products that may contain guarana or similar energy stimulants.

2 pm – Six Vita Wheat crackers with peanut butter and Vegemite. I do not mix the peanut butter and Vegemite on the same cracker and keep them well separate. Why? It's like a relationship between a pig and a dog. They're good if they remain as friends but should never be seen out together.

At evening stop – I award myself with two slices of dried mango. The natural sugars replenish my energy in the short term while I set camp. The preferred mango is the Philippine dried mango and not the sugared variety.

Dinner – I boil the billy for an instant soup while attending to dinner setup and taking supplements. The preferred *soup du jour* in my large mug is Trident, Tom Yum Goong which has rice noodles and a spicy edge. Dinner consists of one of three carbohydrate staples, namely rice, pasta or couscous which are consumed in generous portions. To these I add fried onion and whatever other vegetable is obtainable fresh, ranging from capsicum to carrot and broccoli. I add a sachet of tuna for extra protein to the pasta meal while cumin and chilli are my regular spices with occasional garlic.

For a treat once a week I fry potato chips which get smothered with more than the necessary amount of salt.

If space and availability permits, I will imbibe with two small glasses of cask wine which, as a lay river wine sommelier, I have come to appreciate.

These foods cover my needs and provide enough treats to not be wanting. Energy levels are maintained throughout each day with no need for extras. The bodyweight I continue to lose is making my clothes fall off but that is excess which needs to go—the weight, not the clothes!

The preferred supplements are also worth mentioning as these are an important part of my endurance. The first is magnesium, one of the important electrolytes which is lost through sweating over the day and alleviates the possibility of cramping. The second is branch chain amino acids, or BCAA's as they are better known, 4000mg of which are taken at the end of each day's paddling to help repair muscle, aiding strength and endurance. With respect to comments from the cynic, their effectiveness for me has been proven time and again.

Chapter 8

Swan Cove to Little Bruce Bend

Day 8

Tuesday, April 9

MY BIRTHDAY

Strong wind settling through the day 20°C

After a week of nonstop paddling, my first really big test was this day, my birthday, for the crossing of Lake Mulwala. Despite tourist brochures depicting a lake of placid water suited to all types of watercraft and family adventures, stories found when scratching just under the surface suggested evil might be lurking below. The words of Dan Millman, 'Ships are safe in harbour, but that's not what ships are for' ran around in my mind. I was determined to get on the water early to tick some kilometres off before the head winds turned the lake's surface from fun to fury. It was no secret; sudden stormy weather fronts across the lake had resulted in more than one dead body being dragged from its waters.

Outside my tent, I took a minute to 'smell the gums' and appreciate the unique opportunity to wander and camp so free and safe. The kookaburras wished me happy birthday (I am learning to understand their language), fish jumped and flopped in recognition, and two black swans flew by and waited 50 metres downstream. A light breeze wafted in. I packed up quickly and efficiently, secured my neoprene kayak spray skirt, and hoped I could outrun the forecast 55 kilometre hour winds. A few friends offered advice over social media. 'Stick to the Victorian bank.' Like the obedient children in the Mary Poppins story, I took the advice thoughtfully.

No longer a sceptic, I followed the swans. They led me through a complicated series of backwaters which, in the end, would all lead to the massive body of Lake Mulwala. I could not see beyond the thickly vegetated islands that the 44 thousand hectare flood zone had created. Rounding one of the islands I happened across two fisher folk in a tinnie typically having no luck.

'Lake straight ahead?' I asked

'No worries, mate,' came the reply. 'Short cut's straight on. Just follow the red and green marker buoys across and there'll be no probs.'

With the promise of *no probs* (no problems) I waved off the swans and continued on my merry way. The wind had still not picked up and I liked the idea of a short-cut. Around another island I passed blue sign 2024 and nodded brief acknowledgement to having paddled 200 kilometre from Lake Hume.

Like the light of a new morning, the fishermen's shortcut led me from the quiet serenity of the river's labyrinth to the wide expanse of the lake, but unlike the beauty of a new morning I emerged into a tree graveyard—hundreds of dead river red gum trunks standing resolute against time. Man-made lakes never completely conceal the sadness they endure borne of the necessity for claimed space. It was 1938, after The River

Murray Commission refused to clear the trees, that a group of local men took up axes and cross-cut saws to begin the enormous task of tree-felling. When the lake was filled in 1939, many of the trees had not been removed and now more than eighty years later the five metre tall corpses stand tall with many more that had been reduced to stumps remaining just below the surface. Their cries came across the water with the wind, their stories now no longer audible.

Upon entering the lake, the wind, true to its reputation, stepped up with attitude. Red and green channel markers made navigation clear but placed me in the middle of a two kilometre expanse of water. After days of paddling on calm water, the turbulence of open water had landed me in a giant washing machine. The advice from the fishermen comfortable in their stable boat planing along at speed above the waves was not quite appropriate for this kayaker bobbing around at water level. The now-saturated little voice on my shoulder kept repeating, 'This is not where you want to be!'

There was no choice but to head across to the Victorian bank. With waves breaking over the bow of the kayak I wove through a myriad of dead trees. It soon became obvious why the channel was so important because beneath the waves, the stumps of hundreds of other trees appeared. One moment they were a foot underwater and the next a foot above. It was extremely slow going, it had to be—a flip out of the kayak would have been disastrous. Having ventured so far from shore it was unthinkable that should I capsize with re-entry back into the kayak problematic. People died out here. I did not want to be one of them on my birthday. On high alert, I dodged, corrected, and stroked hard. Life has no guarantees.

With not a moment's respite and anxiety peaking, out of nowhere, two swans appeared up ahead. Humbly, apologetically, I followed them as they guided me though the dead forest toward the bank.

The decision by The River Murray Commission not to remove the trees might have seemed like a good (cost effective) idea at the time, but it has created ongoing environmental and navigational problems. Largely preserved in an oxygen-deprived environment, the submerged trees that never broke down lurk beneath the surface during calm weather rising up like icebergs during windstorms.

The work on the 'John Wayne' type person (in my own mind) had taken a bit of a hit, and I cannot describe the relief when the swans led me to the leeward bank and safer water. It had been a brutal crossing. But although the tension was relieved, the job at hand remained and I got back to the business of true grit.

Along the Victorian southern bank rests Bundalong, as bright as any diamond on Millionaire's Row. Seriously, the lakeside fishing shacks were mansions, adorned with expensive rock retaining walls and modern jetties. My body's energy reserves work on a three hour recharge which was now. Desperately in need of a break, the 'spare no expense' retaining walls offered no choice but to continue paddling. Even though I was close to the bank the wind continued to increase. The banks were cluttered with stumps and snags. Being the posh part of town, these submerged trees, logs, branches, and twigs are given acronyms like CWD (Course Woody Debris) and LWD (Large Woody Debris). With the glare from diamonds of Bundalong shining in my eyes, they were still JS (Just Snags).

Alongside a small park a public boat ramp provided an opportunity for a break. Made of concrete and designed for traction the precious hull of the kayak accepted another crunching slice of treatment as I pulled in. I climbed from the cockpit feeling somewhat unnatural for a bit; like when you take off your skis after having just completed an alley-oop with a double forward and pike. A bite to eat sorted out my swaying feeling. The morning's paddle was emotionally challenging more so than physical but I chose to believe I had just been having fun. When checking my progress on Google Maps it revealed I had smashed out two thirds of the lake's distance during the battle. The choppy waters I was to re-enter shared little resemblance with the tourist brochures depicting calm, ski suitable waters. It had more to do with advertising guru, Leo Burnett's advertising advice: 'Make it simple. Make it memorable. Make it inviting to look at.'

I pointed my kayak into the wind. Once seated, I swung my legs inside the boat, paddled a few strokes and then secured my spray skirt. Sticking to the banks for protection, I continued to dodge stumps and other hidden debris. When rounding the points and crossing the bays, the increasing headwinds threw up waves directly into my face. A different waterscape, but just as challenging as my first day of paddling. Unexpected and unannounced surprises promised grief.

With grit and determination, I gripped the paddle and dug the blades ferociously into the water. Cursing like a sailor at the wind and waves brought satisfaction—I must remember to get a tattoo. The wind increased further over the next hour and a half, reducing the usual stroke distance by at least a third. Even though I could now see the Yarrawonga dam in the distance my destination would not invite me closer. The 30 – 35 knot headwinds never ceased, and with two foot waves crashing over the hull it was too dangerous to take the foot off the pedal. Invigorated, strong, I battled on.

Over the final stretch of the lake, the wind subsided, the waves reduced to ripples, and the sun glistened on the surface. I cruised in a little battered, bruised and elated up to a concrete ramp just short of the weir at Victoria's town of Yarrawonga.

Resting on the grass, I stretched my slightly curled fingers numbed from gripping the paddle. I needed the sun to rejuvenate my body. My memory struggled to recall the full extent of the morning's sights and events with the lake here was so eerily serene in comparison.

'Lovely day out for a paddle,' came an enthusiastic voice.

Coffee in hand, a lady had wandered over as her two children enjoyed the nearby playground.

'I expect hats and sunblock are best sellers in Yarrawonga,' I offered with no hint of sarcasm.

Screams of delight from children, the laughter of those in the café, and the mother's broad smile suggested that life in this river town was indeed a blessing.

With this being the second weir without a lock for transition I assembled the trolley and began to wheel the kayak the short distance into town. My hip and back gremlins, who mainly stayed silent until I pulled the trolley, piped up to remind me why I was still taking painkillers every four hours. Limping along the path, I stopped for a chat, sitting on a park bench with a nice old bloke called Bill. Bill, who was resting his 'weak' heart, remembered in detail all the drownings in the lake, the bodies that had disappeared, and those that had floated to the surface. I continued into town thankful I had not met him one day earlier.

My birthday provided the excuse to drop into the Caledonian pub. It was difficult to manoeuvre the kayak past it. I had to stop. Tucking into a hearty fish meal accompanied with a pint of cider in the outdoor dining area, I overlooked my kayak parked on the nature strip. Life could not be finer.

Pedestrians stopped to admire my precious beast with its red fibreglass deck glistening in the sun. How many kayaks had the locals seen travel through town? Was I just another traveller? Did they appreciate that no two trips are the same? The 'adventurer' tagline had never sat comfortably for me, but different weather conditions, variation of river heights, and seasonal variations did make a paddle along the river a unique adventure. It is these variations that river folk, farmers and paddlers have learned to live with, and something I am learning to admire.

A kinship was developing with other travellers like George Morrison who travelled downstream in a canoe in 1881 and said '...the journey was more interesting and less tedious than the account thereof.' Since then, hundreds of people have kayaked the Murray, to race, for adventure, for charity, or to raise awareness of the river's plight.

Birthday celebration over, I hobbled further down the main street to find Shellite fuel, a small cask of wine and a large cask of water. Two out of three ain't bad and I could survive without the water.

To get back on the river, I needed to pull the kayak a further 150 metres down the road, across the train tracks, through the caravan park, then a further 350 metres to a beach and the boat ramp below the weir. Paddling across the lake was hard. Dragging a loaded kayak through town was tougher. But if I had stayed at home, renovating my house would have been tough too. Working from my office knowing I was missing the sunshine outside would be tough. No matter how tired my muscles were, it was a great day because after years of being 'too busy' I could finally choose my own tough.

At the re-entry point of the river, grandfather and grandson fished side-by-side with their rods dangling almost as an excuse to chew the fat. Their chatter was drowned out by the crashing water from the weir, not unlike the crashing noise from the weir at the Murray's other major storage area, The Hume. Lake Mulwala remains at capacity to cater for agricultural irrigation. But the noise of the falling water here was not in proportion with the flow of water coming out of the high-level weir; and, if there is little going in because of low flow upstream, then there could only be less coming out. Word around the front bar was that Lake Hume's level had reduced to 13 percent.

The wind was still strong enough to move the tree branches, but the riverbanks were high again, providing shelter from the earlier ferocity. The afternoon was a much more relaxed and enjoyable session of paddling. Around four-ish I got to thinking that a birthday should be a relaxing day so after another hour I pulled onto a clay bank to investigate. Definitely a below standard campsite. I slid back out, finding a crowded inland sandy beach further downriver at Little Bruce Bend. There was still space for me, my fire, soup, crackers (I was too full to want dinner after lunch), and wine. I had a pleasant evening lazing back at my fire responding to birthday wishes despite the poor phone reception.

I crawled sleepily into the tent as a group of three young campers from Shepparton with music blaring revelled beside me. Within five minutes they had respectfully turned down the volume. Their music choice had given me a second wind, so once I had realised their good intentions, I called out to have them turn the volume back up. They chuckled about the old man next door: him being me! I found myself laughing as well—the joy of youth is a wonderful thing. As my weary head lowered again it hit the ground. I was now blessed with a punctured pillow as well as a punctured airbed.

My mind was at peace and pleasant thoughts floated in and out. Today I turned 61 yet in my mind I was still 30. The kayak is powering along. It is a worthy beast ...

Distance 2024-1977 47 kilometres
Tough day in the saddle

Chapter 9

Little Bruce Bend to Tarn Pirr Vineyard Bend

Day 9

Wednesday, April 10

A little breezy, but mostly calm 25°C

My head emerged from the tent into a cloudless sky. The river ambled past so quietly and the only movement on land was a thin white wisp of smoke rising with the barest of flutters from my musical neighbour's fading campfire. Yesterday's wind had moved elsewhere to deliver its mischief. A.A. Milne said, 'Sometimes I sits and thinks, sometimes I just sits...' Chewing on my muesli it struck me that my days consist of waking, eating, packing, paddling for eight to ten hours a day before setting camp, cooking, eating, sleeping, and repeating. I found this neither disappointing nor daunting. Rather, the joy of developing a new slide to my life's kaleidoscope of chronicles propelled me onward.

By 8.30am I was back on the river. Snags greeted me from all directions presenting puzzles more amusing than troublesome. The riverbanks buzzed with action as fisher folk and campers rushed to secure their favourite spot for the coming Easter break. Ropes were being thrown over branches to swing off into the river, dads were strategically placing rocks around fire pits, mums fussing over doing twenty things at once, while youngsters hammered tent pegs into the hard ground. I chuckled while watching families, often three generations, building memories together, instructing, arguing, laughing, and throwing out 'high-fives'. There will always be time for work, but there will not always be time for family.

The river twisted and turned like one of those crazy excited children looking for adventure. Each time a bend revealed itself, I was being introduced to another cove, another beach, another sandbar, assembled purely for my pleasure.

Downriver, I pulled over for a chat with another kayak adventurer who had set camp at the ridiculously early hour of 12.30pm. Kent, a young man in his 20s, and recently graduated from university with an environmental forestry degree, had all the mod-cons. Working in a camping store during his study years had helped him accumulate his list of 'essentials' for his unique adventure. Already, Kent had hiked from Mount Kosciusko to Lake Hume, planned to paddle downriver to Mildura, and then meet up with his parents to mountain bike to Lake Eyre. His itinerary allowed for only 13 kilometres per day on account of him collecting samples and seeds in the Murray's flotsam and backwaters. I had not come face to face with a snake so far, but I expected Kent would be saying hello to one before me.

River lesson #54: River snakes do not like to be patted.

Of the 46 known snake species living in the Murray River basin—there is even an eastern-snake necked turtle—the probability of meeting one swimming across the river was very likely. Many stories are told of people trying to hit snakes with a paddle only for them to wrap around the shaft then slide into the boat. In the event our paths were to cross, I planned to work on Newton's principle of momentum combined with fear creating acceleration. I calculated I would travel at a much faster rate than a snake could swim and easily paddle past it or stop if I saw it in the distance. Problem identified and overcome.

Leaving Kent to his snakes, my mind kept ticking.

It would be so easy for a snake to slither into the kayak during the night for a cosy sleep. I started to imagine the point during the next morning's paddle when an unwanted hitch-hiker and a horrified kayaker discovered each other. It did not help that the more common of the snakes living in the Basin are the deadly poisonous tiger snakes, eastern browns, and red-bellied blacks. I added *'check for snakes in the cockpit'* to my morning chores.

I continued toward the outskirts of the thickly vegetated Mulwala State Forest. Images of reptiles had sent endorphins streaming from my brain on a mission of pain and plea-sure. Kilometres passed in rapid succession. Connected to the Mulwala Forest and all on the New South Wales side, the Boonanoomana State Forest and the Cottadidda State Forest followed, creating a natural corridor for flora and fauna alike.

For someone who lives in South Australia and whose capital city carries the name of long passed colonial officials on many roads and places—Edward, Victoria, and Hindmarsh—I was comforted by the park's names and wholeheartedly embraced the words of historian Bruce Pascoe. 'Something like 60-70 per cent of place names in Australia are Aboriginal names. They show how deeply and intimately our old people knew the land, how much they loved and respected the country. It's something we should all be proud of.' The local Ngaralta tribe of Aborigines named the Murray River, *'Moop-pol-tha-wong'*, meaning haven for birds. No offence Sir George, but Murray does not have quite the same ring to it.

Snags in the water had become prominent again. Their re-establishment since laws changed to re-snag has been so quick. Twisting and turning, I paddled on through 25 kilometres of forest, lost in admiration of this majestic green haven where trees extended down to the waterline. In parts of the river, extended limbs reached down to shade me, birdsong echoed in lulls and bursts, and grey kangaroos stood motionless as they considered me from behind river red gums as tall as tales told by the old Australian bushmen. Somehow it was wrong that a town—the town of Cobram—was situated only 10 kilometres away.

A gift in this pre-holiday race for campsites, a secluded sandy beach came into view opposite the 1926 blue sign. WHOA! And right behind that stood the Tarn Pirr vineyard and winery. I pulled in hoping my neighbour's generosity might extend across this narrow section of river. Lucky Lee?

Maybe they did not see me—or hear me yelling out!

Speaking of water... or wine. Because of the lack of intensity in 'endurance paddling,' I had only been drinking one litre of water a day. Boiling water at night worked well to top up my Camelbak, which I stored in the back sleeve of my PFD. The hose from the Camelbak reaches around to my front enabling me to take a drink as though from a straw at any time. The river water in this part of the river was fine to use once boiled, and as towns were not easily accessible, cask water was not an option anyway.

Throughout the day the river had continued to coil around like a harried water snake, but its direction was always obvious, and while there were many snags and fallen trees, the average 50 metre wide span made navigation easy. I was faced with the conundrum of feeling irked by some of the landowners on the New South Wales side. Many have built permanent unused camps that have clear, no entry, no trespassing, and 'f#*@ off' signs. It grates against the Australian spirit to deny people access along this treasured waterway. Meanwhile, the Victorian side is, as always, lined with well-meaning and friendly campers.

A harem of fairy wrens welcomed me with their chirp and dance as I pulled into the beach. Before long a comfort fire crackled away. The gourmet meal of Tom Yum soup, a pasta dish with onion, tuna, chilli, cumin, and garlic hit the spot but sadly there was no wine with which to wash it down.

With the sunset now colouring the sky, the chirps of the wrens were soon replaced by the incessant double hoot of a boobook owl, a bird of prolific numbers across Australia, welcoming me to his neighbourhood. They are also known as a mopoke which is a more accurate a description of their double hoot. Mopoke lost interest in me and continued hooting in his quest to find a mate. Surely, any potential partner listening to that for hours would question the cost versus benefits. But we all know someone like that. My connection with the swans obviously does not extend to boobook owls unless somewhere in that relentless call I was meant to be taking notes. Sleep came before the owl gave up.

Distance 1977-1926 51 kilometres
Easy day

Chapter 10

Tarn Pirr Bend to
Top End Beach

Day 10

Thursday, April 11

Light breeze, blue skies 25°C

When I crawled from the tent, dew covered the fly for the first time; the fly being the extra layer of fabric designed to repel rain, dew, and curious wildlife. A gear inspection revealed that everything left out was wet. The changing of season had come swiftly. I held my hands close to the flames of the camp stove, heated a coffee to warm the cockles of the heart, and gazed up at a petal-soft blue sky full of promise.

Only 1926 kilometres left to reach the mouth.

On the perfectly still water, the morning light beamed through the boughs of gums on both sides. Since Yarrawonga, the banks had become taller and tussock grass that is more resistant to cattle grazing had created an understory. On the New South Wales bank stood the Barooga State Forest. The roads that followed the Victorian bank made for easy camping access for family after family. Some of the camps looked as though they could be packed away in five minutes while others were the semi-permanent squats where true blue fisher folk opted for a more for transient lifestyle. With so much to see including wide sandy beaches on almost every corner, it took a little longer than expected to reach Cobram-Barooga's two bridges. Like towns before it, there was no name or town recognition on the bridges, nor signs along the riverbank.

Barooga sits on the New South Wales-Victorian border with Cobram across the river, and the appeal of both is summed up on the Cobram-Barooga dual town website as a 'captivating lifestyle with wide sandy beaches, towering gums and native bushland'. Well known for its olive oil, the country back from the river also supports beef and dairy production, citrus orchards, vineyards, and strawberry fields. Hopeful of Devonshire Tea, but with no invitation from either mayor to stop for morning tea, I slipped on by.

At morning break, I pulled into a stretch of sandy beach. I pushed myself free of the cockpit, hobbled up to a tree, and slumped down on a thick root.

'Are you okay?' a woman called from a caravan that I would have been happy to call my permanent home.

'Do I look that dishevelled?' I asked.

Her demeanour was one of genuine concern. 'Would you like a coffee and a chair?'

It was hot paddling and the opportunity to relax and enjoy an extra minute's rest sealed the deal.

Jordana pointed to the bank to show me how the river had dropped three metres over the last month. Her husband Jack intervened stating that the length of the watermark up the beach does not correspond to water height. 'It is probably closer to a foot drop,' he said.

Sipping a delicious coffee from the well-appointed undercover camp kitchen., I could not help noticing the elephant in the room; a mound of cut logs two metres high and eight metres around—the size of an elephant! I had to ask.

'Family coming up for Easter,' Jack explained. 'We're going to roast a pig on a spit.'

'Mmm... I hope I'm invited' I joked. 'I expect the paddle back upriver would improve my hunger.'

Now that we had shared a coffee and chat, in true Aussie/ East European tradition, I was considered part of the large extended family. Jack, in his broad accent, extended a genuine invitation and one that we both knew would not be taken up. The conversation shifted to Jack's love of European Carp as the best eating fish in the river. Native to China, and now in waterways across the world, the carp was introduced into Australia's waterways as far back as the 1800s. It was now the most abundant large freshwater fish in the Murray system, negatively impacting on river health as well as native flora and fauna. It is so scorned that it is illegal to return a caught carp back into the water. Most fisher folk bury them, unless they are like Jack who knows the best way to prepare them—I received full instructions. 'Carpe carp,' I mused, with a low level of conviction. As for the firewood, my friend Rose Fletcher later suggested, 'it must have been a monster pig, and a very small forest (now)'.

Now down past Cobram the river had grown noticeably quieter—mainly due to the increase in snaggles above the water and their unpredictable host trunks lying just underneath. Tinnies skirt around with ease, but the ski boats and jet skis would not risk the potential damage to their craft. Overall, I found recreational river users to be respectful, the powered types giving me a wide berth and a wave (of hands) which made sharing the river all the more enjoyable. Out on the wider, deeper sections though it was a different story. The high-powered ski boats carry on with their own agenda, the majority in my observation either not understanding, or caring, about the damage to banks caused by their wakes.

As the river widened, shallow sand banks now reached three-quarters of the way across and even though the kayak drew little water I found it best not to take too many short-cuts. The water was clear enough to observe the thick slimy logs that would remain well underwater during higher water. I snuck up on two young kangaroos springing down to the river. One hit the brakes on the water's edge but the other plunged straight into the water up to its little flapping arms. Kangaroos are not well-known as water lovers but there are many reports of them swimming in the sea and rivers using their legs and powerful tail to swim, and their forepaws to dissuade well-meaning rescuers. Since the river was deemed good enough for the local wildlife, it was good enough for me. In the heat of the afternoon I took an early break, plunging into the warm water. The flow of the river can be perilous during times of flood—but not today.

My intention before retiring for the day was to paddle well past Tocumwal, a short distance downstream, but the river conditions had changed. Fallen tree stumps extended across the river and I had limited avenues for passing. I was not in favour of tipping if caught in their web of branches, not for my displeasure but to avoid getting everything wet that I was carrying. Also, the kayak, with its carbon hull had become somewhat precious. The more robust kayaks made of poly material could race over logs or gravel skidding their bottom without incurring damage. I suppose this is the quandary with many things in life that are built either for work or speed but rarely both.

Rather than dangerous, these puzzles became exciting for the next few kilometres as I slipped, slid, dodged, and wove between exposed branches. My eyes were so peeled to the surface that pink pigs and their families could literally have flown overhead and partied on the banks and I would not have seen them.

Somewhere around the Tocumwal Road Bridge and the Tocumwal Railway Bridge lies the town, but like most of the towns upriver its whereabouts was difficult to discern. I reluctantly paddled on, realising I had missed the opportunity to see The Big Cod, the first 'Big' thing to be commissioned in Australia, way back in 1967. Maybe a big sign announcing Tocumwal to river travellers might currently be under construction.

Overhead the sun was blaring, and some five kilometres downriver a deserted beach had no sign, but it had everything else I desired. I called it stumps, ate two pieces of mango, and jumped into the river like a hot kangaroo. I dried off in the sun on my own patch of yellow sand fiddling with the light plaster bandages that covered my blistered fingers. Apart from the swimming 'roo and its mate, and a small brown kangaroo I called Euro, wildlife today had been reclusive. With my light pace and quiet movement, and with this part of the river having limited vehicle access, I expected to see more. A platypus sighting had still eluded me, even though I had been told that the best way to spot them was from the water. I gazed across the still river hoping to catch a tell-tale ripple when a harem of blue fairy wrens made the kayak their playground. Watching them dart on, around, and under might not have been a platypus moment, but it made the beach even more perfect than when I landed.

As dusk began to descend, I settled into my normal routine at my outdoor restaurant preparing soup and a rice meal for the night's dinner. With the setting sun came a sky of fire, orange then pink, wide, and unbroken. Obligated by Mother Nature's breathtaking seduction of sunsets night after night I had taken countless photos. Never to be taken for granted, the album was filling and it was time to commit future exhibitions to memory.

Questions rolled into focus as I laid waiting for sleep...is real estate as valuable here for its sunsets as beach houses are for sea vistas...are platypuses and swimming kangaroos friends...will a bunched-up pile of clothes be more comfortable than an inflatable pillow with a hole in it...zzz

Distance 1926 – 1880 46 kilometres
Some concentration but easy paddling

Chapter 11

Top End Beach to Kings Landing

Day 11

Friday, April 12

Blue skies, calm, light breeze on the long stretches 26°C

I rose this morning before the kookaburras. It was imperative to get moving early to avoid the inconvenience of expected ski boat wakes. When a boat engine coughed and roared past at the impolite time of 6.15am I congratulated myself on this decision. Seated in the cockpit by 7.15am, I paddled away in glassy conditions. As it transpired, there was no need for concern because *my* glorious river placed obstacles—underwater logs, fallen tree puzzles, and floating debris—in the path of ski boats making this section impossible for them to negotiate. Stretches of wide river complete with log-laden sandy riverbeds unlocked the creaky door of my artistic imagination, inviting me into the world of Vladimir Kush, the metaphorical painter. As the ski boats gave way to fishing tinnies, the sun rose like an egg yolk straining to burst while on the banks, tree trunks transformed into ladders inviting me to relive the spontaneous and dangerous days of my youth leaping from branch to branch in the treetops.

Precious parted the water without a whisper as the sun's rays caught the droplets off the paddle. Time became irrelevant, broken only by the many 'G'days' I threw out to the morning fisher folk who had their tinnies tied to branches emerging above the water. Eager to share the good fortune of this day's serenity I took the morning break a little early when spying a fellow sitting on a sandy beach in a fashion that suggested he had not a care in the world. Melbournite, Danny was kicking back at his favourite river spot. Resting in the shade of a fully rigged caravan we yarned over a cup of tea.

'Just taking a break before heading overseas,' he announced, reclining back in his deckchair. 'Fifty-five and never been out-side of Australia.'

'You going far?' I asked.

'Yeh, Dubai, Paris, London and Italy for our silver wedding anniversary.'

'Twenty-five years,' I confirmed.

'Nah, just six weeks,' he joked. 'Be lucky if the marriage lasts through that.'

Danny and his wife planned to fly out the day after his return from this one week getaway. With a pride that I was yet to understand, he mentioned his mate, Mike who was due to arrive shortly had paddled the entire Murray some years ago. Meanwhile, Danny enlightened me on the ins and outs of life, marriage, children, and platypuscs, the latter which had remained just as elusive for him. He reproached that old chestnut of needing a New South Wales fishing license even when putting a line in from the Victorian bank. Caught by a police officer some years ago, he merrily described how he had escaped a fine due to a loophole. 'Children under 16 can fish without a license,' he said. 'I told the police officer it was my young daughter who had three lines in the river.' Danny is a fictitious name: allegedly!

The spirit of contentment shared by the campers I had met along the way suspended time, summarised succinctly by Bob Dylan:

'This ol' river keeps on rollin', though
No matter what gets in the way
and which way the wind does blow
And as long as it does,
I'll just sit hereAnd watch the river flow.'

I left Dave dreamily contemplating the joy of getting lost out here amongst woody banksias and blood-coloured river gums for days, months, or even years.

A peaceful afternoon and a wide flowing river with few obstructions led me into the famous Sun Country between the Barmah National Park on the Victorian side and the Murray Valley National Park on the New South Wales side. Apart from claims that the sun shines in these parts for 400 days of the year, the area is renowned for the largest stand of river red gums with over 180 sacred Aboriginal sites, more than 250 species of birds and over 900 species of wildlife.

The landscape appeared unspoiled by human occupation and frankly, with so much flora and fauna and history going on, it is a miracle I had room to squeeze through. Unspoiled, yes, but it remains an Australian phenomenon that no matter how uninhabited an area appears, you can always count on finding an empty beer bottle in the scrub.

In another of life's truth, the moment I began to search for a comfortable sandy beach for the night, all suitable options dried up. Not wanting a late finish, I upped my pace hoping for a landing that did not have a clay bank up to 10 feet high. Eventually, in desperation, I settled on a mud flat at the edge of a thick, red gum forest. With water clear to a metre, I guided the kayak through broken tree limbs into the bank, swung my legs out of the cockpit, stood tall, and immediately sank to my knees. A quick scan revealed the entire area had only recently become exposed and dry. Retreating into the kayak was out of the question, so the campsite for the night was confirmed. While moving to solid ground I turned my head left to see a boomer (male kangaroo) standing perfectly still on dry ground regarding me from only ten metres. He stayed for the longest time then turned and bounded off to tell the others. I could see his mob through the forest scrub discussing, most likely, something about white sails in the sunset.

My chosen site showed little sign of man, woman or child having stood before. Without the luxury of a clearing, I removed the empty beer bottle and erected the tent on rough leafy ground before creating a safe fire break to prepare my fire with a choice of the forest's finest wood. Like bush legend, David James Jones better known as 'The Possum'—who lived as a recluse along the Murray River for more than 50 years—I settled in for the night. Unlike Possum who travelled between several bush hideaways shunning nearly all human contact, I enjoyed a glass of cheap cask wine, then hit the sack excited by the prospect of what tomorrow may bring.

Lucky Lee!

Distance 1880 – 1825 55 kilometres
Easy paddling with occasional breeze for interest.

Chapter 12

Kings Landing to War Creek

Day 12

Saturday, April 13

Overcast early, occasional light breeze 26°C

It is hard to imagine that a base of twigs, branches, leaves, and hard clay provided the best night's sleep I had had so far. Even so, I had a slow and bleary-eyed start to the day. With every day until now being busy I had not had enough hours or minutes to repair the hole in the airbed. For almost the entire trip I had used my clothes drybag and, vegan spoiler, my spare kayak lambswool seat padding as an inspired and extravagant pillow. A second piece of lambswool covered the kayak seat to prevent blisters and chaffing. The other recommended seat padding was a piece of eggshell foam which remains upriver near Biggara, probably caught by strainers, and now used as bedding by an enterprising wombat. The lambswool proved more comfortable anyway; the foam, due to the added height had changed my centre of balance making paddling a bit wobbly.

The benefit of a clay bank over a sandy beach is that it records the footprints of visiting critters. This morning revealed koala tracks. Not having heard the male's distinct guttural grunt I expected it was a female that wandered through. To date I had not seen evidence of the introduced Red fox or the feral cat, both partly responsible for the reduced numbers of native mammals, birds, and reptiles. Koalas, their close cousin the wombat, and possums, gliders, and allegedly platypuses are still common, likely possessing their own evasive weaponry. The dinner party that was gathering around my tent each night with knives and forks at the ready was increasing daily.

Since down from Yarrawonga, I had enjoyed using the book, *River Murray Charts*, compiled by Maureen and Barry Wright who travelled the 1424 kilometre stretch of river from Yarrawonga to Renmark in South Australia eight times over 40 years. It has extensive detail of distance, bank style and height, river depth, surrounding forests, and river snag conditions. The charts name bends and beaches together with a host of historical data of the surrounding areas. While having access to this information diluted some of the river's mystery, the forward planning enlightened and forewarned.

While consulting my charts before setting out, a female azure kingfisher flitted into camp to join me. Unlike the ever-present screeching corellas, laughing kookaburras, and whip cracking eastern whipbirds, these little charmers quietly patrol the river and do not usually interact with humans. Known as a symbol of freedom, courage, and adventure, she comfortably sat within two steps of me for the longest time.

Back on the river, the breeze lazily wafted over the river as the morning sun slowly burned the clouds away. Trees and snags rose from the depths along the narrow sections only to retreat as the river widened. The flow was enough that every stump demanded my complete concentration.

Fisher folk were taking advantage of the conditions, tying up to branches extending across the river. 'G'day's' all round and of course, no-one was catching anything. Paddling with eyes peeled past clay mudflats and towering banks, eyes peeled for platypus burrows, I continued on well past my morning break.

Of the two types of burrows that platypuses build along the riverbanks, only one is used by both males and females. The other is used solely as a nesting burrow for females. I could not find either, but my curiosity was growing about other burrows and their inhabitants—Boodies, Rakalis and Eastern Banjos— all of which, judging by the tracks, formed part of the nightly parades around my tent.

At 12.30pm I paddled towards Nine Panel Creek bend. It had no beach but a manageable bank of only two metres high, so I tied the kayak to a thin tree root, balanced as I stood and began climbing. On higher ground, the sight and smell of smoke lured me along the bank in the hope of some human conversation. I waved to a camper in the company of a fear-some sounding dog.

'Permission to enter,' I called.

'G'day, mate. I was the one just upriver fishing in my tinnie when you passed. I've been waiting for you to come in.'

Marcus Aurelius could not have bounded in more stoically and ignoring or at least disguising my hip pain I accepted the offer to slump down beside the fire in one of David Simpson's camping chairs. A fisherman and plumber from Echuca, Dave was camping in a small truck complete with kitchen and coffee machine.

'Looks like you're hobbling mate,' he said.

I gave a brief 'John Wayne' version of the first day. I had time. He had time.

'I've got something that might make you feel better,' he said.

Expecting a good stiff drink, David instead walked me over to a five metre crossing where the river met a lagoon. It was a detour that could have saved me at least half an hour of paddling. Ironic, Australian humour!

I had weighed up the pros and cons of short-cuts already. My quest on this odyssey was to paddle the entire River Murray. Ergo, short-cuts were not on.

'Might have been tempting,' I said, 'but I'm here to paddle it all.'

David nodded that he understood.

'It's not how fast I can travel but how much I can experience along the way,' I added. Whether that proved my undoing only time would tell.

Earlier in the day, Dave had hooked a large yellowfin (aka yellow-belly and in SA, callop) which, like all his catches, he threw back in.

'There's some Murray Cod about, but they're small,' he said, further sharing his views as to why their numbers and size were low in this area.

Back at the campsite, Dave laid on strong coffee, hot cross buns, and fruit cake.

'What a wonderful bird is the pelican,
Its eyes can hold more than its belly can.'

Before I could thank him for his generosity, he explained the reason for the excess was because his camping buddy had to leave unexpectedly.

'Got a T-bone steak if we're still chatting here at dinner-time,' he said.

It was only midday. Still smarting about the pig-on-a-spit I had missed out on earlier, I pledged to time those visits better.

David talked of a planned trip to Japan to visit his daughter who had lived there for eight years. I shared the lives of my own two children, Ali and Bobby, who both lived in England. With so much in common, I asked if he knew my kayaking social media friend, Peter Phillips from Echuca. Of course, David knew him: small world, small river.

Over a second hot cross bun, I raised the topic of the no trespassing signs erected on private properties along the New South Wales border. Was I wrong in thinking the 'Keep Out, Private Property, Trespassers Prosecuted, and F#@k Off' messages were at odds with the peace and compassion of the river?

'They've got a point in keeping houseboat parties off their property,' Dave said. 'The inconsiderate behaviour of boat parties leaves the farmers to pick up and dispose of all the rubbish.'

Another of life's truths: a minority ruining it for the majority.

Meanwhile, across the river, baby boomer caravanners are acknowledged as being environmentally respectful. David told of the practice of leaving old lounge suites on the beaches and also the latest trend of throwing washing machines into the river from the banks of the Goulburn River as a lark.

Our conversation then moved to the other elephant in the room: Brumbies. In existence on the islands around Barmah, plans continued to surface about eradicating the horses.

'They eat the weeds,' said Dave. 'They've been there 200 years and cause no trouble. Let them be.'

The myth of the brumby in popular folklore portrays them as majestic wild horses used in devoted service by the Light Horseman, but many argue, backed by scientific studies, that the horses destroy sensitive and important ecosystems. In my amateur eyes, the forests all appeared in good condition. It saddened me to think they had made such an impact. Fortunately, they do not yet litter beer bottles, dump lounges or throw washing machines!

David's comprehensive local knowledge also helped to explain the aberration I had seen earlier in the day when the silhouette of a four-legged animal had trotted behind a kangaroo who had sat unfazed with eyes only for me. At the time I shook my head and dismissed it, thinking it as unlikely I as seeing a giraffe. As it turns out the trotting foal was every bit as real as the pink pig.

With a full stomach, my impatient river was calling and as tempting as the dinner invite was, the urge to keep travelling was stronger.

Back on the river that flowed through the Murray Valley and Barmah National Parks, I weaved around more snags but enjoyed watching a variety of insect life attending to the moss on the stumps now exposed in these low water conditions. A white-breasted sea eagle scoured the terrain for afternoon tea as whistling kites sang their one and only favourite tune from the treetops. Vying for attention pink galahs announced themselves for the first time along the odyssey. The current increased as the river narrowed and I was propelled along a section called Picnic Point where a caravan park forms a river settlement extending for four kilometres. Cruising past like a window shopper, I admired well-maintained and permanent cabins the size of a 4-berth caravan that were sheltered be-hind willow-choked embankments. Fishing lines dangled from banks retained by stone or permapine logs. Holiday makers cradled stubbies of beer, plastic flutes of bubbly, and ice-cream cones.

Sensibly, the speed limit in the area is contained a respect-able four or eight knots. But behind every display window lurks a blowfly, this blowfly being a young, presumably un-licensed boatie in a substantial motorboat heading straight for me. I veered to the right-hand bank. He followed. Did he think he had to overtake on the left? I gave him time to consider his error, but it was me who yielded at the last moment. I swung into the middle of the river. Greenhorns, eh!

With window shopping hours coming to an end, my focus shifted to finding a suitable campsite. Of course, all options dried up over the next 10 kilometres only worsening as I paddled further. Again, I pulled up on a mud flat. I swung my legs from the kayak, stood tall, and sunk to my knees. *Déjà vu*. Sightings of giraffes never get old but sinking in mud does. This site was too exposed, and I was overcome by a sense of vulnerability, a city-like emotion I had yet to overcome. Reality is that there is nothing unsafe out here in the bush. Maybe a long toothed and carnivorous platypus could creep up but how much could it eat anyway? Retreating to the kayak, I paddled farther into the forest and set camp in virtual wilderness on a little island adjacent to War Creek. Blue fairy wrens darted about to greet me and carp jumped, inviting me to consider Jack's special recipe. Couscous and limp vegies won out. The fire crackled and I missed my guides; maybe the black swans had other travellers to help out upstream.

Distance 1825 – 1779 46 kilometres
Challenging paddling at times but easy conditions

Chapter 13

War Creek to Barmah

Day 13

Sunday, April 14

Calm with an overcast afternoon 23°C

The sniffing, prodding, and footsteps around the tent last night were mildly disconcerting. First came the footsteps, then a little prod against my shoulder. A gentle snort followed. Reacting more out of curiosity than fear, or so I told myself, I reached out and shone the torch hoping the beam would land on a white horse pestering for a carrot. Nothing! Knowing how horses are adept at hiding behind trees on moonlit nights this was not surprising.

Like me, the crows were up at 6am. More precisely because the crows were up, so was I. The constant cawing confirmed their status as nature's most aggravating tone-deaf songsters. One in particular had an urgent message which aligned with the common superstition that if a crow caws at you in the morning, you have averted disaster. Sure enough, when I went to bank to fill the billy I found a series of horse prints imbedded in the mud. Alongside were koala prints and either a goanna or a kangaroo that had dragged a long tail. By the number of various other tracks, I had set up camp right in the middle of the wildlife's favourite watering hole and meeting place. Thankfully, only one had tried to wake me to join the festivities.

The day's travel plans changed when Steve Inglis, a good friend, messaged to say he would be joining me for a couple of day's paddling. Not expecting him until Tuesday, I needed to do a bit of itinerary reorganising if I was to take Peter and Ruth Phillips up on a generous offer they had made of a comfy bed and hearty home-cooked meal. Luckily, Peter graciously offered to not only reschedule but to solve Steve's dilemma as to how to get his car collected from our meeting point.

Knowing Steve's universally acknowledged navigational skills, any landmark less than a small town would prove challenging for him to find me. Barmah proved the most suitable spot to meet, and the caravan park was a convenient place to sleep before paddling into Echuca the next day. The change of plans boded for an easy day, virtually a day off, with Barmah via the Barmah Choke—also known as The Narrows due to it being narrower than any other part of the river and its limited capacity to carry water—being a mere 16 kilometres downstream. Having paddled solidly for the past 12 days, an easy paddle and part day of rest sat comfortably. Only the infamous 'Narrows' stood between me and the easy day.

After a morning of phone calls, my set-in time was later than usual. I took to the kayak just above the mudline and nudging forward slipped gracefully into the river. Stroke after stroke I surrendered to a most picturesque morning but with just a touch of nervousness as to what I would soon be faced with. The chart book suggested caution when dealing with The Narrows—or the Pama Narrows as it is known by the Yorta

Yorta people—and more so in low water. Within a kilometre it was like the switch had been flicked. The river narrowed and the pace of the current drew me forward at unexpected speed.

Decisions had to made on the fly. I dodged around rocks and snags, weaved around recently fallen leafy tree limbs, and glided around sections of shallow riverbed where I could see the rocky bottom through the bubbling water. Somewhat nostalgic, I was playing a part in a game of Space Invaders; an arcade game mastered during my incorrigible youth. And like the game, the antagonists kept coming. Relentlessly growing in numbers and with increased speed they laughed in my face. But I was in charge, confident, and relishing each obstacle as it presented before me. All too soon, and after five kilometres, the money ran out, and the game was over. I was virtually spat out of the Barmah Choke (how many names can one place have?) exhilarated and unscathed.

Like transforming into a wonderland, I emerged into the middle of the expansive 225 square kilometre natural wetlands of the Moira and Barmah Lakes on either side. The waters during times of inclement weather, like that of Lake Mulwala, are renowned for large waves sweeping across the expanse. Today the sun sparkled on the mild surface undulations. The lakes are not only a story book of an earlier life and environment on our planet but a birdwatcher's paradise. Home to over 70 protected plant and animal species ranging from native fish, frogs, and turtles, but the absence of any mention and sighting of a platypus continued to haunt me.

In the distance I could discern tents lining the banks behind a collection of people in kayaks and canoes splashing about. The temptation to explore the lakes was palpable but this call of the wild had to be put on the back burner for a later date. Although the river had been consumed by the lakes its direction was always obvious and after paddling around a heavily wooded mid river island I was surrounded by forest and back on the river proper. Two kilometres downstream from the lakes, complete with a succession of snags, the river widened and cleared for the last seven kilometre paddle south into Barmah.

The caravan park, situated just before the Barmah Bridge, was attractive enough but I pressed on for a further two kilometres in search of a riverside campsite that allowed an open fire. I soon discovered the town runs along the bank and with houses on one side and steep banks on the other a return to the caravan park was the best option. I also soon discovered the difference between travelling downstream and upstream. The current was inconsequential when I was paddling with it, but now a five knot flow changed the balance of power. A short sweat later, I bowed to the river and made my way up onto the sandy beach of the caravan park.

Nestled right next to the Barmah State Forest and only a short drive from Echuca/Moama, the quiet, relaxing, family friendly park offered basic sites that started at $20. For a kayaker wanting to keep their beached kayak within site, this park was a beauty. Inspecting the camp site before erecting the tent, I looked skyward. No large red gums to drop limbs on us during the night.

'We've had to chop down 20 trees so far,' said the cheery park owner. 'Two people died last year from falling branches and one the year before...'

I stopped listening. I could not read whether it was joke or serious. 'The reports of my death are greatly exaggerated' is a quote associated with Samuel Clemens, better known by his pen name of Mark Twain. Stories along the river gathered similar momentum. The bliss of ignorance and comfort of optimism has always worked for me. Having brought up the subject of falling branches I asked our host about having a fire.

'Sure,' she said. 'I'll drop a fire pit to your site. And don't worry about paying for it, I expect you won't be up late enough to use it.'

She pre-empted my next question as every good park owner would.

'Might be hard to find some wood though,' she mocked. 'The locals burn it 'fore it hits the ground.'

By locals, she meant the original owners of the land who had been making fires along this stretch for the last 60 thousand years. The charcoaled remnants of many discarded fires looked far more recent. Despite the warning that I would be hard pushed to find dry wood, she underestimated my new-found hunting skills.

River lesson #153: Collecting wood from under a falling tree leads to not needing a fire.

With a whole afternoon free before Steve arrived, I wandered across the road to investigate the three eating establishments. The hamburger café won. Still thinking of food, I checked into the pub to book a table for our evening meal. The patrons were many and lively and things looked promising. Too quickly every one of my 17 smiley muscles were replaced by a disappointed 43 when the barman explained Sunday night opening hours did not extend past 8pm. I continued the search along the imaginatively named Murray Street to the roadhouse but received the same response.

On the way back a tourist information board on the riverfront displayed a herd of Barmah Forest brumbies and explained their relationship to the Australian Light Horse regiments of the Second Boer War and World War 1. How ironic that they can be celebrated on one part of the river but earmarked for execution on another. I kid you not, at this precise moment I gazed across the river to see a brown horse. It stood on the bank looking in my direction. It waited. I watched. It waited still. I saluted. It turned and walked back into the forest.

On a tree high above the river, a mark indicated the level of the '56 flood. The Big Wet that rose continuously over six months showed no remorse when flooding towns and country-side up to 100 kilometres away from the natural river. Little wonder the old folk who shared that experiences shake their heads in reverence. Incredibly, people who were not even there take on the same tight-lipped shake of the head when it is spoken of. I stared up at the marker. My brows creased, I sucked my compressed lips back into my mouth, and shook my head.

Rule # 124: One must shake their head from side to side when mention is made of the '56 flood.

For a small town, of what appears on the surface to be a population of about six, there was a lot going on. A group milled around the Yorta Yorta Community Hall to welcome an indigenous dance group from Adelaide. The Adelaide crew were celebrating the river through dance on their way through towns down to Goolwa at the river's mouth. I took the oppor-tunity to speak with a local lady about the swans that had accompanied me on Lake Mulwala and which I had not seen since.

'Swans recognise people pure of heart and spirit,' she said. 'They will guide and protect you if they think you are in need.'

Momentarily lost for words, I was awestruck at how per-fectly she had summed up my situation.

'In fact,' she added. 'All birds will do the same.'

I had so many more questions, but the group was breaking up and she smiled and moved on.

On my way back to the park to wait for Steve, an un-pleasant odour assaulted my nose. It was me! Despite washing my person and clothes in the river regularly, I could definitely smell myself. Maybe that was why my swan lady had moved on. It was time for action.

Fresh from a hot shower, a long hot shower, I crossed paths with a couple of old boys. Certain that somewhere on this earth the beer o'clock alarm had rung, 80 year old Bill and his former workmate, 55 year old Bob were kicking back with a cold beer reminiscing. Happy in their own company but eager for a chinwag, Bill was super interested in my adventure. He in turn regaled me with stories of his kayaking and trekking days having also shared travels in the Himalayas, Kokoda, Tasmania's South Coast track, McDonnell ranges and more.

Caravan Park time swallows up days and before long the sun was in its last hour.

Meanwhile, Steve had been on his way since 9am. I later discovered his suspect time management skills had been compromised following a boozy night of revelry. Just shy of 700 kilometres from Adelaide and with an estimated travel time of just under eight hours, he should have arrived around 4.30pm. At around 6pm he called to check our eating arrangements. By this time my hamburger had run its course. Based on his new later than expected arrival time, a pub meal was now out of the question. Our eating arrangements rested solely in his hands.

The headlights of Steve's car cast their beam across the small and mostly unoccupied caravan park at around 9.30pm. What a welcome sight! And just as welcome were the T-bones, salads, and wine. Let the party begin! Talk around an Australian barbeque always incorporates banter, and it is possible that the spirit of the river stretched my tall stories of the odyssey to date just a little taller.

Having annoyed those neighbours who had missed the invitation to our party, we strolled back to the tent past old Bill and Bob's caravans. Now in darkness, no sound, no movement, the cooking paraphernalia remained untouched.

Steve and I sat under moonlight in front of the tent by a rusty old washing machine drum fire pit. The one constant of an open fire is, whether it is cold or not, the heat and flames always draw you in and in no time the smoke infuses any clean smelling clothes with the familiar smell of camping. We continued our chat over old and new times until 11.30pm, way past my paddling bedtime. Just as we were hitting the sack, Steve received a phone call advising that his pregnant daughter's waters had broken. Our excitement died down when Steve discovered he had left his sleeping bag at home. Like all good mates, we bunked down using mine as a quilt over both of us. The weather was warm, and his trustworthiness, chastity, and sobriety sound.

Lucky Steve!

Distance 1779 – 1763 16 kilometres
Soft day

Chapter 14

Barmah to Echuca/ Moama

Day 14

Monday, April 15

Fine and sunny 27°C

Steve had never kayaked before so paddling from the caravan park to Echuca needed as many daylight hours as possible, especially if we were going to cover the 50 kilometre distance to meet Peter Phillips for dinner. We were awake and trying to get away early but only one of us was showing any urgency. While his modest supplies, which inexplicably included his UGG boots, slowly found their way into the fore and aft holds I explained paddling techniques and safety essentials. The sulphur crested cockatoos that had begun screeching from 4am continued with advice of their own. Finally, in consideration of poet, Walt Whitman's more sagely advice, 'If the wind will not serve, take to the oars', we slipped into the water.

Steve was paddling my brother Dave's Expedition kayak which is old but far more stable than the sleek racing types that can tip inexperienced paddlers at the first hint of a swish from the tail of a Barmah brumby. The trick to maintaining balance is to keep a steady consistent paddle stroke and control the foot pedals calmly and gently. But the sight of the Barmah Bridge looming 100 metres downriver and its ominous angle to the current made Steve's breath accelerate so that he pressed down on the foot pedals jerkily. Usually, a left compression steers the kayak left and a right foot pressed moves it right, but Steve's kayak appeared possessed by some bizzarro world villain as it wobbled towards bridge pylons. Swirling eddies and an unpredictable current sent the kayak every which way. Reading that John Monash built the bridge in 1904 from the manufacturers stamp on a bridge pylon was handy to know but we agreed next time we would get the information from a book.

Under the morning sun with no wind, ski boats or tinnies, we cruised along during the first session at an introductory pace while Steve and his kayak got to know each other. The river was clear of obstructions and the current friendly. Not wanting to overdo the workload too early we searched for a suitable break spot to allow Steve to settle his nerves.

We spied a deserted beach at the back of a stand of reeds and pulled in. Steve negotiated the exit from the kayak as it rocked left and right on the flat sand. If the kayak had not rocked Steve's world, then the Ramsar-listed protected wetlands in this part of the Murray had. In parts, you had the sense of paddling along an underground river only to emerge from deep shadows into a big blue sky. And it was so quiet, the only noise was the slapping of leaves in the trees being stirred by the breeze. Steve performed some Brettzel stretches on the ground while I shared my experience of paddling angles and style, using current to advantage, and options for his best seated position. Despite his greying hair, Steve is strong of body and character. He was back in the cockpit with renewed vigour while I pondered how to keep him paddling at a rate that made it possible to reach Echuca by nightfall.

The banks continued high and even though the river widened the current remained helpful. This stretch was a lovely part of the river. Kangaroos drank from the banks, and kookaburras, as though on a mission, shot across the river on a non-deviating path. It was pleasant distractions like these that helped Steve settle into a groove and take his mind off ever-increasing pain in his shoulders, arms, and butt. Conversation meandered and blue kilometre signs passed by unnoticed.

'How much longer, Paddle Boy?' Steve asked regularly.

'When do we stop for a break?' Steve asked regularly

'This is really beautiful.' Steve said regularly.

There was no need to answer. With the weather gods smiling, I was pleased that his first kayaking experience was a calming and peaceful one. Apart from his inauspicious confrontation with a bridge pylon, the day's paddle had flowed with the river and not the usual daily nine-to-five grind. The more time I spent on the river, the more I recognised that river time was a tempo, a tempo I was getting used to.

'When do we stop for another break?' Steve's voice echoed from behind.

I scanned the banks for a suitable resting spot to recharge our batteries, searching for somewhere flat enough for Steve to stretch. Steve and the river fell quiet and peaceful again.

Murphy's law states that when you really need a break to recharge your batteries, all the really good campsites are on the NSW side alongside signs that read 'PRIVATELY OWNED'. The other campsites were hidden on the Victorian side atop of steep high tree-lined banks. We compromised by pulling into a muddy bank. The earth appeared dry but as Steve swung his legs from the cockpit and straightened, he sunk into knee deep mud. It was just another insight into what my daily reality had become. For Steve it was all one big adventure. We sat back on our haunches crunching a meagre snack of crackers with peanut butter and Vegemite, something we had enjoyed together on many hiking trips.

Throughout the afternoon we distracted any thoughts of hardship and pain by counting down the blue signs in blocks of 10. It became less likely we would reach our Echuca appointment and began discussing potential beaches for setting camp. I frequently stopped to allow Steve to catch up, but he mistook these times as bonus rest stops. Every time he caught up, he stopped to chat—funny stuff. I was from a different mould, one cast by a hardworking father which was, 'Talk while you work'. We worked hard and the blue signs passed.

As we paddled closer to our destination, housing development and watercraft numbers increased. More and more houseboats moored on the river, and as we neared the twin towns of Echuca and Moama on dusk, paddle steamers lined the banks.

After checking into the Moama Caravan Park, where my bushranger appearance, rather than the intoxicating good looks of my dreams, earned me two complimentary drinks from the lovely Annie. Out campsite was downriver 500 metres above Cottonwood beach. It was an easy exercise to lug our camping gear to our grassy campsite, but it was impossible to haul the loaded kayaks. After a brief discussion, we resigned ourselves to dragging them out of view. Camouflaged under two trees, I determined it was unlikely they would be tampered with. A short distance away, a young lad of around 18 stood watching. After a few minutes of leaving his fishing lines dangling idly in the water, he reeled his lines in and wandered away. Each time he glanced back over his shoulder at us. We both expressed our views concerning wayward youth and opportunistic enterprises.

A few minutes later the lad was back. Somewhat shyly he strolled over to us.

'Excuse me,' he began. 'I am going to be here fishing if you'd like me to watch your canoes.'

How often we misjudge and, without him knowing, we were quite embarrassed.

'How's the fishing going?' Steve asked.

'Not much yet, but Dad's coming down soon and we're hoping to bag a big one.' This bashful confession only made our private humiliation worse.

Meanwhile, a group of young lads came down to the beach to kick around a football.

Steve turned to me, 'No problem?'

'No problem,' I replied.

Camping and hiking takes you not only to places you would not normally go but introduces you to genuine people who, like me, were taking the opportunity to immerse themselves in nature and embrace the relaxing, tranquil atmosphere. Like Oxford philosopher GA Cohen said, when we go camping, 'there is no hierarchy among us; our common aim is that each of us should have a good time, doing, so far as possible, the things that he or she likes best'. Most campers want to contribute to good times had by all. 'People cooperate within a common concern that, so far as is possible, everybody has a roughly similar opportunity to flourish, and to relax,' added Cohen. The young fisherman was only eager that Steve and I continued to have a good holiday.

A day of solid paddling had taken its toll on Steve, but true to form he had dug in and made it happen. Our original plan was to remain negotiable about time and distance, but with Peter waiting to take us to dinner, I missed that one!

We set tent amongst a collection of other campers which was all too odd after so many days of open space. A large brown owl sat nearby on a post to welcome us. By the time Peter arrived to collect us—it is always easy to identify another paddler's car by the roof racks and stickers—two relatively presentable campers were ready for dinner.

'Ahoy!' I called. 'How did you get through the park's security gates?'

He smiled at my city-boy naivety. 'Those gates are only for the tourists.'

Across river, we cruised along under the bright lights of the vibrant city of Echuca to the stately looking Shamrock Hotel. Incredibly the pub offered 101 different schnitzel toppings, although the peanut butter option on the last page did stretch things a bit.

As a local teacher in town, it did not take long to recognise that everyone in Echuca knew Peter. While he fielded greetings, Steve and I salivated over the many topping options but in the end, it was all too hard and we settled on a choice from the front page. Peter suspiciously chose the plain schnitzel.

Over dinner, Peter confirmed he would paddle with us the next day. Bonus! This was something I had looked forward to since our early contact. A local legend, Peter has paddled the Murray twice, once in low water and again in flood.

After only a couple of drinks, and with Steve showing signs of exhaustion we headed back to our tent for a good night's sleep. I drifted off in the knowledge tomorrow will be more of a doddle.

Distance 1762 – 1716 46 kilometres
Easy for me, hard for Steve

Chapter 15

Echuca/Moama to Wills 1

Day 15

Tuesday, April 16

Fine, occasional slight breeze 22°C

The great outdoors strengthens one's immunity, sharpens focus, and clears the fumes, dust, and other cobwebs from lungs—the lungs of children, that is. An unknown environment, sleeping under the stars, meeting other kids, and an endless potential for new adventures that spill out as quickly as the air from my airbed is simply too much excitement and enthusiasm for one child to contain. I understand it. New adventures require careful planning and preparation, a good dose of excitement and a lot of enthusiasm. But try telling that to my bleary-eyed self when woken from a solid sleep by a tribe of children camped out in the tent next door as they squealed with delight at the breaking of a new day. Their parents remained tucked up in sleeping bags, and judging by the snoring, stayed sound asleep. Now, we all want our kids to have fun—but thinking the entire world should bend over backwards for YOUR kids while YOU sleep... well that was our pleasure. Truth is, we had to be up to meet Peter at 9am anyway. I poked my head from the flap of the tent with a wish to join in the squealing and screaming. No kids in sight. Had the glrrrk of the opening zipper propelled them the next group of campers? Steve crawled from the tent displaying signs of mild swelling on both forearms, as well as wrist, shoulder, and butt soreness. We ate breakfast like we had all the time in the world then carried our gear down to the hidden kayaks at a Steve's pace. No surprise to see Peter had left the rendezvous point and was paddling upriver to meet us.

I faced the kayak to the water, jumped in the cockpit and made two young boy's day when I asked them to give me a push. They laughed as they slid a dishevelled old man in a battle-scared kayak into the river even stopping to take photos which I hoped were for posterity, rather than prosperity. Steve's kayak nosedived into the river behind me. Peter set a smart pace.

Steve worked like a Trojan to match the speed. While his paddling technique might have been lacking, his genuine passion for the outdoors, a steely determination, and his excellent sense of humour left the previous day's hardship well in the past. Peter's sage advice on paddling technique offered relief for Steve's forearm problem and as he had not yet spoken of the first rest stop, I assumed his butt was holding up.

We paddled around Bowers Bend before rounding Corroboree bend, known to the locals affectionately as Chinamens Bend, so named because of the regular fresh food markets operated by traders who had originated from China during earlier times. Officially named Corroboree bend, in acknowledgement of the *real* locals and their Aboriginal heritage, whoever renamed Corroboree 'Chinamens' after the weekend markets must have wrongly assumed that important indigenous ceremonies were only held mid-week!

Within the distance of a punt kick, an enterprising James Maiden had built a public ferry in 1846 to support drovers moving their cattle. Being thirsty work, a public house soon followed, and then a post office which laid the foundations for the town of Maiden's Punt. Somewhat typical of the opportunistic larrikinism of the Australian bushmen, the ex-convict Maiden worked the ferry service at operating times that ceased just as the stockmen arrived, encouraging them to enjoy the patronage. The ferry service and Inn did very well, until a superior rival punt (and an Inn) built by likeable rogue and entrepreneur Henry Hopwood was established downriver in 1854. As years passed, both towns were renamed: Hopwood's Ferry was renamed Echuca after a Yorta Yorta phrase meaning 'meeting of the waters.' Maiden's Punt became Moama, meaning 'place of the dead.'

With the inn just bare remains and no longer serving, we paddled around Shaky Town, known as Yanga bend, and every other bend, until we passed the old wooden Moama wharf upriver from the imaginatively named Echuca-Moama Bridge. Constructed in 1877 and built of iron it was once even more imaginatively named Iron Bridge. Local legend has it that a man's remains are still trapped inside a pylon after a construction accident tragically killed five men. With the sun shining overhead, we were too early for the local ghost tour.

Echuca is old-world picturesque with sleek houseboats moored from steep riverbanks and a line of historic paddle steamers (the largest operating fleet in the World) berthed at the Port: where stands the tallest redgum wharf imaginable. A living monument to the 1870s when Echuca was the biggest inland port and third largest port in Australia, the heritage icon offers the old-world charm of yesteryear, yet is meticulously restored and maintained for today's use. Paddling along its 75.5 metre length (not nearly as long as its 19th century heyday at 332 metres long), I tipped my hat to one of its residents; PS Adelaide, which was originally used to tow barges of red gum logs to the sawmill. So enamoured was I with the steamers that I was compelled to take a photo, which was no small undertaking. First, I had to unclick the three seals of the waterproof resealable plastic phone protector that hung from around my neck. Next, I had to balance myself by bracing my knees against the hull and hoping that a speeding fishing tinnie did not deposit me into the drink. After such a *hoo-ha* I snapped profusely preferring my personalised shots to those thousands taken from a better viewpoint. Then the *hoo-ha* got repeated in reverse, a literal 'pain-in-the-neck' undertaking that discouraged photo taking for anything less than the most breathtaking scenery. Balanced in the shadow of 'Adelaide' I pondered how I might speed up this fiddly process so that when that platypus finally showed its puss, it would hold a grin long enough for me to get a snap.

With the rest of the day's intended 16 kilometre journey expected to be a doddle, much to Steve's delight, Peter, the consummate river authority, paddled alongside enlightening us with an environmental, historical, and political river masterclass. He also explained why the local houseboats were moored on the outskirts of town even though they would prefer to moor at landings nearer the wharf. The local town is committed to preserving the old wharf integrity, much to the houseboat owners' chagrin. This leads on to a more complex problem. The river is owned by the New South Wales authorities and the land in Moama, Echuca's twin on the New South Wales side cannot be moored to because the land is privately owned right up to the shore. The houseboats, therefore, have no choice but to moor in the water on the Victorian side. The Victorian authorities have no control over this and are forced to grant the landing privileges without remuneration. Do I care? Well, yes, just not today. But it may go a long way to explain why Echuca is now roughly three times the size of Moama.

With the river clear and wide, long reaches under cloudless skies, and every other overused cliché you can think of, we reached the blue sign confirming we had achieved our 16 kilometre distance. Master Peter took a jellybean from his cache and said, 'I think there might be a miscalculation, *ahhh*, a technical error.' Steve groaned from the rear. 'It might actually be 16 miles to our collection point.'

The 16 kilometre morning doddle immediately morphed into 16 miles, much to Steve's displeasure. I did not mind because it made the night's campsite destination and afternoon paddle so much shorter, but pain was deeply etched on Steve's face as if some torturer was sitting behind him. Yet it had not stolen his light or sense of humour, the pain only inflaming his will and tenacity.

Eventually, we reached the speed boat ramp that caters for one of the local 80 mile races. The extra distance had made Peter late for an important family function and, while he remained quite blasé, Ruth his long-suffering wife had been waiting in the car for over an hour. As gracious as Peter, Ruth brushed over the fact that the function was being held at their house, unloading food and drinks upon us. If she was secretly harbouring any ill feelings, she would have been a whole lot happier when a speeding wake boat landed the biggest, steepest, and best-curling wave into our kayaks completely swamping them and filling the cockpits with water.

The four hour paddle and 27 kilometres without a break had exhausted Steve and it was with great relief that he loaded his kayak onto Peter's car to be driven 40 kilometres back to his car in Barmah, which I assumed being true river-country would have remained perfectly safe and be covered in fallen gum leaves.

Paddling onto the destination where Steve would arrive for the night's camp and dinner, I encountered a flotilla of speed boats that had all received the same bulletin. As they sped up and down the river, with nowhere to go apart from my trajectory, I bobbed along like I was centre stage at a late-night dance club. As the party continued, waves smashed into the banks demonstrating that Peter was spot on the money when he was explaining how the wash undermines the integrity of the banks. The retaining walls built to counter the impact only added pressure to the banks further along.

Within a half hour, the river bends began to tighten, the width reduced dramatically, and signs limiting the speed to four knots indicated I was approaching Wills Bend Camping Area 1, the spot recommended by Peter.

This spot really did fit the 'dappled light' and 'being as beautiful as the day is long' cliches. Warm sunlight filtered through a canopy of tall gum trees, birdlife erupted from the lush river surroundings, and best of all, the sandbar offered an easy kayak landing. I crossed the threshold of shadows to find the path that led to a massive, bituminised carpark sporting showers and long-drop toilets.

If there is a Wills 1, there must be a Wills 2. A short walk downriver revealed Wills 2, another sandbank, but not as nice a camping spot as the former. When returning, a group of 30 or so brown treecreepers kept me amused. Half the size of a Vegemite sandwich, these tiny birds dashed up and down tree trunks gorging themselves on insects unsuccessfully hiding under the bark.

It was still only three o'clock, so I got busy with my list of tasks: swim, bathe, wash kayak, and collect wood. Steve was due within the next 30 minutes and predictably got lost amongst the labyrinth of dirt roads. With staccato phone reception and one of us entrusting Google Maps, finding the campsite was infinitely more difficult than necessary. I left the beach and stood in the carpark to wave him in.

'Leebo, where are you? I'm here.'

'Stevo, you're not. I'm standing in the carpark and you're not here.'

'Google Maps tells me I'm here. You must be somewhere else.'

'Steve, I'm standing next to the sign that says Wills 1. Can you see the beach and the river?'

'No, it's all scrub.'

By chance, and despite Google Maps, we found each other after I had to sprint across the carpark area to stop Steve from driving off with his kayak and all the provisions he had kindly collected for me. On examination Steve had considered the list I had texted him more improvisational with the result being an unusual selection of goods to amuse me over the next few days. What he did bring though was ingredients for a delicious camp oven stew large enough to feed an entire Irish family and a suitable quantity and quality of wine to wash it down.

Sharing the adventure, laying back in the sand, campfire crackling on a secluded sandy beach, falling stars shooting across the balmy night sky. You wouldn't be dead for quids!

Distance 1716 – 1681 35 kilometres
Pretty easy despite the ski boats

Chapter 16

Wills 1 to Norris Bend

Day 16

Wednesday, April 17

Windy most of the day 30°C

As soon as the morning sun sent the night packing Steve started throwing his belongings into the back of his car. 'I'll sort it later,' he said, hurriedly strapping the kayak to his car's roof and driving off. He was in a hurry to be by his daughter's side for the birth of twins and hoping to beat some of the five-million-strong Melbourne traffic. I waved goodbye with mixed feelings. The last two days in good company conjuring up new and shared adventures had been, despite the weird rations, brilliant.

Alone again, I relaxed under a warm sun with a beachside view with no intention other than to write and catch my breath. I did not take a lot of time to write in my journal, but when I did it offered therapeutic benefits. Although I hardly looked like a writer, the dishevelled countenance of Henry David Thoreau did spring to mind. My hands were weathered and hard, with my broad fingers shiny with calluses. How quickly our body adapts to hardship, feeling relieved that I had finally been able to dispense with the metres of the blister tape.

By 10.30am my joyful river had waited long enough, calling me back in, calling me to continue to its mouth still some 1681 kilometres away. Downstream, steep banks returned and with them came the wind. No sooner had I congratulated myself for attracting a tailwind that had propelled me along for the first four kilometres, than a cosmic shift caused the wind to blow directly into my face. The cosmic shift was merely the river swinging from southwest to northwest. For the first time since Lake Mulwala, paddling became hard going. And now, every time the direction of the river changed, the wind just readjusted itself and kept blowing in my face. Tall gums lined the banks but provided little protection from the wind as its speed whipped up over the hectares of cleared farmland behind. The river continued to meander, but the relative shelter of the sweeping bends was all too brief with long wide reaches now more frequent. A wide river combined with long reaches and strong wind delivers an unwanted gift: waves.

The small comfort of the headwind was the waves coming straight on made paddling more stable. Along the reaches, I kept switching from left bank to the right bank to find shelter and cut the corners short. This distracted me from the grind but brought challenges wrestling the kayak across at a 45 degree angle to the waves. Just when I had had enough of this drudgery, a sign advertising a riverside boutique bar shone through the gloom. *Ice. Cold Beer. 200 metres.* In 200 metres was another sign: *Icy Cold Beer. Another 200 metres.* It did not add up but it propelled me along. Then another sign: *Ice Cold Beer ahead.* I did not need or even want a beer or a cold drink, but the idea of river decadence was enticing. Sign after sign, promise after promise, I turned the bend to see the final sign.

ICE COLD BEER — 'CLOSED'

Lucky Lee!

I laughed out loud because obviously a River Joker was paddling downstream with me. Was the joker a platypus? I had no way of knowing but joy filled my heart at the prospect of this usually shy animal playing pranks on me.

The battle with the hot north-westerly wind continued. Paddling became a grind with flow reduced due to the approaching Torrumbarry Weir. Once down on the plains the Murray is a slow river dropping only one inch every couple of kilometres on its journey to the mouth. That one inch helped little when against the blockage by a weir. At times the wind settled, and this was the time owners of speed boats came to life. They towed no skiers behind them and just roared up and down the reaches. Showing a degree of politeness, the drivers did give me a wave as they buzzed me.

Further downstream, the eroded riverbanks evidenced damage by the motor boats. Permanent orange markers were tied to obstructions in the river to warn speed boat operators and skiers of snags along their 80 kilometre racetrack. This stretch of water had the potential to become my worst nightmare as the combined Easter weekend traffic and Anzac Day celebrations approached. Having the two holiday breaks in such close proximity rarely happens and was something I had not foreseen when planning my itinerary. I could not guess who would be having the more fun.

Today's unofficial target was to arrive five kilometres ahead of the Torrumbarry weir, but with the late start combined with a howling wind, and 'dead' water, that goal faded as fast as the daylight. Finding a suitable campsite was proving elusive. There were either two metre high banks or the shores of the river were lined with tall reeds. What lived in those reeds I was not sure and I did not want to disturb their evening plans. Paddling on past bends, Horseshoe and Turner, I final disembarked at Norris Bend, stepping into thigh-deep water and levered the kayak up onto the bank. The fact that this bend was named implied it was not uncharted, but the thickness of the scrub suggested it was at least well forgotten. With the next bend named Dead Man's Hole I had no intention of investigating further. I settled in despite the disapproval of a mob of 15 kangaroos who turned tail and leaped further into the bush. Corellas screeched from high limbs letting me know my part in the disturbance had been witnessed.

Native grasses made a luxurious soft base for the tent and, with a bit of clearing, Town and Country magazine might have featured the scene complete with campfire and dinner. The fire took me back fireplace preparations of my youth. The surrounding grass was green, but the material underneath remained as dry as tinder and just as likely to flame readily. In these parts, fire can spread like, well... wildfire, and devastate country in all directions. It was only 15 years ago in the hills of Adelaide that I learned that valuable lesson. Being nothing less than an idiot, I had lit a small comfort fire down by my local creek on what appeared as green grass. With the creek so close, I did not expect a problem. But as the fire took hold, the dry grass underneath fuelled the accelerating flames. Now I had a problem. I stood in the middle stamping out flames while jumping left and right and every other direction before bringing it under control. It was not the only lesson in campfire management I had learned, but the other near catastrophic story can wait for another time.

After dinner I boiled the billy and used the cooled water to top up my drinking water, a now standard nightly procedure. I was careful to avoid the blue-green algae when collecting the water and resolved to use sterilising tablets from hereon.

It was a day of endurance punching into the wind. The time spent paddling alone had created a resolve quite different from having another person with whom to share the hardship.

Despite the difficulties of the compounding moments and hours a feeling of satisfaction brought on a smile as I sat on my three-legged stool by the fire. The wind calmed, and the glassy river flowed past under the moonlight, oblivious to me, you and washing machines. A boobook owl's proposals sailed across the river in search of a friendly ear, and I fell to sleep picturing an endless line of brown owls jumping over a fence.

Distance 1681 – 1640 41 kilometres
A hard day into the wind

Chapter 17

Norris Bend to
Sandbar Bend

Day 17

Thursday, April 18

Wind early to light breeze to still 23°C

Each time I stirred during the night the sound of wind blustering through the trees troubled my return to sleep. There were no sounds of splintering or crashing fallen branches but there was plenty of creaking going on. The danger of giant gum branches plummeting to the ground—widow makers— will never be underestimated by anyone who has heard and survived that nightmare sound. Land may be cleared away from the river but closer to the bank trees grow tall and fall. Heeding advice from Lord Baden-Powell during my scouting days I preferred not to set tent under a gum tree. In this thick forest I had little choice. Correction, I had no choice. Broken branches and fallen trees had littered the ground all around me when I set tent. Nevertheless, the night winds conjured images of me waking in the morning as a two-dimensional (2D) image.

In between the branches creaking and hooting owls I had slept solidly. The mandatory footsteps crunching around the tent as I was drifting off was becoming the new normal. When rising from the kookaburra alarm, I investigated for prints. Expertly trained as a lad to discern tracks as depicted on the soles of my Bata Scout school shoes the prints around the tent did not correspond in size or shape. Platypus prints were entirely a different matter. Not to be duped by a water rat, which at 1.3 kilograms is roughly the same as a medium-sized platypus, I had learned to identify the presence of the large hind partly webbed footprints they left on sandy shores. Platypuses have more webbing on their front feet and tend to engage in knuckle-walking when on land. The webbing, which is boon for swimming, makes it virtually impossible for a platypus to grasp objects such as my rations...or ice-cream cones. But they are exceptionally determined creatures that have been known to propel themselves upwards like a giant inchworm to escape enclosures. To my knowledge tracks of the long-toothed platypus have never been found.

After I had dreamed of a platypus with sharp teeth rummaging through my gear bags at Howlong, I learned that the long toothed platypus (Obdurodon tharalkooschild) was a real thing. With teeth powerful enough to crush a small turtle, the prehistoric platypus swam through freshwater pools in Australian forests some 5 to 15 million years ago. I can only hypothesise that paddling along this ancient river has connected me to an innate ancient memory where one metre long platypuses roamed the earth. Carl Jung, the famous psychologist, theorised that we are born with the memories and experiences of our ancestors imprinted on our DNA. We can not necessarily unlock these memories, but it is possible that our most basic survival instincts, such as those I am awakening on this odyssey, might stem from a long time ago.

My plan was for an early get away to Torrumbarry Weir before the wake boats woke. Balancing on a thick slimy partly submerged branch, I slid the kayak down from the bank and entered the cockpit without incident. Small successes such as staying completely dry upon launch were immensely satisfying.

It was an overcast morning and the wind had now settled. The flow of the river was non-existent and if I stopped paddling, I would have literally stopped moving. No free hitchhikers today. Over the hour and fifteen minutes it took to close in on the weir, lush bush lined riverbanks that got lower. Really it was the water level, held up by the weir, which was rising. In the last kilometres before the weir, where a corkscrew shaped river doubled back on itself, the banks were only a metre or so above water level.

The river opened out to lake-sized proportions at the weir and in the near distance, a weird looking floating shemozzle caught my eye. I stopped to observe. The crazy ensemble consisted of a small camouflage army tent secured to three moulded-plastic kayaks that had been tied together.

There are two types of drifters on the Murray. Those who embark on a drift down the river in a fishing tinnie, are mostly self-sufficient and fish and camp while searching for the Big Murray cod; and Simon. I was hoping to meet the legendary 'Simon the Drifter', well known around these parts with a reputation bending towards a lateral thinking amateur philosopher who had opted for a life best described as 'hopeful'. Clamouring around his floating recycling station like a seasoned sailor he made a beeline towards me. Into a light breeze his overhead solar panel charged Ikea one horsepower outboard mower struggled to maintain direction, but he eventually pulled in close enough to bend my ear. Acknowledging a fellow 'adventurer' when he saw one, he shared his fish of the day recipe before unveiling details of his planned grand adventure: drifting the raft downriver, out of the mouth and across the Great Australian Bight before heading north to Broome on the north-west coast of Australia. He expected to be there by Spring, six months from now. Nearing 50 years old, after many years on the river he had only made it this far from Echuca. Not wanting to crush his dreams I reasoned that any procrastination that would see him remain in this beautiful part of the river could not be a bad thing. Did I receive any pearls of wisdom? Nothing that stuck.

The Torrumbarry weir was to be the most upstream of twenty six weirs and locks between the mouth of the Murray and the Port of Echuca, 80 kilometres upriver. When river trade diminished with the advent of railways, plans to build another thirteen weirs between Euston and Echuca were dropped. Now there are Locks 1 to 11 as well as Lock 15; Torrumbarry is Lock 26. No one I had met had been able to explain why the lock numbers had not returned to numerical order, and I had yet to come across anyone lost and searching for the missing ones. As luck would have it, Lock 26 was closed for repairs on account of an unexpected mechanical failure back in February. Out of options, I had to portage. Up 100 metres from the lock, I slid the kayak up onto the bank and went to find Scott, the Lockmaster. Not being in a larger craft with a loud horn I had phoned earlier to advise him of my expected arrival time. And a more jolly lockmaster you would not meet at 9.15am in the morning. Together, we lifted my small, insignificant red kayak, fully loaded, onto his trailer. After a short drive through the caravan park in his 4WD Toyota Landcruiser, we reached a boat ramp on the other side of the weir, and I was ready to roll. But before that I had some very important business to attend to; visiting the park's kiosk to stock up on batteries for my headlamp and purchasing replacement crackers for the turkeys Steve had bought me that were more suited to a dip—

the hummus type not a dip in the river. The visit also removed one more coffee and Mars bar from this world.

The operating weir and lock sounded like a waterfall, albeit a bogus one. The weir controls the amount of water being released downstream. They were originally built for economic reasons to maintain a regular water level for the all-important paddle steamers to transport wool, wood, and supplies along the river. Prior to their creation river hauling was seasonal with many craft being trapped high and dry until the break of the new season. Now the water is held for irrigation and surrounded with controversy by downriver irrigators desperate to ensure an equal share. Because any sane skipper does not want to boat over a waterfall, there must be a lock, a gravity fed chamber off to one side of the weir that allows slow incoming water from above the weir, to bring the water level below the weir, up. Sound simple? The exit gate then opens and if you happen to be in a kayak, you get shot out the other end like a child on a waterslide. All weirs on the Murray have locks, apart from Lake Hume and Lake Mulwala. At these locations continuous river travel is not possible without taking your craft out of the river and transporting it by road to the next available entry point, usually a nearby boat ramp.

As evidence to the broken lock two paddle steamers were moored 100 metres downstream from the weir. They had been waiting some months for it to reopen to enable their return to Echuca. Back underway, the river meandered between the Gunbower and the Perricoota State Forest but the landscape was in a different and odd mood. There was barely any flow to the river, almost as if it was confused somehow; a precious gem set in a tarnished crown. Without flow there was no wake to warn of the snags that were lurking. And so, the afternoon drifted most pleasantly with the banks returning to six metres high, the wind dying away, and the pleasant and metallic whistle of rosellas, on a river as still and as clear as glass. The banks were lush and healthy with vegetation and the inside bends flat and suitable for landing. Fisher folk in their tinnies tied to mid-river branches once again replaced the speed boats and their wakes.

Despite the river's lethargic flow, paddling was easy as I worked my way past Worthy Bend, Masters Bend, McKay Mill Bend, Dalley Ben, Long Bend, Mopoke Bend, Kate Malone Bend, Bonnemans Bend, Scotty Bend, and Halfway Bend until I reached my target of Sandbar Bend. I did not wish to chance a welcome at the next bend: Slaughter House Bend. A family had set a substantial camp on the bank and although I valued their privacy, I was all bended out and it was time to call it quits for the day.

'Permission to enter,' I called. 'It's been a long day.'

Campers John, Cheryl, Jayden and Herewini were so welcoming I was offered a campsite seat and a hot shower. Hot shower? This glamping business is really on the up. The family had commandeered this spacious landing three weeks earlier so that they and their guests could enjoy it over Easter. Many a hopeful camper had driven to the spot, only to turn away disappointed. There is something to be said for travelling light and sneaking on in with a kayak. The two lads were super polite and keen to hear of my adventures, adding that one day they hoped to paddle the Murray themselves. I kept the killer pig story to myself.

John and the lads were energetic fishermen. Bait was cheese cut into cubes and let to dry out overnight before being shaped into worms or other fish delicacies. All used fancy lures, many of which had been sourced from overhanging branches in the adjoining creek lost from lines snagged during higher water. John produced a picture of a 1.2 metre Murray River Cod that he had caught two nights earlier and an 80 centimetre cod he had caught the night before. A man of integrity and teaching by example, he had observed the fishing regulations and returned the fish back to the river. Only cod between 55cm and 75cm can be kept, and there is a strict two-fish bag limit. My observations so far suggested keeping a Murray Cod is sacrosanct and most fisher folk return them to the water regardless of size.

I took up the offer to use their fire for my food prep under more than lighting than cosmetic enhancements can disguise and before I was in danger of wearing out my welcome, retired to my tent. After checking for phone reception—zero—I got down to some starlight journal writing to the sweet sound of a 2-stroke generator.

Distance 1640 – 1592 48 kilometres
A pleasant day's paddle

Chapter 18

Sandbar Bend to Barham Mill Bend

Day 18

Good Friday, April 19

Calm conditions 28°C

During morning coffee with my adopted river family, John shared some memories of his younger years when hippies and folky guitar music frequented the river at Martins Bend near Berri, a town I would paddle past downriver. He phoned his mother who dutifully messaged a newspaper clipping from the 60s featuring a group of 'long-hairs' posing on a stone wall. The offer of bacon and eggs continued the trend of staring hunger in the face of a feast. Australians have an innate desire to extend happiness and goodwill and Easter is becoming another opportunity to celebrate friendship and happiness, regardless of religious allegiances. Wishing me a Happy Easter, the lads pushed me off into the river.

Downstream, piles of driftwood lodged against snags and fallen trees continually forced me to dodge and weave mid channel. After a solid 20 kilometres of paddling through the forests with only blue sky above, I searched for a pleasant place to rest. For another six kilometres the banks were still only suited to swamp wallabies, so I had to settle for a muddy gem. My routine and energy were best suited to a 20 kilometre first session when energy levels are high but one needs to be flexible. John Candy said in the film, *Planes, Trains, and Automobiles* 'Go with the flow, like a twig on the shoulder of a mighty stream'. Suits me!

Between the months of July and December, the flow of the river is usually greater implying that more kilometres can be covered daily. It is not unusual for paddlers to report reaching distances of up to 100 kilometres a day. My current pace suited me just fine. I do not startle the wildlife, I remain intrigued by the unique sounds in the bush, and I can watch for surface ripples formed when webbed-feet marsupials swim and dive.

The camping spots and clearings had become designated for occupation along this part of the river with every bend cleared and named. Today collection of tight bends included Nursery Bend 1, 2 and 3, Social Bend, Cemetery Bend, and a pink galah bend. For a species that is a dime a dozen at home, I had not seen many of the pink galahs in their 'real' natural habitat on the river. They were more relaxed in the less urban setting. Also watching me from the bank was a Swamp Wallaby (a.k.a. Black Wallaby), small, dark brown, and compact. Standing upright and perfectly still I am not sure if it was the same macropus following me down the river or whether there are many identical twins. Maybe not to their mothers but they all look alike to me. We live in close contact with our native wildlife yet rarely consider what an important part they play in our lives. A photograph captures the visual image but lacks the emotion. Fraught with obstacles over time, my memory is still the best tool to make my eyes tear-up. Around each tight bend an obstacle of a different kind came in the form of another fishing tinnie tied to a snag or overhanging branch. They, too, all looked the same to me.

'How're they biting today?' I could never resist casting about for a fishing pun, and most times came across a whopper! Sometimes they were reel.

'They only bite twice a day,' came the reply. 'Before we get here and after we leave.'

I kept asking, they kept replying, and it helped to pass the day.

I paddled on for 15 kilometres until the next break, again forced onto another clay landing, and then a further 10 kilometres in search of a campsite for the night. As I came to the end of the paddling day, the banks on the Victorian side all stood tall at four metres high. Breaking the skyline were Easter campers in tents and caravans with their tinnies moored in the river below. Gazing downriver, the country behind them appeared flat and desolate and it was anybody's guess where they got the wood for the fires they were all burning. The banks were so congested with Easter/ANZAC Day campers there was barely room for a politicians promise. I peered over to the New South Wales side through the smoke fog that now descended over the water. It was uninhabited so I slid into the clay bank with its forest backdrop just down from Barham Mill Bend. With the river only 20 metres wide, I became part of the campers' conversations. A radio with football commentary floated across the water. A radio would have made a handy addition to my kit.

After dragging Precious up onto solid ground, I unloaded and set camp. Getting water for dinner in the ankle-deep clay at the water's edge was less than inviting. Feeling rather precious myself and preferring to stay dry and mud free, I shimmied along a fallen tree bouncing along a branch way too thin. I stretched down as far as I could and when I could not possibly reach any further, the billy splashed the surface and filled halfway. While heating the soup on a fire of forest wood, a grizzled old fisherman cruised past slowly in a tinnie.

'Hey, mate! Do you drink beer?'

Momentarily startled, no doubt due to my recent lack of meaningful conversation, I hesitated in answering.

'DO YOU DRINK BEER?' he said again. 'I'VE GOT A NICE COLD BEER HERE IN THE ESKY IF YOU'D LIKE ONE.'

Lucky Lee! But... I had not drunk beer since 'the operation' and this, together with my unexplained refusal to accept offers of kindness, had me stammering back to his, and my, dismay.

'No thanks, I don't drink,' I said.

What in the world was I thinking! It was a warm balmy night. I had built a thirst strong enough to suck a cactus dry. Where did this, *I don't drink beer*, come from? Very generous, I thought. Very tempting, I thought. Why don't I drink beer, I thought? One beer would not have touched the sides, but I declined, preferring to remain true to my no beer policy as a cancer antagonist, particularly as I had been promoting prostate cancer awareness during the trip. He must have thought I was nuts. I reflected on this man after I reflected on the taste of beer and then reflected on my present condition. With my unkempt appearance, bushy beard, and knotted hair, I was no doubt an object of pity for my advanced age and shabby condition, yet I had seen him as a grizzled old cuss. How interesting life would be without mirrors.

I looked down to the hand that would have held the beer. Around my wrist was a silicon blue wristband. I had been given these bands to hand out along the journey. They carried a message aimed at prostate cancer awareness. Some short years ago I received the gift of prostate cancer resulting in a prostatectomy. Since then, cancer returned, with radiotherapy the next course to send it on its way. While this trip was not specifically a journey of passion, I attached an awareness tag to all social media posts: Pull your finger out and get tested. It was my way to encourage nature's most apathetic creatures: Men!

The tripod canvas chair had stayed remarkably in one piece. It is a thinking chair and I was still thinking about that beer. Then I got to thinking about the drinking culture of the fisher folk in their tinnies, many of whom need a coldie in one hand to balance the fishing rod in the other. Even though the majority had been mindful of the river conditions and speed restrictions, many would be over the limit, well over. Any danger would be mostly to themselves with virtually no-one else apart from me swimming in the water these days. I had not seen a cop for some time.

There was minimal breeze during the day and the heat had taken its toll. With no beer and a sore back, the tent was more inviting than usual for an early night. The sounds of the campers 20 metres opposite did not bother me as I lay in wait of sleep. What noise?

Distance 1592 – 1542 50 kilometres
Easy paddling during hot day

Chapter 19

Barham Mill Bend to Lucky Lee's Beach

Day 19

Easter Saturday, April 20

Calm with afternoon cloud clearing 33°C

The kookaburra alarm went off at 6.30am. I wanted to roll over and ignore it but the branches that poked through the ground-sheet into my back forced an end to an uncomfortable night. During my night of *peace*, a tinnie that sounded of the pricier type roared up and down the river. It was unusual to hear boat noise after dark as most boaties were content to sit back with the other fluid sort of tinny, presumably, to celebrate a day of catching *nothing*. But these particular boaties, who I suspected were under the influence of some type of substance, rocketed up and down in front of my campsite whooping and hollering. Campers on the opposite bank yelled at them to settle down. Eventually, to rapturous cheers, a loud thud signalled the boat had collided with the log that protruded from the river out from my campsite. The laboured noise from the motor and the silence of the revellers suggested they had limped away trying, I expect, to fabricate a good story to explain the damage. Kids will be kids but the boat owner would have needed a good sense of humour.

Breakfasted and packed, I slipped into clear river water before the ski boats and tinnies woke and attacked. So often the river was glassed out before the heat of the day brought the winds. Each of the 26 kilometres through the Gunbower State Forest was like travelling through a serene, four metre high framed wonderland. The forest was part of Gunbower Island, the largest inland island in Australia. It is bordered on one side by the Murray and on the other by the Gunbower Creek which left the river just below Torrumbarry, re-entering near Koondrook.

The 10 or so kilometres on the approach to Barham made for exciting paddling with multitudes of whirlpools and eddies spread over the expanse of the river. Like a cheeky teenager with too much energy, the river wound back and forth, adventurous, unpredictable, and unrelenting. And like dealing with a teenager, Ron Taffel wrote, 'it's not about letting go, it's about hanging on during a very bumpy ride'.

Approaching town, where houseboats lined the banks of the wide river, their kitchen smells of cooked bacon and eggs drifted under my nose. Downriver of the Koondrook wharf, on the Victorian side, Arbuthnot's sawmill was still operational unless someone had forgotten to turn off the machinery—unusual for an Easter Saturday. Started in the 1870s by Alexander Arbuthnot, rumour had it that Alexander was so committed to his work that he got married on the only day he would take off—Christmas Day! So maybe not so unusual.

One bend later, and in sight of the bridge, a broad white sandy beach and a boat ramp beckoned Precious in. The sand had the perfect comforting warmth, so I reclined back to enjoy the atmosphere of families laughing and playing and a few hopefuls dangling fishing rods in the shallows. It looked like a happy place.

I covered the solar panels and left the kayak to take care of itself. The more nautical miles covered, the more relaxed I was leaving the kayak unattended. So far, all the people visiting and living along the river had proved honest, relaxed, and friendly. The first thing I encountered when walking into town was a very Australian thong tree, presumably where thongs go to retire. Labelled, 'Thong Tree', it was covered with thongs (flip-flops for the non-Australians). There was no accompanying historical information, but it appeared to be the place where a single thong goes when it has lost its fellow thong. The quirkiness tickled me. Situated outside the caravan park entrance, the tree stood in a perfect location, given that thongs are standard caravan park and beach footwear.

Barham is a cute country town with three main streets, two supermarkets, two real estate agents and a pub that caters for the whim of every local and holidaymaker. It was an awesome place with an exciting buzz that exuded all the way from the river, through the reclaimed riverside parkland, and onto the streets where people gathered in rowdy excited groups. But the place to be was definitely The Barham Bakery. Self-control was not on the menu, and I had looked forward to this possibility of treats. Checking out the town was quick; just in case anything in the bakery ran out of stock. Not five minutes later a pasty and a coffee landed on my table. Okay, I have to admit it—I also had the blueberry pie. The owner visited my table with a genuine smile and a complimentary sticker: 'Barham-Koondrook ... The happiest place on the Murray'. I'm not sure who conducted the survey or the validity of the claim, but it was getting happier by the minute.

At the supermarket, with super-friendly staff, I topped up on soup, vegies, water, and protein bars. Across the way in the bottle shop, also with extra-jovial staff, I topped up with a cheeky a cask of shiraz. After an hour of so much happiness, I bought a postcard to send to my urologist, Alan Stapleton, so I could remind him that a man dealing with prostate cancer is bound by no shackles.

An hour after docking, I was back in the yak, feeling forlorn at having to farewell the happiest place on the river. Paddling a kayak now 10 kilograms heavier, I paddled towards the Barham-Koondrook Bridge. Built in 1904 for a smidge over £10,000, the bridge's mid-section lifts to allow log boats and paddle steamers through. I slipped by unnoticed. Unlike the imaginatively named Echuca-Moama Bridge, the lack of imagination on naming this bridge remains unresolved some 111 years later. Depending on which map you have, which side of the river you live on, and who you listen to, the bridge is either the Barham-Koondrook, the Koondrook-Barham, the Barham, or the Koondrook. In 1903, after local farmers kicked up a fuss about the rickety old punt causing damage to their sheep during the 100 metre voyage, the powers that be suggested a bridge would solve all ills. But the bickering between states about finance and contractors led to a type of one-upmanship over the name which has never been settled. Perhaps the local newspaper—the Koondrook-Barham Bridge Newspaper established in 1909—has had the final say.

I paddled under the bridge past the waterfront homes, party pontoons, and Tarzan ropes, feeling a little full in the stomach. Whirlpools and eddies persisted until I approached the Campbells Island State Forest where the river narrowed to little more than a creek. During my paddle with Peter Phillips in Echuca he had explained that water does not travel in a straight line and these circular effects that twist and turn are what creates the meanderings of the river. The speed of the river's flow then serves to accentuate the curves of the changing banks.

I blinked twice and yes, the gentlest of wakes disturbed the water, confirming two kayakers paddling along my same route.

I sped up for a chat. Francis and Sally, complete with their fancy kayaks and kit (yes, I was envious), were enjoying a 32 kilometre day trip from Barham to a designated hut at blue sign 1492. With a smile as sunny as the day, I thanked them for their company, wished them all the best, and continued along a creek-like river congested with fallen trees.

It was all very picturesque when I had time to look up and around. But added to a multitude of snags and puzzles, were the wakes of tinnies. Although the boaties politely reduced their speed as they passed, it escaped them that their wake, as with other motorboats, increased as they slowed down. If they had maintained their normal running speed the wakes would have been smaller, and I would not have been bouncing on a pogo stick.

Nine kilometres from Barham, the river traffic eased. The atmosphere cultivated a more ancient feel, and it was not too long before I suspected I had accidently followed a 27 kilometre anabranch known as The Little Murray River (New South Wales) that borders Campbells Island to the northeast. The flow increased as the riverbanks narrowed, and frequent bubbling waves indicated shallow water. I preferred to be on the Murray but here was no need for concern. The Little Murray re-joins the Murray proper downstream at Swan Hill. I did not need to look for swans.

After a morning of warm company and warmer coffee at the bakery, being alone was a salve, a chance for me to appreciate true serenity in this part of the river. A self-described people-person, it was in remote landscapes that I found the most joy and renewed my sense of wonder. This was where I felt in tune with the ebbs and flows of nature. Would this connectedness help raise an elusive and smiling platypus from the bank? The landscape must have resembled that of North Queensland's Riversleigh World Heritage Area where the largest species of platypus ever described was discovered. Was it such a stretch to believe I might make a similar discovery? In this ancient landscape, my mind easily imagined a stalking, carnivorous platypus with a penchant for large prey crossing me over into the realm of fantasy. Blue kilometre signs had vanished, campers had vanished. Across river, tunes from a banjo rang out.

Paddling back against this current to re-join the river proper was not going to happen. That familiar moment when I think I have taken the wrong road yet continue because somehow all roads lead to home, Rome or wherever took over my thoughts. And then, out of the blue, one of my guilty pleasures, the 1498 blue sign rose before me. I was still on the Murray proper. Amazing. The river had changed shape and appearance so often and was so different from my original expectations. It carried more possibilities than I ever imagined and presented challenges when least expected. It really was a calling card of adventure.

The blueberry pie was still in its last stages of digestion so the crackers of the afternoon break had offered no incentive to stop. Time rolled along slowly on this snaggly creek-river and before long the level of the sun under my hat suggested it was time to find a camp spot. Surprise! Surprise! The chart book had not shown the sandy beach that opened before me. Not being one to look a gift-cod in the mouth, I took advantage of rules granting camping in State Forests on the New South Wales side and slid in. The non-clay sandy beach was so unexpected, I named it, 'Lucky Lee's Beach', although I do not expect the name will stick. The 33°C heat of the day was developing into a warm balmy evening. Two pieces of dried mango later I sat on the beach happy with the day's work.

Behind the beach, the three metre high bank was an easy climb so I set the tent high and made the fire low on the beach. Judging by the slick buildings and the harmonised singing, a Christian group occupied the property over the river. A short time later, in another first for me, a group of young lads from the camp, beers in hand, put in on a landing opposite to float downstream—on inflatable pink flamingos. What a perfect way to enjoy a calm warm evening—pink flamingos, like swans, work in mysterious ways.

With the flamingos as inspiration, I stripped down and plunged into the river for a swim as Francis and Sally paddled by. Clearly exhausted, and with a broadening gap between them, the leader explained that she had another 45 minutes of paddling to go before reaching their destination. They were actually very close to the end of their mammoth day trip. The last blue sign read 1498 which meant they only had six kilometres to go. Until this point, the purpose of the kilometre signs had eluded them. This oversight, naivety, or poor river research can result in potentially dangerous situations for paddlers—so say the fun police. Approaching dusk, they paddled off hopeful to make their destination before dark. Their planned rendezvous dinner celebration back at Barmah would of course be happy, but likely a little quieter than anticipated.

I enjoyed an easy prep night of couscous topped with the broccoli I purchased in Barham. Who would have imagined broccoli could be so exciting? The flies did. For the first time, they showed up smacking their jaws and licking their lips. They were most unwelcome. A while later, mosquitoes also came to visit but extra-strength DEET repellent halted their mischief. As dusk arrived, kookaburras sang up a full performance supported by back-up singers of frogs and bugs that I hoped might also feast on my antagonists. What a wonderful day to be alive.

Distance 1542 – 1497 45 kilometres
A perfect day

Chapter 20

Lucky Lee's Beach to Funnel Bend Cove

Day 20

Easter Sunday, April 21

Overcast with a couple of raindrops and

occasional breeze 22°C

The kookaburra alarm call sounded at dawn. As soon as I hit snooze and rolled over an influx of screeching corellas, gifted no sweet voice from their maker, descended to make sure I had no lazy sleep-in. I poked my head out of the tent to speak with the complaints department but there was no-one in sight. Without another person to vent my disappointment, I had no choice but to get up and get on with it.

My routine had become tight. I woke up, dressed in paddling attire, scrunched up my sleeping bag, rolled up my flat mattress, and packed the tent. Then I took everything down to the kayak in preparation for a final stowaway after breakfast. With those tasks complete, I lit the Whisperlite stove, heated the billy for a coffee, and relaxed while I ate my muesli and prunes. The cooking gear was then washed with the left-over billy water and taken down to the kayak. After a final scan of my campsite, the kayak was packed and readied to launch. The weight was evenly distributed across the kayak holds and all the carry-ons had regular compartments. Stowed in the forward hatch for easy access was my mid-morning protein snack. My afternoon food got stashed in the small compartment behind my seat. The entire ritual still took an hour and a half, but it was becoming a lot easier with everything having its place.

When launch time came, conditions got a little breezy with ominous signs of rain. Within the confines of the high banks, the condition at water level was unaffected by the winds as I wandered along the meanderings. The hour was well before the fisher folk had risen and even before the local kids woke for their Easter egg hunt.

Paddling the first 10 kilometres of the day between the Campbells Island State Forest and a slim bank of gums on the Victorian side I reached Murrabit where the Little Murray re-joined the Murray from around the back of the island. Within two kilometres I was under the lift-span, Gonn Crossing Bridge, originally built in 1926 to cater for rail and road transport. As the river widened, glimpses of farmland opened behind a modest corridor of gums that lined the banks. The area is well known for its citrus production with the irrigation supply originating at Torrumbarry. Simon the Drifter came to mind and whether he had progressed past the Torrumbarry weir of if he was waiting for the lock to open. Meanwhile, the river opened wider and with the energy of a new morning I pressed on at a solid pace for another 12 kilometres before taking my first break.

Date palms had showed up in great numbers before Barham, dominating the banks and making it impossible for the native vegetation to compete. How could such a travesty correct itself without human intervention and when would it become serious enough to demand attention? Until now, I had only seen the palms on the New South Wales side of the river but knowing how easily their seeds disperse, it was inevitable they would proliferate along the Victoria banks. Management of their spread had been left in the hands of kangaroos that enjoy the sweet new leaf ends and, most likely, the dates themselves.

After my mid-morning break the river returned to creek-like proportions complete with requisite snaggles. Overall, the river became much straighter but as the current increased, whirlpools showed up when I swung around each bend. It was entertaining and rather than fight the rotating water I stopped paddling and let the nose of the kayak swing around. The whirlpools were usually gentle arcs but some of the bigger ones were more aggressive, with designs to flip the kayak. As more whirlpools passed, time inched closer to my afternoon break. The outside banks reached at least four metres and when cruising along to investigate the landing area of the inside bends, it was all uninviting soft clay. I chose to go without rather than take a dirty sticky stop.

A substantial junction running off to the Victorian side offered a choice of direction, but I reasoned correctly that the river would more likely follow the straighter path. Like the Little River Murray around Campbells Island earlier in the day, this Little Murray River anabranch also creates an island girt by water on the Victorian side. The indigenous Wemba Wemba name for the island is Pakaruk but it is more commonly known as Pental Island. Being so close to each other I would not want to be the pizza delivery person relying on the address stating Little Murray River (Victoria) or Little Murray River (New South Wales). The Victorian Little Murray is 46 kilometres long and at no point connects to its New South Wales namesake. The New South Wales-Victorian border, established in the 1850s, considered the complications brought on by anabranches that leave and return from their host river—as opposed to tributaries that originate from an independent source—determining that the border either side be set from where the Murray's water flow was at its strongest. Early last century Victorians proved to the Privy Council that there was more water flowing on the south side around Pental Island than the north and were awarded the land.

The forests that had dominated much of the landscape to date now suffered at the hands of encroaching agricultural incursion. The tracts of forest that would have provided sanctuary for flora and fauna were now long sparse corridors along the bank. Large expanses of land bordering the river from both sides now had been cleared for farming and while it was sad to leave the forest behind, the use of the land and water from the river for food production is valuable for its societal and economic benefits. But, as most of my journey had been like paddling in a cocoon down three or more metres below the banks, I remained unaware of much of the land away from the river and the magnitude of changes.

Despite the changes of terrain, the river from my position remained as breathtaking as always. As daylight began to fade, a natural cove at Funnel Bend featuring forest-like conditions was too good to be true. The beach was wide and flat with plenty of dry wood for a fire. But plenty of dry wood only occurs from plenty of fallen wood. With rain and winds expected, I scoured the beach and trekked deep into the scrub searching for a safe spot free from falling gum tree branches. There was no such clearing. Finally, I licked my finger and held it to the wind to gauge the direction the limbs might fall, then settled on a flat spot 30 metres inside the bank. Immediately I was accosted by the worst kind of walnut-size sticky burrs. A non-native, these pests planned to use me as a host to spread its seed across the country. Called the American burr by locals, it is more correctly identified as the infamous Bathurst Burr. Forward, back, and sideways, everywhere I stepped another blighter attached itself to me. I vowed from that moment I would hate them.

On the shore, a small comfort fire boiled the billy for the Tom Yum soup that had been a pre-dinner highlight each evening. With the large tin mug in hand, I devoted the time each evening to sit on my stool and rest and reflect on the events of the day. But today, surrounded by enough white feathers lying around to start a pillow factory, I questioned whether the original owner of the feathers or the beast that stripped them of its owner who would wake me in the morning. Choosing one of the larger feathers, I tucked it under a strap on the deck of Precious. To an onlooker this might be a little odd, but to me the feather symbolized freedom and acted as a token of life synonymous to the river. Along the way I had replaced the feather when a new one appeared at my various campsites.

A few raindrops fell over dinner and with the promise of it setting in I ate early and retired to the tent to write up my diary. All attempts to find a comfortable position to write were in vain. Painkillers had been off the menu during the day, but the hip pain flared up each night when crouching down to prepare dinner. There was nothing to do but endure the discomfort, yet I cursed the inconvenience and the possibility that it could continue throughout the whole odyssey. Apparently, journaling is the process of writing things down as a tool to relieve trauma. I journalled: I need to journal a whole lot more. The sound of plump raindrops drummed away on the tent and sleep came before the fall of anything else.

Distance 1497 – 1447 50 kilometres
Nice day, bit of a grind but got lost in time

Chapter 21

Funnel Bend Cove to Beveridge Island

Day 21

Easter Monday, April 22

Breezy early, overcast all day 20°C

I woke to the laugh of the kookaburras and leaped out of the tent before the corellas had a chance to unload their morning weaponry. My leap was met with an ambush by troops from the Bathurst Burr army. Those critters that crunch around my tent at night must have had a big laugh when they piled the burrs with their big heads and fine threads at the door of my tent. As I packed, I brushed down the sleeping bag, deflated airbed, spare clothes, and tent, careful not to drop anything on the ground—which I did again, and again, and again. The army were vigilant so eventually I surrendered and took everything down to the dry mudflat to wrap and roll.

Over breakfast, I inspected the banks for signs of the feather predator but with nothing visible it was obvious it has used a feather duster to cover its tracks.

As I paddled away, a light breeze delivered clean, cool air, devoid of campfire smoke or bacon. I did not know whether it was because the fisher folk had had a big Sunday night or because the fish were full of cheese and not taking baits. During the first two hours, the river and I were entirely alone while meandering through a passage of tall gums that obscured the farmed land beyond a 20 metre corridor. Gradually, people emerged from their tents but unlike the other days there was no waving as I passed. Was I an unexpected figment of their imagination or were they that disinterested? I suspected these campers were city people on their annual Easter camping trips and not yet engaged in the camaraderie shared by the seasoned caravanners and campers I had encountered to date along the river. To the seasoned traveller, I am me, I am them, and our journey is shared. To the city-bred Easter camper, I appear to be an 'other' and just another invisible old white male. The disturbing truth of being irrelevant to the point of being invisible to younger generations flashed before me. But the river deals in powerful magic. Through the meditative continuity of paddling these thoughts moved to a more authentic truth. As ego becomes hollow with age, the void is filled with an inner knowledge and strength far beyond the superficial. My fountain of youth has sprung a leak, but the river keeps running. Optimism? Without question for me, incomprehensible for some, but that is my way. I believe all humans are inherently optimistic. How else can we explain our choices in life to start risky business ventures, embark on daring adventures, or even get married when doomsayers and statistics so often propose caution.

The river changed constantly from narrow to wide back to narrow with towering banks still concealing me three metres below. Fallen trees and snags remained my constant companions. Those remaining upright at the edge of the bank denied erosion and sent their roots down in search of firmer ground.

Over time these root systems have become spectacularly exposed below their trunks descending fan-shaped and ending fixed and determined below the waterline. Giving the impression of an old man's beard (or woman's to be gender-neutral), it was as though I was being observed by wise elders as they imbued an aura of ancient wisdom over the cocoon in which I was paddling. Considering the great height and weight of the trees, it is a miracle they still hang onto the ground and stay upright. Of course, many have not, and instead formed part of my enchanting river navigation. Not to be denied, the fallen gum trees are extremely resilient with small branches sprouting upward from submerged trunks and limbs in a forlorn hope of survival.

Approaching another bend, a line appeared to be drawn across the landscape. In a blink, the trees and forests disappeared. The colour of the country turned red. I had reached The Mallee. This coincided with a new and unfamiliar sound. Irrigation pumps were droning away and drawing water into open channels in a sort of dark-age irrigation. Had we not progressed since ancient civilisations used aqueducts to provide water to fertile yet arid lands? Meanwhile, below the levees, below the land, I was oblivious to what these few pipes helped grow or how much water was being drawn for the purpose.

A sandy beach called me in after I paddled 18 kilometres through the morning session. Basking in the sunshine, I devoured a Growling Dog bar and washed it down with some tasty river water. No king could be more content. The flow had made paddling swift during the morning and even though the chart book indicated many areas of shallow riverbed it caused no issue for the kayak. Determining the best position across the river to take advantage of the flow had been continuously challenging and interesting. The stronger flows on the outside bends allowed for faster downstream paddling but it meant travelling a longer distance. Hugging the inside bends cut the distance shorter but greatly increased the chances of colliding with a log lying just under the surface. I followed the rules.

River lesson #49: Short cuts have consequences.

Back into the groove, over the next 20 kilometres I was entertained by huge carols of currawongs sweeping across the river. The large black birds darkened the sky, blotting out the horizon as they flew into the region for the approaching season. In the dreamy afternoon, an old rickety wooden jetty or, possibly, a disused bridge, rose from an anabranch that returned to the river from the New South Wales side. What and for whom did that serve? With the flow shunting me along too fast, I only caught a glimpse of it. The same thing happened when I was swept beneath a bird's nest—the likes of which I had never seen before—perched in the limb of single tree. The nest was decorated and smooth like the cup of a shiny dried gourd, but as usual I did not have the time, or the desire, to go through the rigmarole of removing my camera.

Arriving in view of the junction of the Murray and the mouth of the Marraboor River, the town of Swan Hill rose from the banks. This was the spot where I would have emerged if I had mistakenly taken the Victorian Little Murray River that encloses Pental Island with the Murray. As I paddled closer a monster crept around from the Marraboor and headed upriver as though we were to engage in some medieval dual. My steed was a kayak, my breastplate a padded life jacket, and my helmet a soft peaked hat. The reprobate that rose before me was the massive paddle steamer PS PYAP and growing intimidatingly larger with every rotation of its paddle wheel. In my mind I was Don Quixote facing the evil giants. I tucked my paddle under my arm. But unlike a battlefield, on the river, there are rules. And, as an observer of river rules, like passing a watercraft on the right hand side, I quickly directed my steed to the side of the river: the side that the Pyap was not! This monster creates a wake that stretches for a kilometre, stirring up hefty sized waves that I was in no mind to tackle. Could this monstrosity be the reason that the platypus—of which this part of the river was originally named—had left Matakupaat.

Standing on the bank with waves splashing against my legs, the PS Pyap looked dandy for its age. Built in 1896 in Mannum, a town downriver, and drawing less than a metre, it worked as a general store along parts of the river not accessible to heavier cargo craft. However, as many of the paddle steamers were apt to do, it spent some years at the bottom of the river before being resurrected in 1977 as a tourist craft that served hors d'oeuvres and wine to amongst others, Prince Charles of England (now King Charles III).

After the old girl passed and the water settled, I steered away from the bank to search for a spot to pull in for a wander around the town. No luck! Pushing along and around Goat Island that sits immediately downriver from the junction, a check of the caravan park on the inside channel also robbed me of an opening to pull-in. I opted to keep paddling. Moving under the Swan Hill-Murray River Road Bridge, which takes longer to say than it takes to travel over or under, I found a perfect rest stop within a kilometre at the James Belsar Reserve.

Throughout the Odyssey, I had developed many rituals such as how I prepared my snacks. A cracker is only to be spread with Vegemite or peanut butter, but never should they be mixed. I did this because, firstly, rations dictate prudence, and, secondly, I do not like the taste of both together. I had also become quite pedantic about the practice right down to the two spreads not being mixed on the knife. This was made easy because the Vegemite tube can be squeezed on direct. There is also an order to be observed. Two crackers with peanut butter to begin, then alternate between Vegemite and peanut butter until all six crackers were eaten. It was entirely possible my regimen verged on becoming anal, but my defence is that order

is key when embarking on a river adventure. Thomas Living-
stone Mitchell who camped here in 1836 did not name Swan
Hill through some hipster disorder and inattention to detail.
No, he named it Swan Hill because rowdy swans would not let
him sleep.

Back on the river, I made a big push for the afternoon. In
the distance, where the river widened, the bank on the New
South Wales side became totally white and bare. After rounding a final bend, the reason became obvious. One hundred or
so sheep followed each other to the water's edge to slake their
thirst.

Along the banks on both sides, trees grew in single file.
There was a certain sadness about the missing scrub, and
the fauna it would have once supported. The river remained
wide, and the chart book's promised beaches never eventuated. With options evaporating, I pulled into a dusty area just
short of Beveridge Island where a modern working-group hut
sat resplendent with all its mod-cons including solar panels,
water tanks and solid locks. Up behind the levee, barren dusty
fields stretched to the horizon. Known as the Swan Hill floodplains, the area has always been devoid of vegetation. Dry
wood, though, as always, was plentiful and in a flash the billy
was boiling, the tent was up, all sleeping gear laid out, and my
night clothes put on.

A platypus hole had been dug into the bank across the
river. I staked it out until my vision blurred but dusk passed
without luck. Then the noises began. While cooking dinner, a
loud grunt, no, a growl, or something in between came from
within a stone's throw. Loud and clear, there was trouble brewing. Taking the torch and my large knife, I crawled over the
bank mindful not to crackle a leaf or snap a twig. I anticipated
a koala objecting to my landing in its spot, or two angry platypuses discussing world domination, or worse, some yet to be
discovered mutant species of wild beast bred illegally out on

these dusty plains. But no, it was two possums getting it off in a cacophony of cavorting.

Of all the camp sites...

Distance 1447 – 1390 57 Kilometres
Easy travels

Chapter 22

Beveridge Island to Wood Wood

Day 22: Tuesday, April 23

Light breeze before calm. Overcast with a
few spots of rain 22°C

The kookaburras were perfectly on time and at 6.30am I opened my ears to their raucous laughter. After eating, drinking and all the other eventful morning chores, I peered over the levee bank and spied two people hard at it—work that is. I assume as they had not used the hut alongside me that they were property workers. Despite a few drops of overnight rain, which possibly only lasted for the half hour I stayed awake to hear them, everything was dry. I had hoped my packing routine would have got tighter over the weeks, but I still did not get away until eight-ish. Rather than fret, I embraced George Harrison's musing, 'Time is now. There is no past and there is no future'.

It all began as a perfect morning for paddling. There was a gentle breeze, the sky was overcast, but the air promised sunshine over the morning. Although paddling through an agricultural region there was little sound. I drifted the 500 metres to Beveridge Island, just taking it all in.

At the junction, the river turned right to run 13 kilometres around the island. To the left ran a cutting, a recognised short-cut, a shortcut the river will eventually use as its preferred path. The only concern in taking the more frequently used shortcut was snagging my rudder on the cables of a private punt that gave access to the island from the mainland. I had spent some time on the phone last night trying to contact the Hazlett family who lease the island and operate the punt, but poor reception made that futile. Afterwards, I had slapped myself for my false integrity of even considering taking the fastest or most convenient route. Murray agreed and rewarded me with the most serene paddle conditions as I set off around the island.

The less frequently used northern route was like stepping back in time. In a snapshot of past river life, old cars that refused to rust lay abandoned on levee banks, time worn water pumping stations housed olde-world pumps, and an old wooden ramshackle hut held strong as though one day it might be called back to service. It was as though I was travelling through a sepia dreamscape that could easily have inspired a Henry Lawson tale. This was the place to be: an April day when the water runs like glass, and where the lack of wind felt permanent as if it had been that way since Ngurunderi[1]created the whole shebang.

Rather than paddling with the usual morning adrenalin rush I continued at a slow steady pace to savour the moment. Not quite a dream but while rounding the top end the soft touch of a hand on my back and then an arm, my grandmother's arm, wrapped around my shoulders and gave me the gentlest of hugs. *Murray, Murray, Murray,* I whispered as tears welled in my eyes, remembering good and simpler times. I paddled on through the three metre banks and the requisite snaggles knowing that I, nature, and Beveridge Island were sharing this quiet moment with the pelicans, ducks, and white cormorants with all of us in no rush to be anywhere else. As the river knows their secrets, so it knows mine.

Out from the island the river opened out and within a kilometre the Speewa Ferry, the first and only punt outside of South Australia, trundled across in front of me. In continuous operation since 1914, the ferry, or punt—in Australia, the terms punt and ferry are interchangeable—looked dashingly modern. My terminological preference is that a punt will ferry me across the river but if some find that objectionable, I suggest a fun, three year course in linguistics. Preferences aside, 'ferry' is the name given along The Murray. The Speewa is government run ferry and it came and went as it does all day and I *'Veni, Vidi, Exivi'd'*. For those non-latin speaking folks, I came, I saw, I paddled on.

Light rain fell as I cruised through the box and red gum Vinifera State Forest, a favourite of weekenders and free campers. I emerged from the drizzle at Nyah—originally settled in 1890 as a utopian socialist community—and began searching for a rest site. There was little indication of the town from the river and as I passed under the Nyah Bridge it became evident the township had passed me by, or to be more linguistically precise, I had passed it by.

Two kilometres downriver from Nyah, I pulled into a beach of past indiscretions, a sandy beach named Gallows Bend. With my eyes peeled for bushrangers or troopers 1, 2, 3, or at least some pretty hairy paddling conditions, my morning snack went down quickly. I set back out through the Nyah State Forest, a virtual continuation of the Vinifera State Forest.

The overall direction of the river through New South Wales and Victoria runs in a north-westerly direction. One advantage of this is that the fast moving bad weather usually originates in the west. While I was yet to experience anything of concern, I posited that the faster I paddled the quicker the bad weather would pass. Conversely, sunny weather moves along more slowly, due most likely to Pythagoras' theorem, or someone of a similar ilk and if I was a meteorologist, a mathematician, and a musician, I could explain it better.

River lesson #23: Paddle fast into the wind

To my knowledge I have no direct lineage to botanist Joseph Banks but the healthy new tree growth at three different heights along the banks at water level indicated germination over each of the past three years. That this sparse and spindly forest could regenerate so efficiently augured well for the health of the river. In an ever-changing and adapting river, how would these mere saplings endure a return to high water which would have some of them submerged? Sam Cooke's song—*Change is gonna come*—calls for a change for the better. I sang my way through the forest in hope and expected it would do no harm for the kookaburras to learn a new tune.

I was wrong to think the irrigation pumps were only a few. Their presence and humming were endless and relentless. As one ended, another began. Eight kilometres upriver from Nyah stands a monument to Jo Takasuka, a Japanese immigrant who battled against the government of the day to start a rice plantation on the flood plains surrounding the region. Established in 1906, the plantation continued operations until 1928 when it ultimately proved unsuccessful. What legacy did that leave for the current farming of water-thirsty crops of rice and cotton, products that can be sourced cheaply from overseas and which have put a drain on the Murray-Darling basin?

Flying close to the kayak, I could have reached out and touched three inquisitive and colourful parrots, lorikeets, or cockatiels. I could not pick the difference between them—as Steve Irwin I am also not—but when admiring these colourful birds and listening to their unique calls I became aware I had lost focus on the hunt for the elusive platypus. A little upstream, where the river contorted and almost cut back on itself, I homed in on what I suspected was a platypus hole in the bank. Immediately after, I paddled past a white and brown log floating in the middle of the river. Informed by learned men upriver that platypuses disguise themselves as logs to avoid detection, I turned ship and headed back 200 metres to observe the suspect. Aha, the platypus laid motionless, suspiciously maintaining its disguise as a log. I slid up to it carefully and, so as not to cause damage or embarrassment, gave it a little prod. I was not really surprised when it turned out to be...a log.

The medium width river served up plenty of bends and turns, and a myriad of snags kept my full concentration. The current ran quickly over the shallower parts and the whirlpools and strong back eddies turned on me with attitude. Every so often, I ventured too close to the inside bank resulting in a bump under the hull as I cruised over an underwater log.

River lesson #77: Just because I can't see it, doesn't mean it won't rock your boat.

My daily plan had been to travel 20 kilometres between the first two rest stops leaving only 10 kilometres to find a campsite during the final session. I took the second break of the day to reenergise before making the final charge for the day. Today's distances were spot on. This deserted sandy beach was flat enough to cruise onto and enjoy the luxury of stepping dry from the cockpit. With a belly full of crackers, I aimed to paddle the nine kilometres to Wood Wood where I could and should and would stop at the caravan park for a comprehensive clean-up. There would also be power points to recharge the external power backup for my phone to cover the shortfall from the solar panel.

I pulled up for a chat alongside a young couple in a tinnie out on a romantic fishing afternoon, but otherwise I had remained pretty much invisible. Had they caught anything? Of course not, and they did not care. Being the day after Easter, the lack of people fishing, camping, and boating was surprising. It was as though the holidays were over for the year, yet the Anzac Day long weekend was just three days away. It suited me: no boats to *wake* me either morning or daytime.

Dreamily paddling along through high banks with tall gums both the township and caravan park of Wood Wood passed by unnoticed, as did the Kulki Kulki Scout Camp nearby. Any ideas relating to a delicious carnivorous dinner and a good scrub and tidy up were dashed-dashed.

Five kilometres past Wood Wood I steered the kayak onto a deserted sandy beach. As I set up the tent, I congratulated myself on being ahead of schedule with a generous afternoon rest to come. It was already 4pm. The reduction of daylight hours at this time of the year was subtle and, with less than two months before the winter solstice, the shortest day of the year, clock time on the trip was less important than hours of daylight. Because I did not intend to paddle by night and set up camp in the darkness, the time to end the day's paddling became determined by the setting angle of the sun.

My campsite sat at a spot close to where the Murray Valley Highway followed the river. The foreign sound of traffic hummed in the background. Distances on the river were almost three times those by road so the 73 kilometres I had paddled over two days, since Swan Hill where my courageous battle with the Pyap took place, was only 35 kilometres away by road. After being isolated and away from suburbia for so long, the disturbance of traffic to ears that had only listened to birds and fake platypuses, was one I would be happy leave behind when the river went bush again.

After the standard post-paddle reward of two pieces of mango, nature provided the ideal conditions for a river swim. My earlier plan to bathe, wash clothes and have a general tidy-up was refreshingly executed. Soup led the dinner courses with a treat being fried chips with salt as the *pièce de résistance*. The main was a base of couscous with chilli, cumin, onion, and carrot. Despite these lavish feasts night after night, the looseness of my clothes confirmed I had lost a lot of weight after only three weeks.

On top of the levee bank, I had enough phone reception to pay my monthly accounts and deal with some necessary chores. Before bed I checked my solar battery only to find it had been incorrectly plugged for the last two days. I only admit this because I am embarking on a tell-all story. I am in no doubt that many elements of my tale may seriously disturb some readers.

A constant thorn in my side was the neoprene boots I wore for paddling. Designed to keep my feet dry and warm, the issue was that nearly every time I got in and out of the kayak I had to step in water. Regardless of the design of the boots, my feet remained soaked all day. Therefore, during the warmth of each midday, I had to remove the boots and tie them to the deck so that they and my feet could dry. Damp feet led to a lurking fungal infection between the toes. Fortunately, tea tree oil held the infection at bay, but the continual pressing of my cold, wet feet on the kayak's steering pads had created a numbness of my toes. Warming my feet by the campfire relieved the numbness. These were neither injury nor impediment and, other than my residual hip problem, my body remained strong and in peak health.

Distance 1390 – 1337 53 kilometres
Casual day

[1] The ancestral Dreaming of Ngurunderi from the Ngarrind-jeri people recounts the establishment of the River Murray from its beginning.

Chapter 23

Wood Wood to Gundagai Bend

Day 23

Wednesday, April 24

Overcast, settling to cloudy 26°C

'Good morning,' I yelled to my feathered alarm clock from inside the tent. Before dawn, and 10 minutes before I wanted to wake, surely *they* would appreciate the early call for a change. They saw the funny side of it. I rolled up, ate up, packed up, took my seat, and slid into the water by 8am. According to the weather forecast it was sunny, but the overcast sky told me otherwise. If you subscribe to personal auras, today's colours of my intuitive plane were shifting from bright happy reds and oranges to more challenging browns and greys. There had to be rain coming and I suspected that would not be the worst of it. This morning's attire included a rain jacket.

The river coiled and turned in all directions and, while paddling was easy, the twisting river brought on whirlpools, tricky, aggressive, rotating bodies of water that required my full attention. Bubbles and flotsam helped determine which way the whirlpool was spinning so I could ride the side current and slingshot right on by. Other times I threw myself straight in, trusting my momentum would see me through. There were plenty of wobbles and paddle slaps to maintain balance. Watching the shenanigans from the bank was a little brown euro. Standing perfectly upright I could have mistaken him for a statue, apart from the way he disparagingly shook his head. Was that for my benefit or with rain on the horizon was he thinking about the '56 flood?

In between whirlpools, I glided slowly to the tapping of Crimson Rosellas pecking out new nesting holes in the stumps left by fallen branches. The melodic bell-like song of those already housed in their cave-like abode rang out as though in encouragement. Male swallows, identified by their long tail feathers, darted across the river in front of me feasting on a morning smorgasbord of bugs. The females, in hot pursuit, joined the speedy manoeuvres with uncanny synchronisation as though it was practised choreography. I called morning greetings to my river friends.

Near the 1334 kilometre marker and with an unyielding attitude, I paddled past the opening of the 700 metre short-cut that bypassed Murphy's Island. I hoped the longer four kilometre route would reveal a similar epiphany to yesterday's Beveridge Island circumnavigation. Possibly dampened by the light rain, the sepia daydream failed to realise. 'No man ever steps in the same river twice,' said Greek philosopher Heraclitus, 'for it's not the same river and he's not the same man.' The long route appeared as majestic as yesterday, but the river and I had marched on.

Meandering a further 17 kilometres I cruised down the long reach toward Tooleybuc, pronounced Tooleybuc for the uninitiated, with solid raindrops gently falling. I powered under the bridge and around the bend to the town's boat ramp. As usual, the town was barely visible from my low point in the river, but to be fair it did sit on a bank 15 metres above the waterline. I pulled Precious up onto a nice grassy bank alongside a concrete ramp which promised seclusion and safety from interference and set off on a 300 metre skip into the town. I wanted treats, I deserved treats, and I was going to have treats.

'Nice day,' I said, quite genuinely to a couple sitting on their veranda.

'Yeh,' said the man while digging into a scone, or muffin or some treat that he could have very soon be killed for. 'I w'z walkin' the dog n saw ya come down in the rain.'

And that was that. The end of the conversation with the remaining portions of his morning tea taking priority. Economical with words out here!

The wee town consisted of a pub, a general store, and a newsagent. Despite the pain, I needed to get my legs moving. With the majority of my day spent sitting in the kayak, I had become conscious that a lack of leg exercise might have a residual effect down the track. I took the one minute walk around town before a raid on the general store.

Having not long left Barham, the happiest town along the river, the grumpy couple running the store were a bit of a shock, for me as a customer and probably for them in having a customer. With the nearby Mallee region being considered as Australia's second happiest place to live, what possessed a couple with such a disposition to live here. Surely there were other more suited occupations—woodchoppers or morticians —not requiring such dazzling charismas. And, at the prices they were charging they should have been 'happy as Larry': a ballpoint pen was four dollars. The hamburger, chip, and coffee machines had not even been turned on. Engrossed in my own schedule I forgot the time was only 9.30am. Obligingly, and possibly because I was now sporting the unkempt look of a bushranger, they came good with my requests.

The town was quiet; they must have been saving their conversation for something! The sky slowly cleared as I took a seat, observing Tooleybuc life from under the store's veranda while watching foot traffic file in and out of the newsagent. Next door, the pub was open and even more surprising was the traffic *it* was generating through the front door. The timing was way out once again for Lucky Lee. The town's phone reception was good, so I updated my status on social media to advise friends of my last port of call should I be lost forever in a whirlpool.

Across the road the old bridge I had passed under intrigued me. It is only wide enough for two small cars to pass—that is, two matchbox cars—despite it being part of a major connecting highway between Sydney and Melbourne. The many trucks that pass through, like paddle steamers, assume complete right of way. I watched as the locals waited patiently, treating it as a one-way road, while the touring caravaners hovered in trepidation. The unoccupied bridge-keepers cottage provided no assistance. The heritage-listed lift-span bridge was built in 1925, presumably for foot traffic and horses, and enjoys the fancy name of Tooleybuc Bridge over Murray River. The New South Wales Department of Public Works had the foresight to give it a name to identify its location should another Tooleybuc appear requiring a bridge, yet they could not foresee a time when two vehicles, let alone two horses with carts would want to cross at the same time. It is no surprise this was the final lift-span bridge to be built of the 583 bridges designed by Percy Allan. Plans are underway, even as my hamburger sizzled, for a replacement bridge to be built. Seeing as though the planning and development had been in progress for four years to reach this stage of stagnation, I hoped the general store was not waiting on deliveries from the Victorian side. Then, on cue, out came my treats. Any compliments I could make would be an understatement and if I could have packed-up another tri-serve to go I would have. The seagulls in attendance, some 500 kilometres from the sea, should have given me a clue. All General Store criticisms withdrawn.

Over the feast it was critical to spend some time studying *The Chart Book* with the next section of river expected to be at best, difficult. A 150 metre section of river 16 kilometres downstream known as Bitch and Pups consisted of two or three mid-river islands—the biggest of the islands the Bitch and two of the smaller being the Pups. The fast-flowing rapids that pelted across the shallow water often made the river impassable, and the snags made safe passage a maybe. Many a craft had come unstuck over the hundred-plus years of river travel; one being from back in 1964 when the Oscar W towed the Gem to Swan Hill only for the boats to be stranded there for eight months. Seeking advice, some ominous, *'hmmms'* and a *'might be tricky'* from the locals provided no confidence for safe passage. After the pickle of Day 1 the prospects of exposed strainers, snags and fast flowing channels sounded menacing. A plan was essential.

The plan conceived was to stop at the marked sandy beach just before the trickiest section. There I could use my afternoon break to investigate the lay of the land and river. If the pass was too risky, and providing the banks were accessible, I planned to set up my kayak trolley and portage around the entire 500 metre area. Simple, sensible, and only slightly speculative.

With a sound plan, a satiated belly, and an obliging river, I paddled along at a reasonable pace between banks that ranging from eight to twelve metres high. Compared to the approach into town, this part of the river was relatively straight, but that did not stop it from throwing in a fair share of overzealous whirlpools. I kept my eyes peeled for blue kilometre signs to judge my distance from 'the Bitch'. They fell short of expectations, like so many other sections along the river, where the blue signs were either non-existent or no longer in the place they should be. The banks started to close in on me. The flow and the number of snags increased. Rippling waves across shallow riverbeds ruptured the surface. I expected I was making good time over the kilometres but with whirlpools swinging the kayak viciously back and forth I just held on. The beach for the rest and exploration must be getting close. Leaning into a 180 degree bend, I was suddenly rocketing towards two islands that rose from the depths like the growling Cerberus. Exposed rocks signalled a shallow underlying reef spanning most of the river away to the left of the first island. At break-speed, I catapulted the kayak towards a narrow channel on the outside bend. A fallen tree suddenly appeared on the surface, and in swirling waters I had just enough time to dodge its branches and swing the kayak into the channel. A large bank loomed. *Deja vu!* I pushed hard, dug my paddle into the rushing water and swung around. The bank wall emerged right in my face, but thankfully without strainers. I shot out of the channel. Within 30 metres the second island rushed at me. I needed to skirt the island on the right hand side again but I could see it was completely blocked with fallen trees. I had no choice but to ignore the chart book's advice, make a snap switch in direction, and slide across the river to the shallow side. Precious took the command and swung hard around, avoiding the island but flying toward the shallow reef. Staying close to the island the kayak stayed true through a narrow gap between island and rocks and then settled. I figuratively scratched my head. *'What the ...'.* With a few deep breaths my composure returned. Then in a vision of blue, I turned the next bend and the numbers 1 3 0 2 emerged to my right. I had missed the sandy beach and paddled straight through the Bitch and Pups. Yahoo!

A wicked example of dry Aussie humour resides at the settlement of Goodnight situated right behind sign 1302. It was named because a farm worker who camped near the bend just after Bitch and Pups would call out 'goodnight' to those on the passing steamers, no matter what time of day. Considering the maze of tangled snags that made travel in low water so dangerous, many of his ominous calls would have come to sorry fruition.

The river settled into a new phase, like that of a teenager now reaching their twenties. Their life was settling but accompanied by plenty of unexpected turns. The sun broke through and euros gathered to wave me along with their little arms. Sections were straighter for longer but interspersed with 180 degree bends and rock ledges on both left and right. In some areas, the odd shallow sections attempted to form a reef resembling submerged icebergs. Humming water pumps broke the natural sounds and rhythm of the river, and tall redgums loomed on the banks.

At around 4pm I began searching for a campsite, passing a couple of small sandy beaches that were already occupied by campers. Running out of time, I pulled onto a mud flat that skirted another occupied sandy beach. To be polite I wandered down to alert the neighbours of my presence and even though their fire smouldered away, there was no-one within *coo-ee*. All their camping gear sat unattended. This had been a common occurrence along the river; campers would leave their camp sometimes for days in the knowledge it would be untouched when they returned.

On dusk, a young couple with their child rolled down the dusty track in a 4WD truck. I strolled back to their campsite and stood chatting to the husband and daughter. The family had been out for a pig hunting afternoon. It resolved the question of what had made the strange grunting noises that wafted across the river as I set camp, dashing my image of a feral long-toothed platypus in search of prey. Over by the food preparation area of their campsite, his partner was oiling and stuffing a chicken in preparation for dinner. When finished she brought it over to the fire wrapped in a cloth.

'This is little Chloe,' she said, proudly presenting her six month old baby. 'Our latest.'

Before I had the chance to gasp in surprise, a series of menacing growls and barks erupted from a cage on the back of the truck. I turned my head to the truck and back to the husband in a single movement.

'Just pig dogs,' he said nonchalantly. 'Cage is locked.'

'You mean you let them out later?' I asked, trying to sound pig-worldly.

'Nah, mate. They stay locked up for the night.'

On cue, another dog ambled up from behind to sniff my leg. As I returned to earth the husband pre-empted my next question.

'He's just our pet. He's alright.'

I left them and the canine security system to their fire and roast chicken.

Settling down in front of my small fire on the water's edge, I enjoyed a hot cup of soup—I was still full from breakfast—before heading up to where I had perched my tent on top of the three metre high levee bank. My personal aura had proved right. The day was filled with mixed emotions, —apprehension, fear, relief, and joy—but it had turned out well. In my experience, worry had never resolved anything that had yet to happen.

Checking back over the chart book the Bitch and Pup islands should have been taken on the wide side instead of in the channels. This simple mistake could have exposed me to real danger. As a lone traveller, I accept a certain element of risk but it was imperative that I did not allow anxiety to cloud my attention to detail.

I did not actually check but I knew, or I thought I knew, the dog cages were securely fastened. I slept with one ear open and hoped there would be no scrunching footsteps around the tent during the night. Sleep came quickly as dreams wandered through images of pigs, bitches, pups, dogs, chickens ...

Distance 1337 – 1291 46 kilometres
Nervous paddling with heavy concentration

Chapter 24

Gundagai Bend to The Wreck of Little Ruby

Day 24

Thursday, April 25

ANZAC Day

Blue sky and calm 26°C

The pig hunters stood like a picture, side by side, mother with babe in arms, and a little one holding her dad's leg. With a heavy sigh, I thanked the skies that I did not get ravaged by hunting dogs during the night. With little chance of critters wanting to roam within sight and smell of these professionals—I did not actually get to see how many professionals were stacked in the cage—the night had passed without a sound.

The family waved me away as I went through the usual routine of backing out in the kayak. Short of aplomb, my preferred motion was to step dry into the kayak, so as not to get my neoprene boots wet, then ungracefully shove my back against the back seat-rest of the cockpit to jerk the kayak backwards shove by shove until it slipped slowly into the water. It does the hull no good, but it always makes me laugh at the foolishness of it all. Exiting is usually a dryer event as opposed to the pull-in to banks that require a step out into various depths of water. It was a perfect day for paddling with a goal to travel 49 kilometres downstream to reach the intersection of the Murrumbidgee River by late afternoon.

Reaching down from the levee bank, a bank of pipes slurped and gurgled while drawing up what sounded like more water than is being allowed to travel down into South Australia. Typical of what I had seen of late, these were no ordinary hose-sized pipes, but closer to the circumference of a car wheel.

Before I managed to develop my first bead of sweat or check for dogs and snakes in the cockpit, I came across a kayak parked on the riverbank along a section of native forest. I stopped to see if anyone was nearby and, after calling, a head rose from next to a smoky fire. A young lass called me in. I was pleased for the opportunity of company and, after a brief introduction, discovered she had not had company since arriving four days ago. The mountain of ashes contained in the rock circle of her fire pit looked all of four days' worth. But the oddity was, there was nothing next to the fire apart from a lightweight shawl, a metal mug, and the barest of rations. This was the opposite of glamping with not even a tent in sight. The weather had been mild during her campout so life under the stars would have at least been comfortable(ish).

'Before I came here,' she explained. 'I met a lovely old woman and her husband in Tooleybuc who invited me in for a cup of tea.'

I suspected the older couple were my age.

'They were so happy when I offered to cook dinner for them,' she recalled with a smile. 'We walked down to the shop and got all the food I needed.'

'You wouldn't have found much in that general store,' I put in. But this was a girl who can see past obstacles.

'What they didn't have, I made up for in the pantry at Anne and Bob's house.'

I waited for the punchline.

'They were so nice and loved me being there. So, I stayed for four days.'

There it was.

Melody is 33, from Zimbabwe, of English descent, and trusts on the generosity of the world to oversee her survival. Friends that she had called on for money or help to support this world lifestyle were, however, ever-diminishing. As an artist, the tools in her metaphorical kitbag helped her to generate income when needed by producing art that she sells at markets. The problem, which was no problem to her, was the metaphorical kitbag contained only metaphorical paint and brushes because she gave the real ones away. As we enjoyed one of my coffee bags, as if to confirm the existence of a benevolent universe, a local fisherman slid his tinnie onto the bank with a bagful of food to wish her well. He also unloaded a piece of valuable local knowledge.

Typical of this time of the year, the flow of the river increases because of the surge of water being released from dams upriver. This extra water is used to meet the demands of an annual 'post-Easter' irrigation splurge. Surge. Increased Flow. Irrigation splurge. I had not seen that in the newsletter. My mind sped back to the Bitch and Pups.

Melody's company was easy, the sun was shining, and there were repairs to be made on the kayak, so with a welcome invitation I pulled up stumps for the day. Until then, I had not given myself permission for a day off in the sun to relax beside the river. The idleness grated but the pangs of guilt to not be lazy and get back in the kayak slowly dissipated. Melody and I continued with our own pursuits for the day, swapping stories as our paths crossed. Her kayak, a Seabird Expedition similar to mine but built of poly material, needed some small repairs that took all of 15 minutes to complete.

'Where did you get this sweet ride?' I asked.

'Farmers always have toys hanging around,' she said. 'I just knocked on a farmhouse door.'

In Swan Hill, with only a few dollars left in her pocket, it struck her that a venture down the Murray would be fun. Her farmer dragged it out from under a blanket of leaves and relieved her of those few dollars. What she now had in her possession was a kayak and a paddle—no life jacket, hat, water bottle or anything else I considered in my materialistic world as essential. I accepted my 'essentials' were leaning toward luxury in comparison, but Melody's lack of kit was flirting with danger. On the positive side, her kayak was far lighter than mine for portaging and paddling.

'The stars are so nice at night,' said Melody during one of our passings.

The elocution of English educated southern Africans is so correct.

'One night I paddled into one of those whirlpools and must have fallen asleep. I think I had been going around and around for an hour before I woke up.'

The little voice on my shoulder piped up. 'Get me out of here while I'm still sane.' But it was overpowered by the little voice on the other shoulder saying, 'Listen, boy... this is what go with the flow is really about'.

The bank across the river was too high to ascertain what was behind it but by the lack of natural vegetation we expected it bordered a farming property. A massive bank of pipes, each with a radius easily large enough to suck up an unaware kangaroo out for a quick dip suggested it grew water thirsty produce. At a whim, Melody paddled across river to investigate the farm. While she was gone, I set up table on a large fallen tree to catch up on some writing. The tree's limbs reached into the river where I could sit and dangle my feet in the water. A light refreshing breeze kept the flies at bay. Serenity ruled. That was until petrol fumes indicated the approach of a tinnie and a group of grizzled men who set up camp on the opposite bank! Of all the lonely vacant spots, what were the chances they would park directly opposite, only 20 metres away. This being Anzac Day, the *fsst* of the beer tops opening was natural regardless of the time of day and every bit as natural as the radio hissing as it was being tuned into the annual Anzac Day Aussie Rules clash between Essendon and Collingwood. Not invasive, I heard only enough to know it was a close and exciting game.

The afternoon moved along as gently as the river. Everyone must have been Easter'd out because there was not another soul on the river. Embracing the spirit of the afternoon, and with that little voice reminding me to 'go with the flow,' I strolled upriver to a sandy beach, waded into the clear water and with the aid of the current, lazily floated downstream. Where was an inflatable pink flamingo when you needed one? The water and weather were warm but after a couple of floats images of an innocent kangaroo being sucked into the irrigation pipe followed by a nasty tube ride gave me the creeps. The pumps were off and even though Bob Dylan advised, 'The pump don't work cause the vandals took the handles' They were electric and did not need a handle to spring into action. I retreated back to my log.

Peering across to where the pumps speared into the river, I looked for signs of the PS Little Ruby—not to be confused with the much larger PS Ruby still in service today—that ended its final voyage right in this spot a hundred or so years ago. There were no signs of the 'old girl'. Many a paddle steamer has been drawn from the riverbed over the years, preserved within the river water before undergoing a complete historical restoration.

The shallowness and the narrowness of the river in this section would make Little Ruby's resurrection unlikely.

Two hours after her journey into the unknown Melody returned loaded up with apples, oranges, lemons, and ... a bunch of flowers. She then unearthed the other boon of ingredients that had been delivered earlier by her friend in the tinnie— eggs, tomatoes, and a variety of vegetables—none of which needed to be saved for tomorrow.

'I'm cooking dinner for us,' she offered.

As she sprinkled my contribution of cumin, chilli, and garlic, I offered to help by fetching my cutting knife.

'No need,' she said, and with a flamboyant swing of her arm, withdrew a long, gleaming hatchet from under her shawl on which we were sitting.

'That should do the job,' I said with eyebrows raised.

'It's useful for so many things,' she said, without the slightest hint of menace. 'Makes me feel safe, too.'

During the process of cooking, Melody became distracted many times. Finally, she managed to set my wooden spoon alight. But that was no problem of course, wooden spoons grow on trees.

'Noooo problem!!!' she said.

With the hatchet in reach, there was no argument from me.

After a delicious feast, I called it an early night and prepared to head off to my tent. Melody, dressed only in a loose-fitting singlet and sheer wrap-around, settled on her shawl alongside the glowing fire, with hatchet tucked underneath. With honourable intentions, I extended an offer for her to share the warmth and comfort of the tent, but she declined. The proposal did come with the offer that she could lay the hatchet between our two sleeping bodies.

The night turned extremely chilly, and I struggled against the cold. Even in my -4°C sleeping bag, I had a restless sleep. When I poked my head from the tent at around 4am, Melody laid fast asleep at the edge of the fire pit. The faint glow from the last of the coals would soon be no more.

Distance 1291 – 1288 3 kilometres
Day off

Chapter 25

Wreck of Little Ruby
to Silver Beach

Day 25

Friday, April 26

Windy and gusty 20°C

At the crack of dawn beneath a sky of fading stars, Melody slept soundly wrapped only in her lightweight shawl. The fire had done its dash and exhaled the faintest single twirl of smoke. After adding a couple of logs the previous four days of coals recharged it back to life. I boiled the billy then sat with a coffee as my host slowly rose for the day. The rug in which she was wrapped was barely more than a scarf and after days by the fire it sported any number of burn holes. She offered no complaint about the chilly night.

While we ate breakfast, Melody unveiled her paddling plans. They resembled something like a dream she had last night, yet I would not underestimate her capabilities.

'I was going to paddle to Mildura then stop,' she said. 'But I have been thinking now of going all the way to the mouth.'

'I'll have a fire ready for you in my backyard when you arrive,' I replied.

A cold breeze fanned the flames but warned of an approaching change. Melody's plans of continuing to Mildura 400 kilometres would be testing. And worse, considering the change of season and her meagre 'essentials', if she persisted in her quest to travel another 1,300 kilometres to Goolwa, her journey might not end well. However far-fetched her plans were, I expected she would still outpace Simon the Drifter.

She said she might leave today... or maybe not. I left her with my jar of Vegemite, which she had taken to, as well as some food and spice. In return, she handed me a bag of fresh apples, oranges, and lemons. I offered her the use of my phone so that she could contact her mother in England, but she declined saying, 'My mother has to learn to stand on her own two feet and not be so needy'.

The breeze that had sprung up showed no signs of abating. The sky had clouded up, but my now intimate knowledge of the river told me the day would clear. Three kilometres downriver I approached a T-junction with both left and right equally inviting. Without reception to check Google Maps and the charts carefully tucked out of reach, I flipped a coin and paddled to the right for 50 metres. It soon became obvious the flow was pushing back in the direction I had come from. The Wakool River was easy to mistake for the Murray. When in flood it carries more water over its 363 kilometre length than the Murray. In contrast, the Wee Wee creek I passed shortly after posed no directional ambiguity, barely adding a dribble to the river proper.

My weather prediction had yet to come to fruition, and with long reaches now replacing meanderings, they served as the perfect runway for the wind to whip up waves. The river was running predominantly north which meant paddling directly into the wind. I took the wind and the waves on the chin. Tough times demanded a constant pace and steely de-termination, and it was not as if I did not have my skirt on. Firmly fixed to the cockpit today, it prevented the kayak filling with water. Kilometre after kilometre I ground my way along the thick tree-lined corridor. Rather than shelter me from the elements, today's corridor created a wind tunnel. I squinted to the sky for some hint of the nice day I had predicted without success and after two and a half hours of intense concentra-tion, I steered Precious to a sandy area on the edge of a bank, completely unprepared for what was next.

Taking a big paddle stroke so that I could slide up to a stop on the shore, the whole river exploded into life. Water splashed in the air. Wavelets crashed into the bank. Something flew over the back of the kayak and landed with a thump. It took a second or two for the cause to sink in, even though it was right before my eyes, larger than life. I had witnessed an explosion of water and fins. Carp everywhere. They are no small fish, and were going gonzo, bashing their heads into a ridge on the bank and feasting on whatever delicacy it held. Is this their most ingenious method to catch worms or shrimp? Just get them off fishing hooks like all the other fish.

After 30 seconds the spectacle faded. I fumbled with my plastic phone sleeve to take a shot, but the event was commit-ted to memory. With time on the river so many happenings had been unveiled that normally go by unnoticed. Taking shel-ter, it rained while I ate; a happening I noticed.

Paddling away and into the afternoon, the absence of blue signs, those same signs I called my guilty pleasure, those same signs I wished would not show up so regularly so as to shorten my adventure, made progress difficult to assess. Despite work-ing hard, the conditions determined it was going to be a long day ahead to reach my goal of the Boundary Bend Caravan Park. Of all the days to choose to cover 60 kilometres instead of the usual 50! I would have told this to my friends, the birds and the animals, but it dawned on me they had chosen to spend the day indoors. Even the tinnies with their optimistic fisher folk were missing. Paddling all alone, it was developing a day of introspection.

The river widened again, the flow reduced, and paddling became slow and arduous. With my head down and driving hard with my legs, I chanced to look up at a blue sign through the tress. Seventeen kilometres to the Murrumbidgee. Head down again, the waves and wind increased. There was little opportunity to raise my eyes to appreciate the surroundings. Instead, I concentrated on the water surface to watch for the varying wind intensity and the squalls appearing on the surface, bracing before they hit me. Stroke by stroke I counted in multiples of 50 to distract the hardship. Every so often I took advantage of a sudden lull in the wind and dug in to gain some extra distance.

On both sides the banks rose up to 25 metres high with rock walls protruding into the river. On the Victorian side, the Piambie State Forest stood thick with vegetation but on the New South Wales side, the northern side, there was scant coverage. In different circumstances, the forest may have been pretty, but today I only lamented how little the surrounding landscape was alleviating the wind speed.

Desperate for a break, I tied up onto a labyrinth of tree roots and scrambled up a bank to a flat landing. River water never tasted so good. Crunching into a cracker with Vegemite, I gazed across to the opening of a creek. Only it was not a creek. It was the opening of the Murrumbidgee River, one of two main rivers that flow into the Murray. It is the second largest water source to the Murray, but it appeared small and insignificant, more like a vein than a major artery. The subject of much controversy, irrigation demands combined with poor catchment rain had decimated fish and wildlife numbers with many sections of dry riverbed along its course. In a country undergoing increased desertification due to extended drought and heat, and with water the limiting factor in so many agricultural and domestic pursuits, never had the plight of the river rung truer. It was unbelievable that back in 1858, paddle steamers operated up and down the Murrumbidgee going as far as Gundagai, some 1250 kilometres upriver.

The wind had dropped a little, so I got back into the kayak for an excursion into the tributary. Very quickly it narrowed and filled with snags. My intention was to find out whether the Murrumbidgee had a flow of its own or if the flow was entering it via the Murray. The snags emerged so thick and gnarly across the entire surface, that I called an end to the investigation and turned back. The flow was negligible either way.

Where the two rivers converged, turbulence bounced me across some waves, but at least the sun had come out which bode well for a more pleasant afternoon. My chosen destination, Boundary Bend, was described in the chart book as 'pleasantly situated on a large curve in the river', and if my calculations were correct, just a mere 14 kilometre stone throw downriver.

I put my head down and got back to business. My eyes were drawn to one particular deck sticker. It represented a shared dream, but sadly my friend, Geoff Fabian died before its realisation. A keen surfer and all-round sportsperson, he had had designs on paddling the length of Murray before he died at the too young age of 41. I was pleased that I had been able to bring Geoff's memory along for the journey, his attendance represented in our shared symbol affixed to the top deck where I could see it every day and every stroke during the odyssey. Following his passing and up until his funeral, several family and friends reported strange occurrences, including me who received a mysterious and unexplained symbol on the face of my phone. The symbol just as mysteriously disappeared at midday and neither I nor the phone company could identify it or restore it. Until then, Geoff had shown no higher powers of communication to the supreme controller that I was aware. This was apart from calling 'Send 'em in Hughie', between wave sets. And no, Hughie did not help, or maybe he did. Who knows the temperament of waves? I have honoured that symbol as a bond ever since.

Leaving the Murrumbidgee behind, my mind quieted, but the wind roared again. It whipped up waves in the reaches and unexpected squalls threw the kayak about. The more I thought it could not get worse, the more it proved me wrong. Added to paddling against gale force winds, was having to dodge shallow sections that barricaded three-quarters the width of the river, and in ever-increasing wave heights, rock islands sprung from nowhere threatening to send Precious to the bottom like Little Ruby. Due to the shallow bottom the waves sprung high and only two metres apart, both thick and fast. The kayak ditched and dove. It could have been fun, but it was not.

Just before the bend of Boundary Bend, I bobbed past an opening to a shortcut, but without hesitation, I maintained my integrity to the odyssey to stay on the river proper. At the start of the Boundary Bend's five kilometre loop, a mass of irrigation pumps gurgled but this time their offensive noise was all but drowned out. Two rock islands materialised through the white caps. In calm conditions they would have been picturesque. Today they were obstacles. Halfway around the loop, weather conditions became so fierce they were verging on danger-ous. Geoff would have been in his element in these surf-like conditions. 'Not now, Geoff,' I called to the wind. The waves and their intensity increased. Geoff was not having any of it. Instead, I imagined his smiley face calling on Hughie to send more in my direction.

'No Geoff, not now,' I called more loudly in case he had not heard but mostly as an emotional discharge. This disagreement of timing continued for some minutes.

Ahead, two men in a tinnie were also being smashed. Their boat had been only one of three I had seen on the river all day. Travelling faster than me, they slowed down to either check on my safety, or verify my sanity. I looked at them, thinking the same. But then they were not yelling at some mythical controller of surfing waves.

My goal to reach Boundary Bend was slipping further away. Without confirmation that a suitable landing area would be available, the consequence of paddling further on in darkness to find a campsite was not worth the risk. As the storm grew more extreme an honourable pull-over would preserve self-respect. This was not the first time I had missed a planned stop at a caravan park with a general store and facilities for a good wash up. But the main appeal of the caravan park was being able to enjoy a substantial meal after such a tough day.

At five o'clock, and only two kilometres short of my initial target, I pitched the kayak onto a beach and leaped out. I cracked open the front hatch, snatched out the blue resealable plastic container, ripped open the lid, and delicately removed two pieces of dried mango. Chewing them slowly, deliberately, and happily, a strange feeling washed over me. There was neither relief nor satisfaction at the day's progress. It was more like a knowing that this is a day like any other and will fold into the journey like the obstacles of any travel experience. With the forest surrounding me and the storm still raging, I collected wood and set the fire in a pit for safety and protection. The fire burned strong and warm, and the soup hit just the right spot.

In darkness and on dry ground, the intensity of the day's events faded downriver. I felt strong and well-recovered. It was just another day on the river with trees in the river, snags and logs everywhere, gnarly low-lying rock islands, 25 metre cliffs, waves over the kayak, fresh air coming in at 30 kilometres per hour, wind in the trees above the tent, leaping carp—Whew!

Goodnight, Geoff. Until we meet again.

Distance 1288 – 1230
58 f'n hard kilometres

Chapter 26

Silver Beach to Yungera Island

Day 26

Saturday, April 27

Blue sky, breezy at times 25°C

The kookaburra alarm echoed through the forest at sunrise, and I sprang out of the tent to see what the day would deliver. My prediction for deteriorating weather conditions following the passing of Easter was actualising. The previously warm to mild conditions were turning cooler due to the Southern Ocean influence while simultaneously generating winds from the north. Living within kilometres of the Murray mouth, and as a keen surfer, common knowledge is that the winter swell is supported after Easter by light northerly winds that replace the soul-destroying south-westerlies of the summer.

With freezing hands, hands that struggled to dismantle the tent, I acknowledged the inevitable seasonal shift in over-night temperatures. Autumn was transitioning into winter. For the first time I dug my jumper from the dry-pack and, while enjoying muesli and prunes, lamented the loss of coffee due to a malfunctioning fuel-stove pump.

Shavings of silver glistened from the shallows as I prepared the kayak. Deciding to keep this spot a secret, I made a mental note to self to return one day to lay a claim should my rise to stardom be delayed. Sliding into mirror-like calm conditions, it was the polar opposite to yesterday's battlefield.

The two kilometre paddle down to Boundary Bank was as simple as the slide onto the grassy bank next to the boat ramp. The bend, situated on a long sweeping double curve with huge sandbars on either side, was named because it was where two properties originally had their boundaries. From the boat ramp, I climbed three metres up the bank, crossed the Murray Valley Highway, and strolled across the park to the caravan park and general store. It was well stocked with fishing gear, coffee, and bacon and egg sandwiches. Under different circumstances, I could have landed there last night but lugging all and sundry across the road to the park would have proved problematic. I will never know whether a hot shower might have alleviated the hardship.

The general store was operated by an energetic and friendly young fellow who made it a pleasure to stop in. While waiting on a bacon and egg sandwich, and coffee, he kindly charged my phone. Being well ahead of time, I took an hour to rest on the bank, reporting my progress via social media, making a couple of phone calls, and thawing out in the warm sun. The birds were back out enjoying the sunshine and being some- what busier than me. If I had a property out here to sit, ponder, and enjoy sunshine, surely there is something more imaginative than Boundary Bend: Bacon and Egg Bend, Hands still freezing cold Bend, Imagination Bend.

I set back out into a light breeze that came and went but, otherwise, the river remained smooth under a piercing blue sky. Banks rose to eight metres, and the river stayed wide, but with endless 180 degree bends the overhead crows would have reached their destination long before me. Exposed rock islands rose from the river in a variety of fascinating shapes, their glistening formation spectacularly covering half the width of the river. Sticks thrusting upward a metre from the islands acted as sentinels alerting river travellers to the imminent danger just a few centimetres away. Having seen trees growing in the middle of the river and on the small islands, it was not inconceivable that some of the sticks might have once been small trees since succumbed to drought or flood. For the fallen trees prostrating across the water, the river was wide enough that I could paddle around.

On one tight bend, an obvious sign of a curved fish trap above the water line indicated the area was once an important source for food. In his award-winning book, *Dark Emu*, Bruce Pascoe describes the intricate rock walls that indigenous people used to corral fish to be captured in wicker nets or speared. Praising the traps, colonial travellers reported their existence as far back as 1860. With not even a yabby in sight, I moved on.

After another couple of hours of peaceful paddling devoid of my guilty pleasures, a picturesque sandy beach tempted me to stop and enjoy a real break. Feeling suitably recharged from the protein bar, I waited as a tinnie carrying a couple cruised in from downriver.

'G'day, mate.' I waved.

'G'day, mate.' A true-blue colloquial reply.

'You're in for a real treat.' They spoke in unison.

Ice Cream came to mind.

'If you think the river is nice here, you'll be amazed at the scenery just after Euston.'

Could the scenery get better? The calm river, glistening rock islands, and natural bushland of this morning's journey would be hard to beat. I was happy to forego the ice cream on the promise of more spectacular views.

Long stretches between bends did not make for the most interesting paddling. But the sweet distraction of the Manie State Forest and Yungera Island's spindly tree scenery made me feel like an effigy travelling through a painting. The spindly redgum and black box trees interspersed with native lignum formed part of a recovery project to re-establish the river's wetlands and billabongs. Apart from offering designated areas for camping, the restoration of the natural flora had contributed to the return of threatened species. Blue-billed ducks, white-bellied sea eagles and painted honeyeaters were on their way back, and as though I had forgotten to mention them, a threatened growling grass frog croaked my way. My attention was drawn to the New South Wales side of the river.

Problem: Goats!

As the day wore on, more and more goats appeared until entire herds confirmed that numbers were out of control. All it would take is for one of these blighters to develop a taste for human flesh and there would be carnage on the Mallee, the likes never seen before. The sleepy town of Euston downriver might already be significantly sleepier. The Victorian joint town of Robinvale needed to blow the bridge NOW before these evil beasts grew webbed feet and learned to swim. The New Zealand faction movie, *Black Sheep*, chronicles how rapidly these situations can escalate. But there was no way to send a message. I vowed to keep a keen eye on stock numbers and report any mischief to the relevant authorities.

With the blue distance markers still absent, I pulled in for another break—on the Victorian side. The chart book indicated a further 14 kilometres to tonight's planned campsite, a destination chosen so that I could be within a 56 kilometre paddling distance of Robinvale-Euston the following evening. At 3.45pm I pushed off with still plenty to do.

My daily destinations on this trip were never preordained, with distance over-ruled by the unknown weather factor.

Syncing to the river, I paddled to a rhythm: no time, no schedule, just my breath, the motion of the paddle, and one eye searching the banks to see how many goats might be watching me. I paddled past inlets, today high and dry, shortcuts that in higher water would offer a labyrinth of fun. Skirting around more rock ledges, dodging reefs, and avoiding snags, I pulled into camp at 5.15pm.

I looked forward to telling my fairy wren friends stories of kangaroo and pelican sightings throughout the day but tonight they had deserted me. The currawongs had also been noticeably absent from the skies. I suspected this had more to do with the landscape than me. Date palms had disappeared from the banks for the time being and *Schinus Molle*, the tree that grows by the back door of every old stone country house to keep flies away, and better known as the South American introduced pepper tree, had retreated in favour of native casuarina trees. How ironic that pepper trees were so valued in the Australian outback yet left to grow unattended in the scrub become so invasive at the expense of the native flora.

River lesson #247: 'Visitors Welcome' is not an invitation to move in.

After camp set-up, I sat on my 'thinking stool' remembering back to schooldays and calculations from Nostradamus, Newton, and Noodleneck Jackson, from my grade two class. I had been advancing the kayak by a metre with each paddle stroke which meant, having now travelled over 1,000 kilometres, I had paddled over one million strokes. Not necessarily thinking of the wear and tear to my body of one million strokes, the same persistent hip problem bit as I had hammered in the tent pegs. As before, it was not painful while paddling but re-emerged when out of the kayak and bending. It had not reached an intensity where I needed to take painkillers or rub in Voltaren cream, both of which remained tucked away in the medical kit. Having stopped for my regular breaks throughout

the day, I had escaped the numb bum that came when paddling over two and a half hours. Otherwise, my body remained
tip-top, and despite the progression of age implying escalating
limitations, I was in no rush to legitimise that claim.

I stirred my dinner with the charred wooden spoon, which
despite its trauma continued to serve dutifully, unlike my
second set of sunglasses that went west during yesterday's
slog around Boundary Bend. The clunk of the paddle knocking
them free of their elasticised rope sent them flying but I put
zero priority on retrieving them in those waves. English is a
strange language, I pondered, while writing my diary between
stirs. Sunglasses like binoculars are a single unit, and yet gram-
matically they become a pair. Marcus Aurelius said, 'Very little
is needed to make a happy life: it is all within yourself, in your
way of thinking'. An unexpected enjoyment of this trip was
the unrestrained freedom to think. The only previous times
I achieved this was during long runs in my youth where my
mind would open a chasm for lateral thinking, wide, serene,
and uncluttered. But life got busy and, somewhere, I forgot to
prioritise these simple but important pleasantries.

Tonight's campsite sat on a nameless beach at the 1180
blue mark and judging by the surrounds, it was not unknown
but a popular camping spot. I had again set the fire in a pit
and sat thinking of how unexpected it was to be alone at such
a beautiful site on the Saturday of the ANZAC Day weekend. I
pulled on my jumper even though the fire was giving off good
heat. My beanie made an appearance for the first time.

Thankfully, the camp was set on the Victorian side and not
on the goat side; nevertheless, I slept with one eye open and
listened for the slap of webbed goat feet on the bank.

Distance 1230 – 1180 50 kilometres
Good day

Chapter 27

Yungera Island to Robinvale/Euston

Day 27

Sunday, April 28

Breeze early and overcast, clearing throughout

the day 24°C

Rumi, the 13th century philosopher said, 'The morning wind spreads its fresh smell. We must get up and take that in, that wind that lets us live. Breathe before it's gone.' The morning's life-giving air might have been tied to ruminations, but I hoped the 'wind' stipulation was not necessary. The robust breeze that tussled the leaves above brought recollections of the aftermath from only a couple of days ago. Precious and I slipped into the water under threatening skies.

A westerly rose, and with the river wide and unsheltered, a few cheeky waves slapped me across the face. Because wind travels continuously around the globe, I rejoiced in knowing I was breathing the same air Rumi had once taken in. The forecast had predicted cloud clearing to a nice afternoon, but for now I paddled under a sky so grey it made the river look oily.

The paddling began with the typical morning gusto as I settled into a driving rhythm. Within a few minutes I started to hum my song of the day. Wilbert Harrison's, *Kansas City*, soon came to life. The original lyrics required modification, only because I did not know the original words, but the tune was delivered with, at the very least, enthusiasm.

Well, I might take a train
I might take a plane
But if I have to paddle
I'm going just the same
I'm going to Euston town...

I was alone on the river with nobody listening, or at least I thought so as there were no coins being thrown in my direction.

Ten kilometres downriver into the Belsar Island State Forest, a protected wetland similar to Yungera Island, a 300 metre cutting connected the river via a direct route rather than its meandering three kilometre loop. The opening to the loop was overgrown with young saplings, and the cutting now appeared to be only a flood or two away from becoming the river proper. This is how the river rolls, ever changing, and ever growing: The Murray is a living entity.

As the morning progressed the weather came to agreement with the prediction. The breeze shifted to a tailwind before dropping entirely. Working its way west toward South Australia, the river twisted and turned between north-west and south-west. North-west again being the afternoon's general direction. It was easy to tell I was within a coo-ee of the Euston-Robinvale weir because the water level rose to land height making for typically lower banks. Paddling through the forest the high banks of the past few days were gone altogether and the land now folded down to the water's edge. Gone were the beaches, and trees extended back right from the shoreline. It felt quite majestic winding through the green enclosure, clear of snags and fallen trees, with the sun sparkling on the water and the birds in full song. I had missed this type of landscape.

During my afternoon break, I phoned the Robinvale Caravan Park to confirm site availability and a suitable landing beach. With both confirmed, and rations running low, the need for a town was now. I did not really fancy another night of couscous and onion. It had done the job but with that onion being the final vegetable on board, I considered my meals were Spartan enough.

After a long hard push, my resolve was again tested as I approached a cutting that would have meant I could reach Robinvale within 15 minutes instead of having to paddle the 12 kilometre trip around Bumbang Island. Approaching the fork of what locals refer to as 'the nine-mile,' that little man on my shoulder whispered into my ear again. But it was not the little man, it was an actual voice. From the bank, a young couple signalled for me to investigate something floating in the middle of the river. Seeing only a plastic milk container, I commended their commitment to keeping the river litter free, but as I reached to grab it the offending container started travelling across the river under its own steam. Snatching hold of the container, I placed it across the kayak skirt, quickly discovering that attached to this container was a cord that was attached to a hook which was in turn attached to a fish! One thing a kayaker in a fully laden kayak does not need is a flapping fish on their lap, so I high tailed it across river, fish in tow, and pulled alongside a fallen tree on the bank. Handing over the line, the young man took control and pulled in, almost, a large European Carp. Within arm's reach it shook loose, free to bite a bait another day.

The little man whispered again in my ear but the decision to paddle around Bumbang, or not, was as obvious as 'to be, or not to be'—and by fortune without the same dramatic over-hanging consequence. I could see the caravan park but could not bear to have my current go awry nor any enterprise of pith and moment be compromised. The return journey would be little more than a grunt and a sweat to cap off this weary day.

The river surrounding Bumbang Island Sanctuary was quite narrow. The island itself consisted of masses of thin spindly gums with some of the more significant trees sporting names of significant people. There is reported to be over 750 trees displaying scarring for canoes and other utensils. With respect, I did not to stop for investigation. Access is discouraged unless permission is granted through the Murray Valley Aboriginal Co-op. After rounding the back of the island, a large wetland off to the left resembled like the river proper, and an obvious trap for younger players, but a quick check on Google Maps kept me on the round and narrow. I completed the loop as dusk fell and sprinted the last two kilometres towards the Robinvale Bridge. The caravan park sat just short of the bridge and, while not a surprise, it was disappointing after having checked with the park, that there was no beach to pull into. Concerned that travelling further downstream in semi-darkness to the Euston Caravan Park might produce the same result, I paddled close to the metre-high grassy bank and called out to a group of revellers in the hope they were sober enough to impart their local knowledge.

A group of 50-plus year-olds with drinks in hand gathered on the bank. I was to go no further. Egged on by the group, two burly volunteers, Metho and Skeg, helped me hoist the kayak onto the bank. Then thinking better of it, they hauled the kayak further up placing me on a site adjacent to theirs.

I raced off to check in at the reception desk only for the manager to suggest I consider a quieter spot. Apparently, my white knights were prone to unruly behaviour, especially as this was their final night. What followed was a heated discussion between the manager and his wife about the fee I needed to pay. Eventually they agreed on the off-peak rate of $29 that I had been quoted over the phone. After thanking them, I let them know that I was happy to take my chances with the neighbours. In fact, some good-hearted camaraderie was exactly what I needed.

The small, modern, picturesque park had open sweeping areas of well-manicured grass that stretched all the way to the one metre bank at the river. I strode past the cabins, all 5-star, and most importantly for the weary, smelly paddler, the amenities were also first class.

Eager for a good scrub, I quickly erected my tent. Metho delivered a beer complete with stubby holder because... well, that is what nice people do. To return the niceties, I drank the beer and accepted a generous invitation to join them for the evening's drinks and BBQ. But first, I needed a shower and clean. My newly grown beard could have been better groomed, or even shaved off, but it had served the purpose of sun protection. Plus, I did not have a shaver. And I did not want to shave.

Looking and feeling more presentable, politeness demanded I make a contribution, so I skipped 400 metres to the supermarket to check out the produce. Now 6pm on a Sunday night, Ritchies IGA supermarket was pumping. Farm workers of every imaginable nationality swarmed the place resulting in line-ups at every one of the ten or so checkouts. The mood was so festive, that while I waited in a long checkout line, I opened a packet of chips and offered them around. When I reached the checkout girl, I held out the packet.

'Would you like a chip?' I asked.

'Umm, no thanks,' she replied, as though it was the first time that had ever happened.

'This crowd is amazing,' I continued, expecting it might be her first day. 'It's Sunday evening.'

'It's like this all day, every day,' she said, without any hint of amazement.

I wanted to stay there to enjoy this all day every day. I left, eventually, in a jolly mood fascinated how the argumentative mood in the caravan park's office could be in such contrast. Having first checked the park's social media reviews, they were not all bad. But those that were, cited a lack of empathy toward their clientele, an observation that was starting to look accurate.

Armed with rations, but more importantly food and drink for the party, I joined the unruly revellers. The focal point was the fire. The flames leaped and cracked as I was introduced to at least 20 people, the names of which most escaped me, although most of the ladies' names were Anne. The party was the brainchild of a group of family members from various regions around Australia who preferred social catchups rather than meeting up at the inevitable funerals. A central location would be chosen for a party once a year. As my luck would have it, Robinvale drew the card.

Chef Peter provided the BBQ meat of lamb from his own farm. The fact he could determine, by name, which of his sheep was on my plate did test my digestive empathy, but I ate on. With mutual enthusiasm, further promises of catching up when passing through some of their home towns were generously offered, including the use of a hot shower on a houseboat moored at Customs House on the SA-Victorian-New South Wales border—if needed! By the end of the night, I think I had called all the ladies Anne as well as most of the men.

At some unknown hour, full of hospitality, I found my tent. Sleep was deep.

Distance 1180 – 1124 56 kilometres
Long day and testing, although being stronger, not too difficult

Chapter 28

Robinvale/Euston to Happy Valley

Day 28

Monday, April 29

Blue sky, no wind 24°C

I woke with my nose pressed against the side of my tent, a little dusty after the night's gaiety. I unzipped the tent flap and looked out to an orange sky with hints of Arctic blue. Clearly the weather gods had heard my promise not to drink anymore wine. To be truthful, I had made that pledge on previous occasions. I headed off on foot to fulfill my morning task of gathering more provisions from the supermarket. Over the next three to five days paddling to Mildura, opportunities to buy replacement rations would be scarce.

I read the historic plaques as I passed. After World War II, Robinvale—which wore its pride on every carefully laid out and well-presented street—became a soldier settlement district with blocks set up with grapevines and citrus trees. It was named after Lieutenant George Robin Cuttle, the son of a local landowner killed in action in Somme, France in 1918 during World War I. The adding of the Latin term, Vale, literally means 'Farewell Robin'. The French town of Villers-Bretonneux, where he and the Australian regiments fought to liberate the French is Robinvale's sister city. Maintaining its military link, in 1949 many fruit growing blocks were established by the government and offered to soldiers returning from World War II duties. The town also has the largest Jehovah's Witness Kingdom Hall I had seen this side of the black stump.

Passing through the checkout that had line-ups already, I gravitated towards the in-store bottle shop to buy a small cask of wine. The shop assistant informed me that they were not allowed to sell alcohol before 8am. I was not the least bit fussed. The promise to the weather gods was out of my hands. However, whether someone buys alcohol at 7.30am, 8am, or 9am, I think they—or we—share the same questionable character. The church was still closed on my way back to the caravan park so my chance to repent before hitting the river was lost. Only later, while paddling, did I reflect on my general state of dress and grooming expecting the bottle shop staff probably considered me a tragic candidate for rehabilitation, or worse.

My decision to spend a morning in the sunshine writing up my diary and posting my movements on social media was removed when I returned to find the kayak already loaded onto a carpeted boat trailer. Whatever I said or did, my party friends obviously did not want to hear or see again. After quickly loading the new rations, then loading myself into the kayak, Skeg drove me or more correctly, paraded me through the caravan park and down to the boat ramp. What could go wrong as the trailer backed down into the water with the kayak pointing downwards ready to slip away?

A crowd of surprisingly chirpy friends gathered with glasses charged for a champagne farewell. Cameras flashed and video footage rolled. It was going to be a classic John Wayne farewell.

Cheers went up as I made a perfect entry into the water, and with a wave I paddled off with one final amusing memory to complement those of the previous night.

Under the bridge, down a couple of kilometres, and around the bend, a gleaming light shone above the Euston Club. The twin town of Euston, across the bridge from Robinvale is the elder of the two towns, and thankfully was still there (for now) despite the inevitable goat strike. A tug, not unlike a magnet pulled me ever closer until there was no choice but to slide onto the club's own sandy beach. The waitress enthusiastically took my order for a strong coffee and a chocolate muffin: the perfect antidote for a big night. Received less enthusiastically, was my warning of the imminent danger posed by the vicious caprinae (goats). Pretending to not hear me, the waitress, like Zimbabwe Girl, had been fooled into believing that faith and providence would provide safe harbour.

The club boasted a nice aspect on the river so, taking advantage, I stayed put whiling away a couple of hours to write; albeit with ears and eyes peeled. Over a second coffee, I called the lockmeister of Lock 15 to inform him of my arrival at approximately 11am. This news was met with great enthusiasm. But it was so nice on the club's balcony watching the sun glistening across the river that I stayed put and whiled until almost noon.

Slipping back into the river, the sheen of the water was ruffled by the flapping wings of a pair of ducks taking off. I trusted them like swans, but the direction was obvious and wide. What should have been around the next bend, turned out to be around five kilometres of bends and then another and another through the Euston State Forest. Feeling guilty at how few kilometres I had achieved, I paddled hard and fast but the low-flow zone typical before weirs did its best to put the brakes on. I did my best to expend the energy provided by the muffin and coffee, arriving at an open lock with the patient lockmeister ecstatic to see me.

'G'day, mate,' he said, as I paddled into the lock. 'I was expecting you an hour ago.'

'Sorry, the Euston Club put a chocolate muffin in my way,' I called back, out of breath. 'Had to eat my way through it before I could pass.'

Transition through a lock in a boat was not foreign to me, yet I was uncertain how a small craft like the kayak would respond to the water movement once inside. The lockmeister sensed my apprehension.

'Just grab onto the ladder when I start to let the water out,' he called above the noise of the mechanical gates.

When all the churning water underneath settled, I yelled 'Been busy?'

'Yeh mate, you're the second boat in nine days.'

Now I could see why he was eager and excited for a chat. He explained that the weir is held at full capacity to provide for irrigation and for upriver skiing. He also confirmed what I had earlier read on a website, that the lockmeister's role in addition to facilitating travel through the weir, consisted of maintaining the grounds and reporting on river conditions. While formal qualifications are not critical, extensive on-the-job training is.

Holding tight to the slimy rusted ladder bolted to the concrete inside wall, I lowered my hand from rung to rung as the water level dropped. The gushing water slowed, and loud metal clangs rang out as the lock gates began to open. It was like a new river was opening before me.

'No worries, mate, all ready to roll,' the lockmeister called down.

'Thanks, mate,' I replied. 'We'll have that coffee next time I paddle down.'

'Good luck, you're gonna love this section.'

And he returned to his office to sit by the phone to wait for the next call to action.

Although the exit procedure went without incidence, apart from being shoved back and forth when the turbulent water released from the weir met the river proper, I ruminated on the chances of successfully negotiating another 15 locks and the potential embarrassment of flipping over if caught out by a rogue wave. As I paddled off, I began calculations on the numbers of visitors the lock has processed since it opened in 1937 based on one every nine days. Being the last weir and lock built on the Murray this would be the easiest to count. The sun was shining, the birds were whistling, and I lost interest at 50, or 100, or ...

Into a new river, the banks grew large again with rock walls and red cliffs up to 50 plus metres high. As if in a whole new world pelicans proliferated, trees grew tall, the water shone like glass, and I was gliding through velvet. Long sandy beaches up to 400 metres long and spectacular rock reefs imposed on the river. From time to time, rocks popped up mid-river but rather than acting as minefields they created a sense that the river was from a different era.

Twenty kilometres later a rock reef extended across three-quarters of the wide river. At high water, the reef might not have been visible but today it sat proud, glistening in the sunshine. Behind its rock barrage huge deposits of sand had settled resulting in a large mid-river island. I skirted around its side through the channel that rushed around the rocks, pulling over on the beach to admire this river gem. It was named Success Reef, not because of any success, but because the PS Success had problems negotiating the rocks and narrow channel way back in the 1800s. I sat like a king, lazing back with my protein bar and water bottle.

As I approached a second reef two kilometres later, it gave the appearance of extending the whole way across the river. At the last minute I shot into a small fast-flowing opening to the side. The scoot through the rapid-like channel grew instantly exciting when I was forced to deal with the root labyrinth of a strainer parked right in the middle. It was tight and the rear of the kayak brushed the booby trap after a dig of the paddle and an arm fend-off. I spat out alongside the tropical-like beach of the sandy island behind, all calm and serene as though I might expect a waiter standing there offering me a cocktail. Peering through clear water to a depth of two feet, more scattered snags, fallen trees and swizzle sticks lurked just beneath the surface.

After 34 kilometres of scenic paddling, an overnight stay at Happy Valley beach looked and sounded too appealing to pass up. It had been a lovely day's travel, although the lack of kilometres covered was a little disappointing. The relaxing hour or longer spent in Euston caused the shortfall, but admittedly contributed to one of the most relaxing days I had spent on the river. The old adage of being 'about the journey and not the destination' was never more relevant. I sat on the beach to enjoy my two pieces of mango and chewed over that adage. 'Journeying equates to a life lived' I reasoned. The concentration required when paddling meant I was in the moment virtually every moment of the journey. But does this not place destination, goals, and achievement as the means to the end rather than in the reverse? One cannot be without the other. Maybe falling asleep in a whirlpool for an hour could help.

Later while stretching my tired limbs by the fire, all peace and serenity was shattered by the grating sound of bleating goats on a stretch of moonlit barren land on the opposite New South Wales bank. The destruction they had caused to the native vegetation was sad to see and, being rapid breeders, I could only imagine the problem would get exponentially worse. Without a natural predator, and in such large numbers surely controlled culling was needed to maintain some level of control. From flora to fauna, species native to Australia appear meek, mild, and trusting enabling the invasion and devastation by introduced species.

There is something about an open fire that flicks the 'contemplating' switch. I thought about the time it took for First Nations people to build boats from the scarred trees 100 metres upriver, I thought about the PS Ellen that 96 years before had sank right in front of me, and I thought about my children, Ali and Bobby.

Distance 1124 – 1090 34 kilometres
Lovely day's paddling

Chapter 29

Happy Valley to Retail Bend

Day 29

Tuesday, April 30

Sunny to cloudy to overcast 24°C

The bleat from a goat startled me awake. It sounded too close for comfort and near enough that one of us might be breakfast. I carefully unzipped the tent to check the coast was clear— clear to the other bank where a small herd stood watching me. Not coy like a pink pig but sizing me up for a family roast. Well, they had better be quick because with all this paddling there was less of me each day to feast upon.

Happy Valley? For whom?

Despite meagre phone reception, the weather app forecast winds up to 20 kilometres per hour during the day. I shut the phone down without opening the news app. Priorities had changed out here. World news had become less important to me the longer I spent on the river. Although societal expectations were to keep up with world events, they rarely affected

my daily practices here or at home. Besides, using sensational-
ism as a viewing tactic and giving priority to trivial news items
disturbed me. I was not missing it. Of more interest was the
20 kilometre per hour wind forecast. I was in the kayak by
7am hoping that the rock islands and rock reefs marked in the
chart book would not spring up through the waves anticipated
along the many long reaches.

The only thing awaiting me as I slid the kayak into the river
was a whole lot of perfectly calm water and, of course, the little
swallows as they swooped over the river with never so much
as a 'good morning' returned. I charged up to make as many
kilometres as I could while the good weather lasted. I dodged a
rock ledge before sweeping through Carina Bend, past Danger
Island where a squadron of startled Australian pelicans took
flight like a fleet of Boeing 737s, their webbed undercarriage
running wildly on the water before tucking them behind. With
their long neck tucked back and their heads rested on their
shoulders, they soared above me as I paddled further south-
west past masses irrigation pumps waiting patiently until it
was time to start their daily work.

On the longer stretches the river widened, reducing the
flow, but paddling in slow flow compared to digging in against
wind and waves was preferable. Like yesterday, massive yellow
sandy beaches appeared around nearly every bend, with some
stretching out to 500 metres. Rocks and rock ledges covered
up to three-quarters of the river in places. The solid rock banks
that jutted out of the water gave some warning of what lurked
underneath, and I gave them a wide berth. The ledges, always
captivating, slowed my progress as I lingered to admire them.
At times like this, I was grateful for the lower water levels,
as the rock formations would have been missed by anyone
travelling in higher water. Pelicans in squadrons of 10 or more
rested on the many midriver islands and fallen trees. Always

facing into the breeze, they expelled the odd hoot but otherwise cared little for my passing company.

The sun rose high enough to spill its warmth over the river, signalling it was time for the morning break. I pulled into a sandy beach at Pound Bend, ripped out a protein bar and sat contented with the strong morning's work. Conditions had been perfect for paddling but with wind predicted I laid back to catch my breath in preparation for the heavy work to come. I became lost in the sky, watching castles, dinosaurs and kittens disguised as drifting clouds. As a youth I had often whiled away my time watching clouds. Back then I never considered the past or the future, my only desire to do what felt good at that moment. My heart filled with joy and gratitude for the clouds that were still overhead, most likely on just another rotation. How many years had they been going around and around waiting for me to stop and appreciate them again? I could not recall seeing anyone of late lying around in the parks or on the decks of their houseboats looking skyward. It would be sad if the pastime of cloud watching had been lost, although I imagine there is a computer game to take its place.

Back on the water, an occasional breeze was enough to keep sweat from my brow. Long wide stretches presented ahead. Even the meanderings were lengthy. The flow suffered from the width, reducing paddling speed until the odd occasion when the river narrowed. With the kayak full of provisions from the Robinvale stock-up, paddling was more of a drag than usual. I had added 15 to 20 kilograms of weight but there was comfort in knowing it diminished the more I ate and drank. Water is the enemy of weight. With every litre weighing one kilogram, the five and ten litre bladders made the kayak inch through the water like it was dragging a bucket.

Knowing I had fallen short in distance recently, I popped a couple of painkillers to numb the reoccurring hip pain and dug deep to make my daily average of 50 kilometres. After 20 minutes, I did not feel the pain, but I became so drowsy I could barely stay upright. So many times, the temptation to pull over and catch some sleep washed over me. I dared not pull over though with goats of many colours lining the banks.

Gulps of cormorants soared above but, in the trees, covering every branch sat masses of corellas quietly chatting. To stay awake I began teaching them a new word. Afterall, corellas are a subspecies of the cockatoo. Working on the hundredth monkey phenomenon—the rapid spread of new behaviour from one group to another—I called out the word 'crazy' each time I passed a crackle of corellas. C-R-A-A-Z-E-E, I called expecting that each crackle downriver, through collective consciousness, would progressively imitate their new learning until corellas over the whole river would begin to speak. It was entirely possible the painkilling drugs had altered my consciousness but at the time my theory seemed plausible.

It was still early, and just after Spark's Reef, a blue marker signalled that I had completed 50 kilometres. In search of a suitable campsite, I paddled on past Ki Bend and then another four kilometres before I found a sheltered beach with good kayak access, no vehicle access, equal amounts of sun and shade, flat ground for my tent, and no bleating goats or towering trees with fragile branches. It was 3.45pm and the wind blew up almost immediately. Sticking to the Scout motto of 'Be Prepared', I lit a fire and cooked an early dinner. With rain forecast for the next day, I packed all my gear back into the kayak before retiring in readiness for a dry getaway.

In the early evening, lightning flashed, thunder rumbled, and rain tumbled. Having anticipated the storm and with the kayak packed and sealed, I drifted off to sleep feeling snug and smug inside my little cocoon of a tent.

Distance 1090 – 1036 54 kilometres.
Nice day, but a drag with poor flow

Chapter 30

Retail Bend to Big Tree Bend

Day 30

Wednesday, May 1

Storm clouds clearing to cloudy, breezy 22°C

When the kookaburras called at the break of day, I yelled 'good morning' then poked my head from the tent to witness the damage from last night's storm. Everything was dry. The thick dark skies confirmed today's forecast for further storms around midday may not be so charitable. The river was glassy and I was anxious to get in and enjoy the conditions while they lasted. A malfunctioning fuel pump for the Whisperlite stove removed the option for coffee. It had been tasting more like ground ground of late so 'care factor'—zero. It saved time.

The first two kilometres proved why the Murray has remained an inspiration for artists and poets. I slowed down to admire sections of exposed rock and rock shelves that offered safe harbour for land and aquatic wildlife. With the rocks creating a major hurdle for motorised river craft, this quiet spot would have been ideal to see a platypus. But now almost one month into the paddle, I was beginning to rate these little drifters in the same observation category as river trolls and mermaids.

The first obstacle for the day was at Retail Cutting where the river proper had taken a new path. The opening to the old eight kilometre section at the current water height was thick with saplings, reeds, and overgrowth and would from now be inaccessible. The new route was narrow, fast-flowing, and also thick with snags yet comfortable to navigate. I drifted smoothly around the next bend when the sight of bubbling water on the surface in the middle of the river set off an alarm. I ripped the kayak sharply around to the left narrowly missing a nasty five metre wide rock ledge lying inches under the surface. Precious was not happy with the 'narrowly' and squealed as she got another scratch in her gel coat. Fortunately, kayaks are easier to manoeuvre than wool carrying river barges like the Florence Annie, in the 1890s. So many barges and steamers ended their lives at the bottom of the river because of the damage sustained from rocks, reefs, snags, fire, and bad weather. Florence Annie survived the hazards on the Murray only to end on the Darling River where she sank around 1912.

Through the entire morning's paddle of dodging and weaving, the river behaved like a petulant child—unreasonable and bad tempered—desperate to hold onto its youth before reaching the stability of adulthood. The rain was holding off, and the wind remained mild, yet the fisher folk were absent again, appearing to have pulled up stumps the moment the autumn weather began to slide in. Goats brazenly lined the banks and it was likely that Euston was now gone. I wanted to report their large numbers to the Kulkine Police Station on the cliff high above, but it closed: in 1870!

Darting through the channel of another rock and sandbar configuration just short of Brett's Bend, the sandy beach behind the rock barrage called me in for my morning break. If only I had paint and easel to capture this scene...and if only I could paint. The river back from this island to the ravaged town of Euston is referred to by the locals as Ninety Mile Bend, which from point to point can be covered by road in 30 miles, or less by crow.

After a short break, I slid back into the river to take full advantage of the optimum conditions. Magnificent birdlife was again part of my daily scene but on this heavily overcast day they restricted themselves to the banks where they peeked out from behind trees and bushes. The river's meanderings provided temporary relief from the winds but there were still plenty of long sections to whip up some white caps and excite Fabs. Just before Tapaulin Island, the imaginatively named Tapaulin Cutting shortened my planned route by seven kilometres. Once again, the old section of river was choked up with trees and undergrowth resigning the original loop to a backwater. What would one have to do to own this newly created island? A choice piece of real estate girt by river, a renovators delight!

Under barely enough rain drops to whet a whistle, I cruised past Adelaide, Mulberry, and Brown's Bend. For my second break of the day, I slid into a long sandy beach at Le Bruns Bend. Finally, I could relax and stretch the legs. I removed the six crackers from their packet and salivated over the Vegemite and peanut butter that would soon join them. As though a lunch bell had sounded on a cruise ship, an elderly couple caravanning nearby jumped to life. Side by side, holding hands, they barrelled along the sandy beach to greet me. After the usual niceties, and excusing myself for eating in front of them, the gentleman took a stick and went down on one knee; a practice that is disappearing with that generation.

'You'll need to be careful, son,' he warned. 'Not far from here it can get pretty dangerous with the water so low.'

I watched as he used the stick to draw a map in the sand.

'Now, when you come down the river here, there's rocks to the left, here, and an island over here...'.

At each 'here' he drew another circle but before I could relegate the map to memory, the soft, dry sand closed in on itself.

'We've been coming here for years,' his wife chimed in with another story. 'One year it was so shallow down there, I walked right across the river with the grandchildren.'

Not used to receiving so much information my eyes started to glaze over. I recalled my own father advising me not to believe everything I heard and only half of what I saw. The old gentleman's voice came back into focus. I think he might have actually continued talking all along.

'So just take the channel and she'll be right.' And he drew one last circle.

People like this gave me the warm and fuzzies. Genuine to a fault.

Three kilometres downstream, I reached the funky rock arrangement he had described. A puzzle for sure, with a complex narrow rock and snag configuration, shallow sandy riverbeds, and a large thickly vegetated island. From a distance the channel to the left of the island looked tight and I could barely make out the channel to the right. Did the old boy say left or right? I was sure he said left. How could she had walked across there with the grandkids? I expected a rush of water, but the flow was quite moderate. The reason was soon obvious. The channel to the right opened out 15 metres wide and I pushed through and past the island without a care in the world: apart from being curious whether this island might also be for sale. Lucky Lee!

Within four kilometres another island popped up behind a three-quarter-river rock ledge. The islands and rocks continued to bring endless excitement and, if my camera had been operational, I am sure all potential home movie night friends would have been equally excited.

According to the charts there were many settlements and homesteads along the river which, due to the height of the banks, had gone by unnoticed. Picture-worthy, they told a tale of early settlement that could be better appreciated if on the bank. I found far more beauty from the river itself with all manufactured structures paling into insignificance. Another person may travel the Murray and come back with 100 pictures of buildings, pumps, towns, and bridges. It is intriguing how we are all so different—and yet the same.

The afternoon session required a bit more effort as I pushed along longer reaches down through the Mallee Cliffs State Forest. The waves tried to rise up, but they were of little consequence as I worked the leeward banks before cutting across the river to shortcut the bends. The little rock surprises midriver continued to keep the paddling interesting. Pumps with huge water pipes that guzzled masses of water from the river were so prevalent I moved to the other side of the river to avoid being sucked in, rolled about, and spat out into a dam. I was aiming for the small settlement of Nangiloc. Judging from its online reviews, the hospitality at the local pub was on a par with the likes of Raffles and The Wahgunyah (except for Sundays). If my luck held out, it would not be closed for renovations. But more attractive than beer and burgers was a sandy beach just before Police Bend. Reputed to have the biggest river red gum tree in Australia, and even the world, I pulled in. A lover of tree candy, a giant red gum always got my camera finger itching. Chewing two pieces of dried mango, I backed up along the beach with my phone camera at the ready. I backed up and backed up for as far as I could go but still could not fit it all into the frame. I took a picture of the trunk of the biggest red gum tree in the world.

River lesson #48: Big rivers make big trees and small cameras make small pictures.

The day's distance totalled 68 kilometres but when factoring in the 15 kilometres of short cuts through the cuttings, I had paddled 53 kilometres. Water in the rear kayak compartment was increasing daily and, even though only minor with nothing at risk of damage, the time for attention had come. After inspecting the hull, it was evident the repair work from Day 1 was breaking down. Out came the repair kit and with great technical, mechanical, and engineering mastery, I applied duct tape. But it would not hold. Plan B: wait until Mildura in a couple of days when I could have a closer inspection.

The fire crackled away, the night had a balmy air under the cloud cover, and the beach had a resort feel (in my mind). I opened the iPad for some Augie March music. It was a pleasant way to cook up but, with no offence to the band, it was the last time I would spoil the natural sounds of the river.

My phone reception was good enough that I could attend to the usual chores and check the weather forecast for the next couple of days. Today's forecast had proved all threat and no action, although rain was forecast again tomorrow. I hoped cleric Charles Caleb Colton was right when he said: 'Those that are loudest in their threats are the weakest in their actions.' Being exposed in the outdoors was not the best time to test his theory so after dinner I packed up the kayak with all but the tent and sleeping gear. And later, while scanning on my phone, I discovered a once in a lifetime opportunity! The island at Tarpaulin cutting, a 34 hectare property with river frontage, only 15 minutes from Wentworth, with a population of herons, was for sale for one dollar short of $500,000. Developers are not making any new islands, they say, and one could do worse.

As I lay in my cocoon, poring over the charts for tomorrow's adventures, it struck me that I was now within 1,000 kilometres of the mouth. Of the end! After 30 days in the kayak,

I had become lost in the adventure, lost in the beauty, and thinking of the end in around 20 or so days was not cause for celebration. Those blue kilometre signs, my guilty pleasures, the chocolate of my river, would I expect, start to lose some of their lustre.

Distance 1036 – 968 68 kilometres (less fifteen for cuttings)
Waiting all day for rain that did not come

Chapter 31

Big Tree Bend to Bonnie Doone

Day 31

Thursday, May 2

Overcast with a light breeze 22°C

The thick layer of rain cloud diffused the light but did nothing to dampen the raucous laughter of the kookaburras. I shot out of the tent to thank them for waking me. But no, they were laughing about the few items I had left out overnight that were now damp from a combination of light rain and the new season's dew. I shovelled down a quick breakfast, eager to slide into the calm glassy water, uncertain of how long the conditions might last.

My path meandered north along the Kemendok National Park on the New South Wales side, where the 58 thousand hectare Mallee Cliffs National Park adjoins its eastern boundary. The Park is not visible from the river and survives without permanent waterways. Rather than that being an impediment it thrives, being home to 32 threatened wildlife species including bilbies, numbats, and mallee fowl, and four threatened plant species that does not include Bathurst Burr. Even if I could have paddled across the land Flintstone-style to infiltrate the park's ten-thousand-hectare predator-free fence, public access is strictly controlled with educational facilitators and researchers having priority. Foxes, feral cats, and the curious are not welcome.

From the river, high cliffs rose behind green forested banks creating an avenue that included long sandy beaches, shallow reaches, and polished rock shelves that lurked just under the water line. The peacefulness of the still morning air and the glassy light-brown water under a full overcast sky made for a surreal image as though I was looking through the smoky filter of a camera. The many banks of irrigation pipes reaching into the river were not operating at this early hour. Swallows came out to greet me, but under the overcast skies all other birdlife stayed inside to do the chores. Their sensitivity to changes in barometric pressure is reportedly the basis for their inside knowledge and unlike me they know when to stay indoors. After two and a half hours and 20 kilometres of cruising, I stopped at the designated tourist campsite of Sand Bar Bend, a 180° bend in the river also known as Forest Bend.

Across the river, four kangaroos shared a morning tea of their own. The photos—in this case taken by an iPhone—never do the wildlife justice. Looking at the pictures over morning tea, they did not capture the softness of the roos' red to greyish fur, their fluid and graceful motion as they balanced on their small front legs and tail, while swinging their hind legs forward, or the way they nipped off the grass with their front teeth before grinding it side-to-side in their jaws. It looked like pure enjoyment. My memory held greater detail.

With the weather showing signs of growing more irritable, I paddled off ahead of schedule. Once settled, I took a deep breath, then a deeper breath through my nose. The smells of the river and forest came to life: some subtle, some strong and demanding of attention. Aside from barometric awareness, land animals have more developed olfactory glands than birds, but which, if any apart from us humans, could spare the time to enjoy the bouquet of their environment for pleasure rather than for survival.

PD Ouspensky wrote, 'When one realises one is asleep, at that moment one is already half-awake.' I had lapsed into cruise mode and awoke not quite cognisant of what and where the last few kilometres had gone. I was at the mouth of a 50 metre cutting, where three fisher folk saluted me from their tinnie for choosing the longer four kilometre route of the river proper. When I passed the opening on the other side of the cutting, all three men erupted into cheers. I suspect a bet for how long it took me to cover the four kilometres proved more fruitful than the fishing, for one of them at least. More impressive was how they had managed to moor their houseboat into such a shallow snaggly cutting. My bet would have been on whether they could get it back out.

A couple of stone's throw inland is Nowingi where the Victorian government had planned to locate a toxic waste dump. The community's united front against it prevailed. Local people, who call their region 'Victoria's food bowl' were rightly concerned and annoyed, some outrightly defiant. Bumper stickers with 'No Toxic Waste' appeared on many cars and trucks, and posters with the same message got attached to fences, buildings, and trees. Perish the thought that leakage would find its way into the river, but locals were just as worried about their reputation around the world. Food grown next to a toxic waste dump was not a good look for some countries: including this one.

Living at water level had acclimatised me to changing river conditions. Currents in channels, eddies, and whirlpools had become obvious by the movement of surface froth and flotsam, whereas shallow water, undulating riverbeds, and approaching winds were visible by their various disruptions on the surface. The sound of wind overhead in the trees was not always indicative of conditions down on the river. Shiny water is a kayaker's delight, but patches of opaque water indicated wind. These patches, distinctive by their size, position, and intensity, usually provided fair warning from breeze to gusts. After a month on the river, I could quickly determine whether to tackle the wind, skirt around it or head for leeward banks. Waves spoke for themselves.

The breeze came and went without influencing the cadence of my paddling, which had become so rhythmic I could have timed myself between blue markers. I continued with the same relaxed pace, the same pace of the sheep that kept land barren on properties on the New South Wales side. Now and then, a few would stick their inquisitive heads over the top of the bank—white-woolly faces sharp against the green and brown tones of the landscape—curious about the aquatic red creature gliding past their doorstep. Sheep have face-recognition abilities and can remember up to 50 other sheep faces for two years. They also have a particular talent of remembering which human faces lead them to food. Donna Mulvenna said, 'We want ewe to know, we are happy for ewe, but without any food, ewe are forgotten.' I said, 'I hope goats don't have the same ability'.

Over the weeks, small pains in the arms and shoulders have come and gone, each time disappearing when I concentrated on correcting the slightest of bad habits that crept in while paddling. All day, every day, I became familiar with my body's messages. During the usual afternoon's moderate pace I could concentrate on the form and integrity of my strokes to improve paddling efficiency. My usual low-angle paddling style was ideal for the less-tiring endurance paddling, but every so often I switched to the high-angled style where my hands were held steady at shoulder height. Used in the powerful sport of sprint racing, the technique using the same cadence had little effect on my overall pace. The longer low-angled strokes suited me with the kayak gliding along smoothly in the manner for which it was designed. With my body now more conditioned after long days of hard paddling, I switched between high and low-style paddling for amusement and usually came first in the race call that went along with it. Of course, all that went out the window when the wind howled and the water got lumpy.

The landscape slowly changed as the afternoon progressed. Rocks and rock ledges all but disappeared although with rock banks spearing into the water I maintained a careful watch for little surprises. Rain fell lightly a couple of times but only for short periods and provided more interest than dampness. The occasional log popped up in the middle of the river and while none resembled platypus logs, I did spy my first slender white spoonbill moseying around in the shallows. Bird feeding hour had come.

Further along, the long sandy beaches were replaced by reeds that covered, or more precisely, blocked entrance to most of the banks. Fifty metre high red Mallee Cliffs marked the end of the forest giving way to a two kilometre section of river known as Devil's Racecourse. The racecourse ran over a low riverbed but had no effect on driving the kayak though. Branches that had fallen from high above jutted out from the banks providing excellent springboards for darters filling in time. Easily mistaken for cormorants, the darters—that amusingly swam with their heads barely above the water as opposed to the other birds that float—were fascinating to watch as they dived from their branch to spear fish with their long sharp beaks. Then, in some fancy underwater manoeuvre, they detached themselves from the live fish before gobbling them down their slender necks.

During the afternoon, a widening river led me into the Gol Gol State Forest on the New South Wales side. The breeze remained moderate but by sticking close to the three to four metre high banks, under watch from patrolling whistling kites, paddling was more comfortable. The elements, combined with the length and width of the river, generated a moderate swell that rolled upriver and underneath the kayak. Thankfully the wind direction was on my side so as not to turn the swell to waves.

The river drew me 10 kilometres north before turning 10 kilometres west. Orange buoys tied to fallen tree limbs signalled a section of river that hosted another of the 80 kilometre ski boat races, this one downstream to Mildura. Shortly along, with the number 793 barely detectable, a 'mile tree' stood opposite a large assemblage of houseboats moored on a bight where steps dug into the bank led to the settlement of Karadoc high above. The surviving 'mile trees' date back to the 1800s when numbers were carved into their bark to inform the working boats captains of the miles from Albury to towns downstream (as opposed to my guilty pleasures, the blue signs which specify the distance upstream from the mouth of the river). The tree carvings, 50 centimetres in height, become less identifiable each year as the regenerating tree bark creeps back over the wound.

My original plan for camping tonight was at Bottle Bend just short of 50 kilometres for the day and within a day's paddle to the major town of Mildura. But with Bonnie Doone around the next bend reminding me of the iconic Australian movie, *The Castle*, my patriotic duty demanded an extra five kilometre push where my 'vast river experience' told me I would find a sandy beach. Two things surprised me: firstly, the spelling of the name should have alerted me to it not being the place referred to in the movie; and, secondly, reeds occupied the bank of the said sandy beach. Precious gave a squeal as I hauled her up into the reeds and over broken branches. The loud complaint was a touch dramatic resulting in, at worst, a scratch. I stepped out into easily managed ankle-deep mud.

Up on the levee bank the ground was clear area with plenty of wood for a nice campfire. The Bonnie Doone station on the opposite bank was not the small Victorian holiday destination of Bonnie Doon where gold was found during the mid-1800s gold rush. Also, unless the swans had really led me off-track, it was not the Californian wine region of Bonny Doon where headaches have been found since the 1980s.

The light rain was sporadic and did not demand an urgent setup or dinner preparations. Sitting on my tripod stool, which was stoically trying to hang on until the journey's end, I peered over at a stately homestead with its manicured lawns and noisy machinery. Later, as smoke wafted from their chimney and the sound of chinking wine glasses floated across the river, I hoped they were enjoying the night as much as I was.

Distance 968 – 915 53 kilometres
Moderate to easy day

Chapter 32

Bonnie Doone to Mildura

Day 32

Friday, May 3

Light breeze to moderate.

Overcast to sunny 22°C

I crawled from the tent on daybreak to see droplets from last night's rain glistening on the leaves that hung heavy from the extra weight. The scratch around under trees for dry wood to start a fire disturbed a few bugs and lizards but with a handful of kindling and a match a fire grew strong to warm my hands and boil a billy. With today's destination a mere 34 kilometres away, there was no hurry to get going and before long I sat on the three-legged stool enjoying a morning coffee. I breathed in an air of contentment with this being the last day of my solo journey for a while. My brother, Dave, will join me at tonight's stop in Mildura and, while there have been many positives of travelling solo, I looked forward to sharing the adventure and the tall stories that would eventuate.

Over the last month, I had never been far from help, but endurance and survival had challenged me, at times without notice. With every decision and consequence my own, it was satisfying to reflect on the resilience required for the price of independence. There had also been times when my mind wandered, sometimes into the realm of fantasy, and sometimes to achieve perspective. I took a stick, went down on one knee, and wrote in the sand, 'I am happy, and there's no better time to be happy than now'. I stood and looked back. The sand had closed in on itself, relegating my epiphany to memory.

My relaxed morning's leisure had gone on too long. The tent had to be packed wet as did much of the gear left out overnight. Also left out, and now wet on the outside were the indispensable dry bags, still in order despite designs from long-toothed marsupials that lurk in the dark recesses of the wild. After a quick gather and pack, I slid the kayak back out through the scratchy reeds and into the water at the respectable business hour of 9am. The only commitment I had was to reach Lock 11 at 2pm, the fixed time for downstream transits. Being one of the busiest locks on the river, it had a schedule of 'on the hour' for downward travel, and 'on the half-hour' for upward. I was advised to be on time due another craft having a regular 2pm scheduled transit.

The light breeze was not enough to disturb a bride's hairdo as I paddled north for 20 kilometres. Orange snag markers appeared on the many fallen trees. Stunning high red cliffs inspired the name of the settlement above...Red Cliffs! But Red Cliffs has a much greater history than its modest name might suggest. Following World War 1, the government of the day established Australia's largest soldier settlement dividing 33 thousand acres of mallee scrub into blocks to be taken up by 700 returning soldiers and nurses, some of whom had served in Gallipoli. The fight did not end at Gallipoli though, with the harsh conditions of the Mallee severely challenging the new custodians who were battling both physical and psychological scars. I tipped my cap as I passed.

Ten kilometres later a large houseboat came upriver driving on the wrong side of the river heading for the substantial landing of Trentham Estate Wines. As though I was invisible, or maybe because at 10 am people get thirsty, it cut directly in my path and pulled into the landing. How rude! Was it that inconsiderate drivers are not confined to roadways or was it that these 5-star hotels on water drove like house bricks. I pulled a grumpy face at the skipper—you do not need a skipper's ticket to drive a houseboat, obviously—as he pulled to a stop almost running over me.

Minutes later, I sat on the bank chewing on a protein bar and acknowledged how my grumpy face had passed immediately. It needed more than that to change my relaxed demeanour after 31 days of unification with the river in a bond of serenity, patience, and harmony. Having spent part of my career working in the retail sector, I had quickly learned how necessary it was to 'let go' when a grumpy or abusive customer unloaded onto a defenceless retail worker. Preferring an optimistic approach, I focused on the majority of happy, thoughtful customers. And for those grumpy folk, I hoped their moment of poor humour was the worst thing that happened to them that day. Hope is better than resignation.

Turning west at the picturesque settlement of Gol Gol, the breeze rose up to inform me that the 12 remaining kilometres to the Mildura lock would not be without effort. Paddling into the breeze was welcome though, as a bit of hard work sat comfortably with my current strong physical state. At Mildura's twin town of Buronga, the scenery switched to grand homes complete with sweeping green lawns and opulent boat houses. In contrast to the Victorian side of the river, which retained its natural beauty, Buronga was a parking lot for expensive ski boats and jet skis moored to impressive private pontoons.

Lying in the heart of a citrus and grape growing region, business must have been good. I had expected on this Friday afternoon that motor craft would be out for a joy ride but maybe the buffet at Trentham Wines estate had taken priority.

As I got closer to Mildura, the quantity of houseboats and small paddle steamers increased with many more moored in the marinas both left and right. Paddling under the George Chaffey Bridge that forms part of the Sturt Highway connecting Mildura to Buronga and, more importantly but not necessarily, Adelaide to Sydney, snappy modern buildings and the sweeping parks of Mildura dominated the banks and stretched down to the water. Having lost all sense of time, I was within a kilometre of Lock 11 arriving with half an hour to spare.

The weir and lock arrangement in Mildura is different from those upriver with one and the other being either side of a mid-river island. You can walk along a pathway around the lock (while it is closed), take a stroll around the island, and then wander over to the weir. The river entrance to the lock is along a channel retained by rock walls. Back from the banks, impeccably maintained lawns brought on a picnic like atmosphere. With the weir releasing its crashing water from around the other side of the island, I looked forward to an easy transition. The gates of the lock were closed and the only thing to do was wait for the other rivercraft joining me for its regular 2pm appointment.

Unable to disembark from the kayak due to the slippery moss on the rock walls, I sat patiently watching tourists eat hot chips, cream buns, and slices of watermelon. What were they waiting for? Watching a lock open and close is hardly entertainment. I reached for an apple I had had stored up front since Zimbabwe Girl and, after taking a bite, found it had gone soft. I threw it to the seagulls who regarded it with disdain, preferring scraps of chips and cream buns. What were seagulls doing way out here anyway? Had they been begging for chips since Mungo Man, the original owner of Australia's oldest known human remains some 42,000 years ago, inhabited the sand dunes of Lake Mungo? A horn blew from behind.

At precisely 2pm, PV (Paddle Steamer, or Paddle Vessel, for the pedantic) Rothbury smashed its way through the water towards me and thrust her huge bulk through the opening to the lock. My insignificance became evident in both size and importance.

Unlike regular boats that send out a V-shape wake from behind, paddle steamers emit a wake from behind their rotating paddles working from both sides of the craft. Depending on the size of the paddle steamer these wakes—that generate waves at right angles to the bank—can continue to roll along the river for a kilometre. With PV Rothbury generating waves at a metre high, the approximate height of me sitting in my kayak, I crawled behind to cover the 30 metres into the lock. Once both inside the lock, I expected the turbulence to settle. It did not. As the growing crowd on the bank rushed to get a better view and the passengers rushed to the outside deck, I now knew the reason they were there. To see me, in distress. I bobbed up and down with swell coming at me from every direction. If anything, the waves being generated off the chamber walls were growing with excitement. I sat still realising how risky it would be to paddle over or even take hold of the chamber's slimy metal ladder. Was that a compassionate voice I heard through the turbulence?

'Come on, we're wasting time,' yelled a female crew member from the rear deck of the offending monster as the lock's gates closed. 'Grab onto the boat.'

Jesse Jackson said, 'Never look down on anybody unless you're helping them up'. This woman had obviously never heard of Jesse Jackson. The vessel's deck stood a metre above the water and out of reach. The hull was visible underneath the deck but a metre inside. The three-metre paddle wheel consisting of a series of fitted blades remained immobile but precariously close. I breathed deep and kept my cool, informing her of my intention to continue at my own comfortable pace. Passengers crammed the deck to witness either my survival or my demise.

Just as the water began to settle, the lock gates opened and the Rothbury churned up the water leaving behind its huge wake. After waiting for a couple of minutes I ventured out safely. The spectators on the bank walked away as though their home team had lost a final in the dying seconds. Outside the lock, the PV Rothbury turned and headed around the island so that its passengers could check out the weir. The unobstructed river was open and calm for me to continue.

Dave had organised a cabin at the Apex Caravan Park, three kilometres downriver from the lock, so that we would not have to negotiate the lock's transport timing in the morning. Suspecting the Rothbury would be bearing down upon me any minute on its *tour de force*, I sprinted with Olympic speed to the beach across the road from the caravan park.

The sun was shining, the wind had dropped, and the birds were whistling. The long, wide beach divided a luscious, grassed park from the river where around 15 small groups and couples lazed about soaking up the sunshine. I took my crackers from the kayak, fished out the peanut butter and Vegemite, whipped out my spreading knife and sat facing the river as the PV Rothbury made its way past. It was 3pm. Even from my higher viewpoint, it gave the disproportionate impression of a cruise ship in a bath.

Sitting safely on the shore, I was about to take my first satisfying bite when a voice from behind made me jump.

'She's a beaut, ain't she?'

A weather-beaten old man with a three-day growth came from behind me. Dressed in an ill-fitting, long-sleeved once-white shirt that was tucked into old baggy suit trousers, his ensemble was topped off with an old felt hat from the 50s. Not a camper, a hobo, or a drunk, but a genuine Aussie bushman, one of a dying breed: literally.

'I was 'ere when we slid 'er into the river,' he said proudly. 'First of August 1909. Worked on the riggin' for Mr Anderson. Log boat in those days.'

I listened. What had today become fancy tourist paddle steamers *were* originally working vessels, but the dates seemed a little sketchy. I was being primed for something, money I expected.

'In the off-season, we'd load 1,600 bales o' wool up on the ol' girl 'n drop 'em down to Morgan,' he said, holding his gaze on the 'ol' girl'.

'Must have been plenty of work on the river in those days,' I replied in more of a statement than a question.

'Worked 'n the shearin' sheds mostly,' he said with his eyes wandering downriver after the boat. Then, looking back, 'Can't spare one of those biscuits can ya, mate?'

How rude of me not to have offered.

'Sit and have a couple with me,' I said.

I smeared peanut butter and vegemite across a selection of my finest crackers. Sitting quietly, apart from the loud chomping of the crackers, he gazed out over the water. I could see his memory filling with stories of his past along the river.

'Sheared for Mr Keir, head honcho in Sydney, out in the sheds between Punyelroo 'n Swan Reach,' he said. 'Look out to the right 'n the sheds 'r still standin'.'

'Aren't they used anymore?' I asked.

'Git most of their felt from t' other side of the world now,' he said, shaking his head.

'You've lost me, I'm afraid,' I replied, thinking it must be nearly time to go.

'Rabbits, laddie. We sheared rabbits for Akubra hats. Millions of 'em.'

Hang on, Akubra hats *are made* from rabbit fur, but ...sensing my doubt he carried on.

'Little blighters, we'd each shear fifteen 'undred a day. 'Nuff to make a hundred hats,' he said, proudly. 'You'll see the ol' sheds jus' after Punny.'

I sat thinking for a moment, and when I turned back, he was wandering off slowly down the beach, yellow perspiration stains decorating the back of his white shirt.

I wandered over to the caravan park, checked in at reception and grabbed the key. Not wanting to bother with setting up the trolley to transport the kayak, I carried the contents bit by bit across the 200 metres to the cabin. From past experience the kayak would be safe left on the bank, minus the paddle, until Dave arrived to help me carry it. Once again, my throbbing hip made itself known, but it was now in competition with a swelling that had developed behind my right knee.

Not my biggest day as far as distance, but through the constant effort against time and adversity, weariness washed over me. Sitting on my cabin balcony, I gave a big wave to the passengers of the Rothbury, hopeful for a win in the next final, as it returned upriver.

Feeling a million dollars after a shower, a hot shower, I laid out the tent to dry and washed my sweat-stained clothes ready for a fresh start tomorrow.

It was with a big hurrah that I welcomed Dave, my niece Soraya, and her daughter Elise. The conversation went differently than I had expected.

'Hello, brother,' I said with hand outstretched.

'What's happened to you?' he replied, stepping back. 'Where 've you gone?'

I looked down at my bare chest a little self-consciously.

'No. We can't have this,' he said. 'We need to buy food.'

As we unpacked the car his face took on an incredulous look. It was the same look as when river folk contemplated the enormity of '56 flood?

'Don't expect me to be ending up looking like you,' he said.

Having a car meant easy and quick access to town where we stocked up on indulgences. Feasting and drinking to health for longer than necessary, we shared a vibrant conversation about the adventures so far and hopes for those to come. The soft bed was very welcome, yet I wrestled with the pillow and quilt while trying to relieve my mind of pigs, platypuses, and plans but most of all my old bushman mate and the fifteen hundred bald rabbits released from the shearing shed each day.out Punyelroo way.

Distance 915 – 881 34 kilometres
Effort day completed by mid-afternoon

The River Murray settles onto the flatlands from the Snowy Mountains looking so sweet and seren resembling more of a creek than a river. Once inside the river, the cold clear water that shoots out fro the grade three rapids upstream requires attention to detail even for the experienced paddler. From th location the river marks the border between New South Wales and Victoria.

Looking from the Biggara bridge I took my first paddle strokes with more than 2 million to come. Cocksure but naïve, I had intended to wear a top hat over the journey. Fifteen minutes later I had lost the cocksure attitude.

The Hume Dam marks the end of the upp Murray. Established between 1919 and 1936 t dam holds in excess of 6 times that of Sydn Harbour. This picture shows the reservoir at 19 per ce capacity before it reduced to 9 per cent during my tr

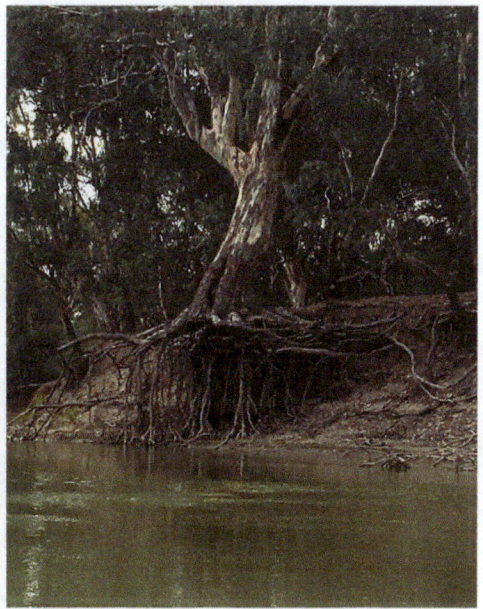

Blue signs every 2 kilometres indicate the distance in kilometres to the mouth of the river. Not wanting the journey to disappear I looked away but they were my guilty pleasure: they were my chocolate.

Known as strainers, the exposed tree roots of gum trees are fixed, many and deep. The sight of these age-old trees clinging to life is thrilling but the thrill is gone in an instant if driving your kayak into the inescapable labyrinth in a rushing current.

Many a sunset brought internal applause while I enjoyed a well-earned soup by the fire at the riverbank. During 'The day of the swans' the river was a mirror from dawn to dusk.

Downstream, in the lee of the Yarrawonga Weir, the gentle passing of knowledge from generation to generation continues as it has on the river for the past 60,000 years. It's hard to imagine such treacherous conditions in Lake Mulwala only a kilometre upstream. With this being my birthday I pondered the yin and yang of life and the necessity for both.

At the campsite of John and Jordana I witnessed the impressive reserve of wood (obviously brought from home) prepared for the upcoming Easter celebration with family for a pig on the spit. Despite the sincere offer to join them I wasn't tempted to travel the four days back upstream. But I was entrusted with John's secret European-learned technique to prepare the perfect Europen Carp meal which fortunately required less wood.

One of the many remnants of another time on the bank around Beveridge Island where time itself has stood still. Not a river shack, it might well have been home to a family of 6, 8 or 10 or even the family of Andrew and Margaret Beveridge and their 6 sons and one daughter who came to the region in 1846. On a sepia day when fantasy and fiction meld together another likely visitor may well have been Ned Kelly who was raised in Beveridge just north of Melbourne.

John holds his catch of a 1.2 metre Murray Cod before its return to the river. The next night he caught a smaller cod of 800 centimetres which was also returned to the river. The bait he was using was … a secret.

River guru Peter Phillips of Echuca stands smiling alongside myself and Steve Inglis despite being an hour and a half late for a function at his house. Peter's imparted knowledge of the river improved my experience no end for the rest of the journey.

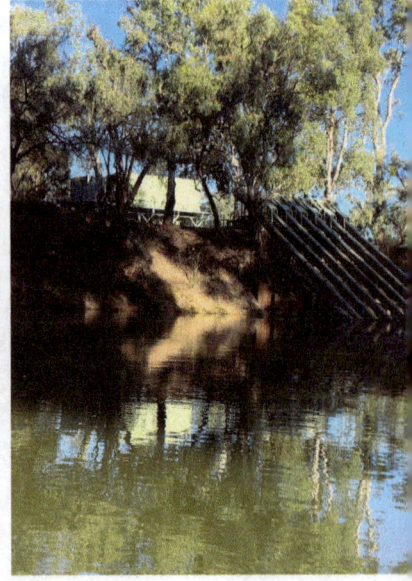

The paddle steamer P.S. PYAP was built in the river town of Mannum and originally used as a floating general store. It is now used for tourist cruises and even though over 30 metres long it can float in as little as 1 metre of water. These facts were not on my mind when it rounded the bend at Swan Hill headed in my direction.

Continuous banks of water pipes drawing water for irrigation hum away relieving the river of more water than reaches South Australia.

The picturesque sights of rock ledges and mid-river sand islands between Swan Hill and Mildura provided endless admiration as well as careful management. At times during this low water, they would reach across three-quarters of the river leaving only channels of rushing water for my progression.

Long yellow sandy beaches can stretch for 400 to 500 metres along the river and up to 75 metres back to the forested bank. In times of higher water they will not be visible and cause endless problems for inattentive houseboat travellers.

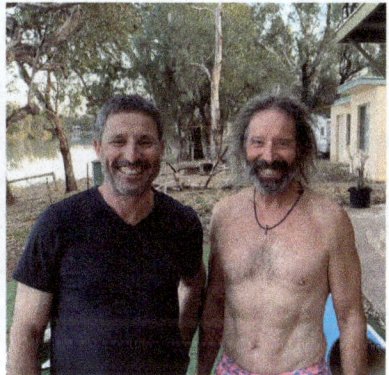

By the time I returned from the supermarket in the morning the 'family' had decided I would be launched back into the river on a boat trailer; but only after I had been paraded through the caravan park while seated in the kayak. Champagne glasses clinked as I successfully remained upright while paddling away.

My brother Dave found me in Mildura, happy but only a portion of my former self. The bushranger appearance might explain some of the gasps from people when I came upon them unexpectedly.

Nearly everything carried in the kayaks is used for evening and morning meals as well as camp set-up. The routine to re-pack the kayaks in the morning with everything fitting snugly back into the hatches was quite precise despite the messy appearance. This picture shows Dave organized a little quicker than me.

Brothers Steve, Geoff and Dave Inglis happily enjoy a morning coffee while Malcolm Cheffirs cooks up breakfast. Their bright and happy expressions changed dramatically over each of the 40-plus kilometres during the day while paddling from Morgan to Blanchetown with Dave and me.

One can only imagine an epiphany rose from the ashes of our festive night in Blanchetown when our hosts Anthony, Peter and Wayne decided that carrying the kayaks down 20 metres to the bank required energy better used for other activities.

The cliffs of Big Bend seem endless and with reeds occupying the opposite bank, there were few opportunities to pull in for a break. Rain fell continuously from midday and it was dark and cold before we could locate a suitable campsite. The cliffs were spectacular.

Downstream, in the lee of the Yarrawonga Weir, the gentle passing of knowledge from generation to generation continues as it has on the river for the past 60,000 years. It's hard to imagine such treacherous conditions in Lake Mulwala only a kilometre upstream. With this being my birthday I pondered the yin and yang of life and the necessity for both.

At the campsite of John and Jordana I witnessed the impressive reserve of wood (obviously brought from home) prepared for the upcoming Easter celebration with family for a pig on the spit. Despite the sincere offer to join them I wasn't tempted to travel the four days back upstream. But I was entrusted with John's secret European-learned technique to prepare the perfect Europen Carp meal which fortunately required less wood.

Lake Alexandrina at 26 kilometres long and 20 kilometres wide leaves a person in a small kayak quite vulnerable. Water conditions, described as 'soup' by Brad, thankfully remained favourable all night. The fog began to lift sometime after 8 am.

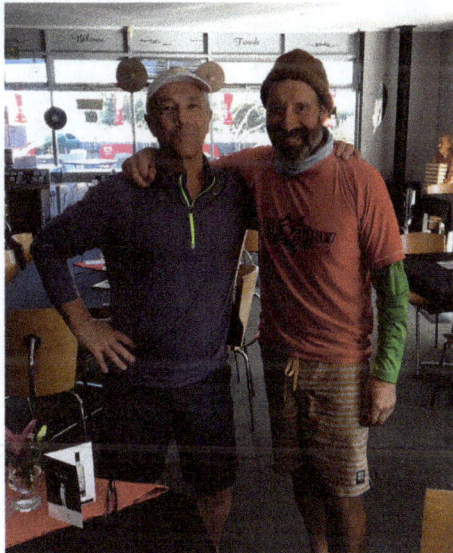

After a long night crossing the lake Brad looked like he was just warming up. He left the café after a quick coffee to go to work.

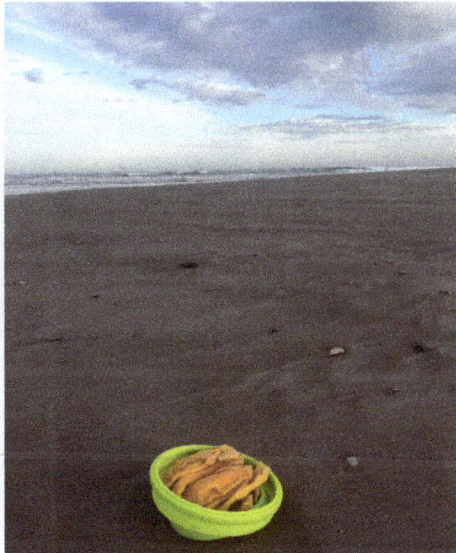

After 52 days I stood to watch the river spill its bounty into the sea. I contemplated paddling out but with strong winds and a 3 foot swell I ate 3 pieces of mango and decided I'd had enough adventure for the time being.

PART II

Mildura to the
Murray Mouth

Chapter 33

Mildura to Horseshoe Bend

Day 33

Saturday, May 4

Overcast with light wind 22°C

I was happy when the caravan park kookaburras signalled an end to the frustrating fragments of sleep and wake. There is the slimmest chance that sleeping on hard ground with a flat mattress might become my preference. I breakfasted alone as Dave, Soraya and Elise slept until the smell of coffee brewing brought forward contented morning groans and eventually the morning faces we all have but prefer not to exhibit as social media selfies.

The first job of the morning was to repair the leaking hull of Precious. As he did after the carnage of Day 1, Dave took control sanding back previous repairs that had lost their integrity before applying more of the ever-effective Five-minute Araldite. He worked much more efficiently than at Lake Hume without an inquisitive small brown dog licking his face. Word on the street is that water in Lake Hume has further reduced to nine percent of its holding capacity.

As he demanded, Dave drove us into town to stock up on supplies lest he should wind up looking like me in the coming days. The town of Mildura has grown large since my last visit 35 years ago when I remember little more than empty streets, pizzerias, and bars; and not necessarily in that order. The city has doubled its population to 32,000 whereas its little sister, Buronga, just across the river has just over 1,000 (and a lot of nice riverfront houses).

One of us was in no urgency to recognise the connection of paddling, daylight hours and distance yet my anxiety was soothed by an indispensable 45 minute bakery break. In addition to the extra rations a trip to the local camping store equipped us with a sealed egg holder as well as a new air-bed to replace my 'flatress'.

Dave's intention was to remain with me to the mouth before his return to work on May 22. At the current average of 50 kilometres per day the distance of 881 kilometres could be achieved. But Dave had not paddled lengthy distances before and the battle of determination versus fitness during these ever-shortening daylight hours as Autumn would be his challenge. Back at camp, Dave worked to balance his kayak for both convenience and weight distribution as I had done during the first week. That was all such a long time ago.

'I'm just gonna take this from the front section to the back.'

'Didn't you just move it from there?'

'Yeh, but I think when I moved the sleeping bag it changed the balance.'

'What about the egg holder?'

'That can stay with food, but I'm having second thoughts about the sleeping bag now.'

Dave's methodical attention to detail requires patience but it gives me comfort when seated next to him in his plane. At

1.30pm Soraya and Elise slid us backwards into the river to begin Part 2 of the odyssey.

River people along the journey praised this section between Mildura and Renmark, a three day paddle, as the most beautiful along the Murray. Our initiation to this beauty was an afternoon wind that blew up into our faces. In less than perfect conditions we hugged the banks to escape the stronger wind along reaches of the wide-open river. At a modest early pace Dave worked on his technique while enjoying the distraction of the greenery enveloping our passage. After 11 kilometres we stopped at Chaffey landing off the town of Merbein for a protein break and catch some breath. Steady, steady, there is still a long way to go.

Our paddling plan was set some months ago with an understanding that I would place no pressure on Dave to complete daily distances beyond his comfortable capacity. I was not bound to any time agenda yet for Dave 'The Journey' and 'The Destination' were entwined and at odds with each other. Even at this early stage it was difficult to assess whether his enthusiasm or his doggedness drove his pace.

The wind continued and after only another five kilometres a mutual nod of heads determined this would be our camp spot for the night. The experience of a nice beach 'just around the bend' or 'just over the next hill' when hiking is usually met with disappointment and we agreed, if just this once, to yield to Yhprum's Law, known since 1974 as the opposite of Murphy's Law. Ergo: everything that can go right, will go right.

'Only two pieces of mango?' asked Dave.

'That's enough,' I said. 'It's our reward.'

"We've got two kayaks and lots of space and we don't need to ration.' he pleaded.

The setup was smooth with Dave happy to fall in with my established routine. The regular evening meal of soup followed by 'couscous surprise' was as per normal but, having witnessed my weight loss, the challenge put before me now by Dave was to put some meat back on the bones. I have had no one to observe my before and after with the only indication of the extent of my trimming down being the fit of my clothes. Looking into the mirror yesterday and considering the initial shock from last night's guests, the point was valid. But I had been eating an overflowing frying pan of food every night and was not sure I could even eat more. The extra space now available in the second kayak offered the answer and we now had fancy extras like eggs and apples.

As the fire burned through the evening, plans were proposed and re-proposed with the absence of any real intention to comply. Mainly talking for talking's sake and in the excitement of being by the fire, under the stars beside the river, I extravagantly poured us a *third* glass of wine. When we squeezed into the two-man tent I pressed down and discovered a renewed comfort between me and the hard ground.

Distance 881 – 865 16 kilometres
Challenging paddling over the short distance

Chapter 34

Horseshoe Bend to Jackson's Reach

Day 34

Sunday, May 5

Sunny to overcast with a building breeze 20°C

With total disregard for my new mattress, the kookaburras invited Dave and me to the new day well before acceptances. Although we were busy the morning came together at a much slower pace than usual. With two of us working together the fire was reignited and the billy was soon boiling away. A caffeine adrenalin spike changed it all. Like a well-oiled machine we assumed complimentary pack-up tasks with only a nod of the head and slipped into the water within the standard 90 minutes at 8.30am.

A glass river below and synchronized swallows above welcomed Dave to the adventure. The one plan from last night we did observe was to ease Dave into the regimen of a full day's workload. We would paddle only 32 kilometres today to Lock 10 at Wentworth and camp just below the weir. Dave felt good, or so he said, and by the time we had travelled through the bends and curves, past beaches rock walls and pumps, and under Abbotsford Bridge, we pulled in for the morning break opposite an exposed rocky ledge imposing on the river: a 20 kilometre morning session.

Before leaving, I rang the lockmeister at Wentworth to advise our likely transition at 2pm. Clouds began to roll in as we began our final 12 kilometre paddle to the weir and with that a westerly breeze aimed directly at us. The river was wide and the water flat although along the longer reaches a rolling swell came up towards us. A few hopeful fisher folk in their tinnies roared past in the hope of hooking that unlucky fish before somebody else got it.

Ahead of schedule we could travel without any urgency to achieve our goal. I relieved Dave of the need to push too hard for our appointed time and paddled on ahead intent on amusing the lockie with some friendly banter while we waited. As I got closer to the weir, the lure to witness the flow-challenge Darling River took over. I had time. The Darling is the major river joining the Murray and its significance is recognized by the label given to the one million square kilometre catchment area as The Murray Darling Basin. I could not see very far along the 2740 kilometre Darling that stretches all the way to Queensland but what I could see consisted of dry riverbed.

River lesson #11: It is preferable to paddle on a wet riverbed rather than a dry riverbed.

Talk, talk, talk! Now known as 'a conversation', the end result is the same: inaction. I had read about the current situation while in Mildura and I shared the hopeless sentiment of the report. It lamented the power of The Murray Darling Basin Authority, an 'independent' body established in 2008 to oversee the sustainability of the waterways for irrigation and the health of the river to protect its flora and fauna. With politicians, land holders, water rights holders, and environmentalists each tugging in different directions the poor Murray Darling Basin Authority is but a toothless marionette. Reports of corruption and poor management continue to surface while politicians meet along the river wearing their Akubra hats as fish lie dead in stagnant pools upstream in the barren Darling River. Maybe a flood will come to wash away all the secrets. I put my camera away without taking a photo.

I wanted to paddle into the Darling for posterity's sake while I waited for Dave but not only did I not want to lie aground for three years as did the PS Jane Eliza in the 1800s but it was counter to the spirit of Dave and Lucky Lee's adventure where we unite like the rivers to reach the sea and taste that last piece of dried mango together. I travelled to the bank opposite the Darling outlet and sat waiting for Dave so we could paddle up to the weir together.

The wait was so long I became concerned Dave's kayak had developed a technical problem. I rang the lockmeister to apologise for the inconvenience of our potential lateness. He laughed.

'He's waiting here for you.'

'No, he's behind me,' I replied, all-knowing.

'Well, there's someone in an orange kayak waiting at the gate.'

Not only is Dave's kayak yellow—pointed upwards at both ends like a Viking kayak and resembling a banana—but he was also behind me, so I knew it was not him. I was surprised though that another kayak on the river had escaped our information vine. News travels fast out here.

'Must be someone else,' I said. 'You better let them through, and we'll catch you after.'

There was a short delay.

'If your brother's name is Dave, he says to hurry up.'

I cannot repeat exactly what I said and the lockmeister and he probably did not hear because he was laughing too hard.

Awkward, messy, hilarious! Dave had passed by on the other side of the river while I was obviously not watching and called out while I was obviously not hearing. I paddled like crazy only to receive mock abuse from the lockmeister who was not worried in the least.

Full of information about Wentworth and its surrounds we were informed of the Rabbit Plague of 1933 when estimates of a billion marauding rabbits reduced the land to dust. I quickly calculated that would provide fur for over 66 million Akubra hats if they could be herded into a suitable paddock. With Australia's population being six million at the time it would mean there would be 11 hats per person. They say Australia was 'built on the sheep's back' yet in 1933 it could well have been fashionably attired on a rabbit's back. Australia: A nation of many hats. Indeed!

I must have been swirling in a whirlpool when I came to. The lockie had switched talk to the weir. It maintains the water level at capacity only ever varying by five centimetres either way; except in times of flood when a section of the weir is opened for river craft to travel up and downriver without the need to use the lock. Looking much too young he quietly shook his head in reverence.

'The '56 flood,' he said. 'The town is built on such low banks they race to get sandbags when a wake boat passes.'

Dave and I nodded our heads in recognition.

With a smooth exit from the lock we found a sandy beach and rather than pull up stumps for the day we broke out the afternoon crackers. Now, I did not want to be picky, but Dave piled the peanut butter and Vegemite on in lashes and taking things a step further applied both to each of his six crackers. This was a serious breach of rationing, and I grabbed the crackers in case he went for a seventh. It is about the journey. I let it pass.

Over the late session accompanying Dave's groaning, pre-sumably indigestion, kangaroos and goats came out to cheer us along as we slipped around several rock ledges protruding into the river. We passed more hopeful fisher folk in tinnies along the tighter meanderings. Relaxing with dangling rods in the water many young couples were enjoying the extended time between bites with intimate one on one conversation—apart from the passing groaning kayak.

The hours rolled away with conditions so agreeable for paddling. We had travelled much further than planned and at 4pm we jointly agreed to push past a sandy beach with the intention to end the day at the next one just around the bend. Five kilometres and 45 minutes later, with Dave's indigestion now echoing along the river, we slid up a muddy bank in the Wallpolla Island State Forest.

Far from the typical forests upriver we had landed on a designated campground all laid out for regular visitors. By the amount of available wood, visitors had not been many. With little more than a nod of the head Dave set the fire, I erected the tent, out came the three-legged stool, and in short time we enjoyed soup as the river flowed by under our admiring gaze.

The day's distance of 47 kilometres was far in excess of our easy paddling plan. Dave works hard—he is a powerful and determined beast. But his groans suggested a reigniting of old injuries rather than indigestion. As I waited for sleep to come, Dave slept. But the depth of his breathing had me thinking of ways to curb his physical eagerness without curtailing his mental enthusiasm.

Distance 865-818 47 kilometres
Some moments of extra effort

Chapter 35

Jackson's Reach to Lock 9

Day 35

Monday, May 6

Blue sky with no wind and a glassy river 24°C

I opened one eye. I heard nothing but silence. I opened the second eye. Still silence. What a strange morning. The kookaburras had slept in, and the corellas had crept away so as not to wake us. I unzipped the tent the cold of the new morning struck my face. The sleeping bag was warm and my eyelids became heavy. Dogs, cats, horses, and most likely platypuses can sleep with their eyes open. But not me. An extra 20 winks or even 10 washed over me but before even one wink, at precisely 6.51am, a large black messenger in the form of a crow began its daily news report.

Dave sprang from the tent and before the crow had finished scratching its blackboard he had the fire going and a coffee in hand. Coffee bags are tastier than instant, but it still tasted like dirt. Even so, standing with a warm cup in hand, watching the smoke drift over the river, the experience alone was worth the effort.

We got busy and after the standard 90 minute pack up pushed Precious and The Banana off backwards into the river. The dent our kayaks made as we paddled was the only disturbance to the picture-perfect reflection of the surrounds on the water. In conditions so serene conversation was an unnecessary extravagance we moved along in silence through the forest lined meanderings in our own private river. Many anabranches ran off to the left and right, most only accessible in higher water, with those at our level thin and swampy. Even during higher water, these anabranches would be more suited to poly kayaks like Dave's which are tough enough to travel over rocks and snags without being damaged. My Precious snubs her nose at such skid row distractions in the same way royalty does when waving in obligation at the peasants from the closed tinted window of a Rolls Royce.

The whir of a tinnie motor disturbed the silence from time to time with all heading upstream in that typical impatience of the occupants to get the best secret spot. Chatting with the occupants of one craft, as is the common practice of the brotherhood along the river, we learned the tinnies were coming from a caravan park named Fort Courage, owned and operated by the Wentworth Angling Club. They enjoyed more success fishing upriver and through Lock 10. I think they were just going through Lock 10 for the jokes!

After an easy 18 kilometres, we pulled into a 'private' sandy beach on the New South Wales side for our protein bar break and, due to the new rations at the brother's insistence, we also had an apple. Yeh! Living the cuisine dream. Behind the sandy beach there was a substantial permanent setup developed for entertainment by the owners boasting shelters, tables, toilets, storage sheds and lighting. Even a permanent fish cleaning sink with running water stood optimistically by. After half an hour of recuperation we headed back into the water enjoying the same glassy conditions as earlier.

Three and four metre high banks kept us in our river cocoon with little connection to the countryside above and beyond. A short distance along, however, the trees stopped and the barren banks turned to red. Curiosity got the better of us, so we parked on a wide shallow bank and climbed up to see what this new country looked like.

'What do you see on your side?' asked Dave as I reached the top ahead of him.

'Saltbush,' I said. 'What's on the other side?'

'Saltbush.'

And that was that. We had entered the land of endless saltbush which extended to the horizon on both sides and supporting nothing but saltbush. It was as if a distinct line was drawn across the countryside. This landscape was so familiar from my many holidays in the Riverland region, but I never expected to witness such a dramatic environmental change at such a precise moment. Back in the water, the river changed little apart from the meanderings lengthening between bends and a few longer reaches but in such perfect conditions these stretches, while less interesting, were easily managed.

We agree to an early second break with fatigue and pain catching up with Dave. But where were those nice sandy beaches when you needed them most? Finally, we dodged around a couple of stumps and negotiated our way onto the bank of a small muddy anabranch. More and more reeds had begun taking over the sandy beaches to the point it was becoming nigh impossible to find a beach that had not become overgrown. These reeds, being native to Australia, are a filter for the river and would receive our greatest respect if not for the fact they were so inconvenient. Like seaweed on a beach, all that is needed is for them to become a viable economic product and our pristine river beach would be returned. More seriously though, visible through shallow water an underwater weed menacingly known as Killer Algae now lurked below, showing its un-native face with an imposing coverage reaching out from the banks in the slower flowing water. Not the insidious blue-green algae, it has the deceptively enchanting appearance of a fern-like aquarium plant. The solution is obvious I told Dave: more plants in more aquariums. Forget the fish; the plants look attractive all by themselves.

This session of 20 kilometres must have brought on an appetite and I watched on incredulously as Dave had seven crackers with Vegemite and peanut butter instead of the designated six. Comfort in food can show up at the strangest times. Over lunch, and with minimal phone reception, a scratchy call to the lockmeister at Lock 9 revealed he closes the lock at 4.30pm. Our relaxed day of paddling meant we were caught half an hour short of time to pass to the other side. Our night would be spent on the up-side of the weir. It was only 10 kilometres to the weir so, apart from the onset of dusk, we were in no rush.

A short distance along from our stop we passed the modestly sized opening to Frenchman's Creek which houses the inlet regulator to Lake Victoria, South Australia's water reserve. The lake helps control water during floods, releasing it when flows upriver are low. Covering an area of 12,000 square hectares—or 17,000 soccer fields, or three times the collective area of all the Monopoly and Scrabble boards ever produced—this lake is not available for recreational purposes. Entry into the creek is prohibited. Lake Victoria is the smallest of the four lakes along the Murray with Lake Alexandrina occupying 65,000 square hectares, Lake Mulwala 43,000, and Lake Hume 15,000. Morosely, like the other lakes, it gives the impression of a tree graveyard where flooding has drowned the trees of the original natural landscape.

Further downriver the substantial opening to Wallpolla Creek gave the impression that it was more of a lake than a creek. Birds and wildlife abounded. I chalked that up as another good place to explore next time. Kangaroos had turned out in large numbers along the bank during the day, but it was the birds that stole the show. Pelican squadrons lazed around in abundance as were gulps of cormorants blocking the skyline when they flew in their own haphazard formation; whistling kites called to us with one flying to its nest proudly displaying a fish in its talons; darters as always; and the odd parrot flew by to show off its striking plumage.

Within 300 metres of the weir, our choice in finding a landing spot led to a compromise. A metre high bank with a little grassy knoll looked promising. We pulled in around tree strainers, hopped out into water up to our waist and dragged the kayaks up onto a well-used and popular campsite to the side of a dirt road. Neighbours to the left and right within 20 metres were unavoidable and brought a stark change from the seclusion of beaches and forests upriver.

The hunt for firewood was more difficult but not for the more experienced such as us—or so we thought. It turned out the campers around us were equally experienced. Never a real problem, though, and a strong fire burned with a billy boiling for soup in no time. Dave is a stickler for having dry neoprene paddling boots and they would always occupy a place around the fire, usually in the smoke zone if one can ever determine where that is for any consistent period of time. One friendly older neighbour from Barmera, a town downriver, came over on sunset and chewed our collective ears for a while before we made the mistake of saying another word and he chewed them for a while longer. A short while later a yell inviting us to tea came through the trees from his caravan campsite.

'You boys wanna cup o' tea?' he called in the same brash manner that the grandfather upriver spoke to his grandson.

Not quite an invite and more like a demand. We could have been on the other side of the weir and still heard him.

'We've just made our soup,' Dave yelled back. 'We'll come over afterwards.'

'Suit ya'self,' he yelled back.

Within 10 minutes his voice again pierced the darkness.

'I've just put a log on for ya,' he yelled. 'Tea's out on the table. I'm goin' over to see some friends.'

So, we were to make a cuppa at *his* caravan, take a seat by *his* fire, and enjoy our *own* company. What? Laughing, we went over to his expansive, purpose-built caravan campsite, boiled his kettle and did enjoy his cuppa and fire, less a biscuit which we greedily guessed might be on the cards. As we left, with him nowhere in sight or earshot, we doffed our beanies in celebration of the bland generosity that will disappear from the Australian culture within a generation.

We were still laughing with joy as our heads hit the pillow or, in my case, the sack of clothes that had replaced the pillow that holds no air.

Distance 818-770 48 kilometres
Easy day

Chapter 36

Lock 9 to Bluey Bend

Day 36

Tuesday, May 7

Calm increasing to storm before settling 20°C

'You're gonna get blown from here to Kingdom Come'

We woke to the gravelly prediction of our elderly neighbour keen to deliver the latest weather report. We peered from the tent expecting him to be standing before us. No, with stars still in the sky we could see him over at his caravan fussing about and securing anything that could be blown away. Our meagre phone reception had already alerted us the prediction of winds of up to 40 kilometres per hour yet as we emerged to greet the day—or more correctly, night—conditions could not have been more perfect. Nevertheless, we ate and packed in haste eager to take advantage of the fine weather while it lasted.

The entry into the kayaks down a metre from the bank was precarious but successful with neither of us wishing for a morning swim. We paddled off leaving our neighbour shaking his head as though a repetition of the '56 flood was looming. We arrived at Lock 9 a minute later with gates wide open and green lights inviting us in. We were the first customers for the day. Above us on the concrete bank stood the lockmeister, 8am coffee in hand, and the jokes started immediately.

'So, you guys sorted out your differences then,' he began. 'Found each other this morning okay, did ya?'

Ah, so the lockmasters chat with each other up and down-river. Droll, very droll, as Officer Dibble would say. They have been very friendly, contrary to the grumpy reputation river folk habitually honour them with. They have always been willing for a chat, and apart from our need the keep going, I am sure we would be invited to lunch, dinner, and their first-born if the opportunity arose.

The lock dropped us four and a half metres and as we exited, the experience of entering a new river world was as exciting as all previous transitions. With the river no longer held artificially high by the weir, the bank's new height from down in the kayak brought on a different visual perspective through changes in light, colour, and depth. In addition, the return of the river to somewhere nearer its more natural state brought on a feeling of tranquillity that settled over our little micro-environment. The local inhabitants returned to the banks and trees. It was getting harder to sustain hope but their appearance sent visions of the elusive platypus. A kookaburra laughed at my optimism. I called back, 'Your laughter reaches my ears, but hope comes from my heart'.

We paddled for the next 17 kilometres along much longer stretches of river in calm windless conditions and water inside four metre white banks. Passing Ned's Corner, with its high yellow banks, the line of trees on the top was no disguise for the saltbush plains that swept from it into the distance. When the river direction turned from southwest to northwest, we took the opportunity to break for sustenance and for Dave to top-up on painkillers to relieve the increasing pain in his back. He has continued along without complaint but with the high paddling style his fixed-angle blade paddle demands, his back and shoulders during the latter kilometres of each session were screaming. The preferred low angle, endurance style paddling was not possible without creating more problems with the potential for a wrist injury. Additionally, in the back of our minds, we constantly calculated the distance per day we must travel to enable him to reach the mouth before heading back to work. Without question his body health will determine the ultimate conclusion.

A breeze sprang up while we rested. Heading away, enveloped by the Wangumma State Forest, the coverage did little to alleviate the strength of the developing wind but the blue skies offered hope for a return to our calm conditions when the heat of the day subsided. It took some digging in and Dave with a newfound and pain-free threshold led the charge as he worked himself into 'the zone'. We pushed into the wind along much longer reaches for another two hours enjoying the challenge and admiring the scenery but most of all appreciating the absence of humming irrigation pipes that state forests forbid. Spectators had lined the banks for much of the last 15 kilometres and although they were not able to clap or cheer their support was appreciated. Ranging from kangaroos and emus on the Victorian side, to goats, cows, and sheep on the vegetation-stripped New South Wales side, they kept their gaze as though we might suddenly spring from the kayak in the middle of the river and either eat them or convert them to some strange religion; both of which have their pros and cons. The kookaburras that were busy early during our meandering snuck away as the wind increased. Snags and trees in the river reduced significantly as the day progressed but, with the river wide, at no time did they affected our progression. We stopped for the second break before the final session charge to Lock 8, nine kilometres downriver, where we would soon after set camp. There we would discuss the erroneous severity of the weather prediction by our gravelly-voiced old friend up-river. We laughed at the urgency of him tying everything down around his caravan. Reception was fine so the lockmeister took our call and would be ready for our transition.

The final assault became more like the final insult as the wind reared up as soon as we took off. We had been advised to expect winds up to 40 kilometres per hour, so the only sur-prise was when it came. And that time came on quickly. Once again, Mary Poppins came to mind, and as the banks were our friends and we kept them close along the long stretches. The banks not only provided leeward protection but a respite from the waves which had grown much more menacing in the deeper middle of the river.

The lockmeister was waiting to send us into our new river. Being only a two metre drop, we could see the river from over the top of the weir as we paddled closer—hardly a need for the weir at all. As we came out into the new world the storm grew in ferocity and, thankfully, our destination of Shoal Beach was a mere five kilometres along the reach and around the bend. Thick dusty clouds began to roll in and conditions grew treacherous. The distance of five kilometres was now a long way away. We passed a group camping mid-way along the reach who, by the look on their concerned faces, knew more than us about the approaching weather front. Heads down we drove forward, expecting conditions could not get worse. Rounding the bend, a thick orange weather front blocked out the horizon. Still well into the distance, we shared a nod in congratulations of beating it. We were nearly at the beach and so close to our destination. The horizon was suddenly at our front doorstep. We were swamped in a matter of seconds, the front darkening the sky and blasting us with orange sand and dust. Paddling was impossible so we turned to the sandy beach and falling as we exited the kayaks, dragged them to a small clump of young gum trees.

We could only hear each other by yelling and, through this, we agreed to erect the tent within this group of small trees close to the bank. This would avoid the danger of the larger trees behind the beach falling on us. We erected the tent with great difficulty, pegging it down and loading it with our belongings to keep it stable and safely in place. As we collected wood in the vain hope we could have a fire at some time later, we turned to see the tent somersaulting down the beach intent on us having a campsite further back and, maybe, if we were not quick enough, in the river. The beach, fortunately, was 400 metres long which gave us time to chase the tent and carry it back. The wind by this time had subsided slightly. A fire was out of the question, but we were confident of having safe shelter for the night. Crackers and tuna inside the tent would do for dinner.

There is a lot of our father in Dave. Content as I was to endure this night and mark it down to experience, Dave's mind worked towards broader solutions. Returning from a walk downriver some 400 metres he reported a designated campsite complete with a wooden table and bench seats, compliments of Victorian Parks and Wildlife. Reluctantly, for I had already had my two pieces of dried mango, I had to agree with his proposed move. We carried the erected tent with its contents along a dirt track and set it up in a clearing by the table and fireplace but far enough away that embers and trees would not disturb our hopeful repose. We then paddled the kayaks down and slid onto the sandy beach in front of the campsite. Within moments, Dave was attending to one of his true passions. He likes fires. And, he has a tried and tested methodology. Old coals will become new coals very quickly once a new fire encourages them. The best way to build a coal-producing fire, he claims, is to burn the largest log he can possibly drag over then surround it with smaller pieces to keep it burning. Happy as I was with modest fires in the forests upriver, Dave's roaring infernos brought results to nullify the cooling nights that May was bringing upon us.

The storm had passed but the wind coming upriver remained constant. Without indicative signage we named this campsite Bluey Bend. Firstly, because the wind *blew* so hard and secondly—in honour of all the red-heads that enjoy the Australian nickname of 'Bluey'—because of the thick red dust that invaded our afternoon and settled over everything. The fire was set a little too far from the table for heat but, with ingenuity, a piece of corrugated iron was found and placed at the fire's edge, serving as a windbreak and a heat reflector. Large logs previously arranged for stools served as further windbreaks. I would not let Dave burn them. Taking advantage of the table for more comfortable food preparation, we enjoyed a treat of fried potato chips as well as our soup and main course. With a glass or two of our cask wine to wash it all down, we wanted for nothing.

During our after-dinner chat green-eyed spiders, whose eyes glowed in the dark, roamed the grounds mistaking our fatigue for vulnerability. Lurking in the darkness and just out of reach, the eight-legged vultures circled around waiting for the opportunity to have a piece of us. When it was time for sleep, we tip-toed to the tent careful not to break their hearts or anything else. The zips were closed tight.

Distance 770-727 43 kilometres
Easy to very hard

Chapter 37

Bluey Bend to Lake Victoria Station

Day 37

Wednesday, May 8

Clear with cloud building, breezy 20°C

After holding onto branches with their little feet during the wind yesterday and overnight the kookaburras must have needed a sleep-in. Dave and I were happy with the late wake-up call at 7am. I packed the tent and even though we had pitched it in the clearing with 30 metres clear on all sides the vacant land was littered with small limbs that had fallen from the surrounding trees. Meanwhile, Dave kicked up the coals that were still glowing from last night's inferno and with the billy boiled we enjoyed hot water on our muesli and prunes.

Over coffee, and with the convenience of the camp table, we attempted to fix the Whisperlite stove using the seal replacement kit purchased upstream in Albury. When we fixed it at the time it only needed one O-ring so the choice to buy the Annual Maintenance Kit for 25 dollars rather than the 65 dollar Expedition Service Kit was sound. Rookie error!

River lesson #36: When one seal perishes, all others will follow.

As we slipped into the river at 9am a light breeze cooled our faces and when the conversation turned to today's weather prediction neither of us had anything to offer. We knew of yesterday's wind with rain expected tomorrow but neither of us had checked today. Without phone reception we were at the mercy of Mother Nature herself. Fancy two grown men leaving themselves open to the vagaries of nature. The worst that could happen was stories for the grandkids.

The river was wide with long bends and long reaches. For now, the tight meanderings had left us. The breeze direction was unpredictable, swinging around and not in sync with the direction of the river. It is difficult to predict the wind direction when down on the water. At times I could hear howling in the trees yet on the water total calmness, at other times it would channel up or down the river and in a different direction to what I observed from the trees above. This morning it came from the west, yet every bend threw up a surprise as to whether it was at our backs or in our faces. It was light and of no consequence anyway. With blue sky above, the water glistened on the many rocks sitting proud mid-river and, as we dodged the small outcrops, the fallen trees and underwater snags provided more entertainment than difficulty.

The further we travelled, the clearer the river became of these obstructions. Replacing them came long sections of reeds blocking access to the beaches as well as many areas where young gum saplings shot up close to the waterline. All this new growth suggested the river was reclaiming the banks that had been changed to beaches over the past low water seasons. Having moved through Wangumma State Forest we slipped quickly through the river corridor of Lake Victoria

State Forest before entering the 6330 square kilometre Murray Sunset National Park. We had paddled 17 easy kilometres when we pulled up to an open sandy beach for our first break.

Dave found a new lease on life and, springing from the kayak, he dug into its hatches bringing out protein bars, boiled eggs, and apples. Where will this extravagance end? Previous days I was not seeking more than a protein bar but now seeing the extra food I happily munched it all down. On the surface this cuisine dream might not excite a gastronome but some-where down the track, when I would tell a yarn to grandkids, they would know it went down better than a crunchy water rat being gobbled down by a long-toothed platypus.

As we paddled away, I was comfortable that the extra food did not add any weight to the kayak. After all, I had just trans-ferred the food from the kayak hatch to my belly.

The Murray Sunset National Park is a thick but spindly forest and provided good protection from any breeze. The dif-ference in environmental protection between a National Park and a State Forest is clear. No boats, no campers, no visible camping sites or access roads: access to the banks was limited by land and river. Further inland the park offered many great walks and natural scenic attractions. Another spot to visit on the 'to do' list. Over the next hour and a half, the water began to creep its way up to where the trees met the edge of the bank and the flow slowed to a dribble. The seven kilometre grind to Lock 7 used up all the morning break feast. Along a lengthy reach a sign featuring an X-shaped white cross appeared on the trunk of a tree. Peering diagonally across the river, another appeared. Known as the Saint Andrew's Cross, this signal alerts river craft that a channel exists between the two from point to point to avoid running aground on an underwater sand-bank. No problem for a kayak. Soon followed a green beacon mid-river signalling for us travelling downstream to pass on the 'port' side, or 'left-hand' side for the less nautical. It unnecessary for us, but we followed the directive seeing as though the dredge, Manno, that had served to help construct many of the local weirs, lurked somewhere under the shallow water. The floats strung out to alert craft not to approach too close to the weir came into view and we directed the kayaks toward the lock. The transition through to the new world river was without incident or joke.

Spilling out two metres lower we entered the shallowest section of Murray. That is, apart from the beginning that had slipped to the dark recesses of my memory vault. The level is so low that transition up or downriver is not possible for larger craft such as houseboats, riverboats, and paddle steamers, many of which have been stranded for extended periods of time attempting to reach the lock from downriver. Even we were advised by the lockmeister to steer clear of the wide sandbar directly out from the weir. We did not. After dragging our kayaks across to the narrow channel, we gave the lockie a wave and paddled on.

Within 500 metres, the Rufus River emptied its available contents into the Murray. This was the same water diverted into Lake Victoria vie Frenchman's Creek a couple of days ago. Whatever they did to it during that time is a mystery, but it came back out the colour of iced coffee. The new colour dominated the whole river. More succinct than this insult, The Rufus River has a much more sinister history dating back to 1841 when at least 35 Indigenous Australians were shot by police and volunteers who were sent to protect the crossing of 6.000 sheep and 500 cattle into South Australia. Known as The Rufus River Massacre, reports from the 'settlers' told of 'marauding blacks' numbering in the hundreds, intent on murder. Standing defiant with rocks and spears, no account has been produced to date from the local Maraura people's perspective. Queen Victoria had sent instructions some time earlier that 'both natives and settlers were equal subjects under her Crown'—evidently taken as a suggestion rather than an instruction.

Time and again the shallow beds on the inside bends caught us out and we found ourselves having to stick to the outside bights to stop being caught on the bottom. Fortunately, it was all sandy bottom through these parts and the kayaks suffered no damage when we strayed. Within another kilometre, the next river spectacle faced us: groynes. These take the form of a line of wooden posts erected in earlier days across the river extending from the bank to all but the outside channel. They are a version of a breakwater in the sea and were originally covered in brush, resembling a brush fence. Remnants from early days as a method to maintain the depth of the channels by arresting sand and silt drift, they remain in the river as just posts with a safety beacon, usually, on the outer edge to indicate where groynes finish and the channel begins. That these have been left in disrepair and navigation through this region is nigh impossible for anything but a tinnie or kayak, the ineffectiveness of the groynes to benefit travel by paddle steamers of the day is obvious. While we considered paddling straight over, any remaining wires still connected to the posts spelled trouble.

The river narrowed, meandering again, and contained by three to four metre faded yellow barren banks. There was a great wilderness appeal to the density of the smaller spindlier trees above as we glided between the Murray River Sunset Park and the Lake Victoria State Forest. The Murray River Sunset Park, Victoria's second largest national park, is home to 600 species of plants and 300 species of birds as well as the native Buloke woodlands. During 2018 alone, the Victorian Government revegetation programme assisted in the planting of more than 300,000 various seedlings in the park.

We stopped for the afternoon break at a sandy beach after only another five kilometres. The sun, disguising the coolness of the day, demanded a wash and swim before we feasted. The Rufus showed its true colours. Not only had it changed the colour of the water, but it had seriously affected the water temperature. It was ridiculously cold, headache cold, and I rose quickly from the water after diving under. The wash and swim were brief, and I detected the other party having more of an English wash.

Throughout the afternoon, wildlife numbers increased, and coming in closer for a visit. Spoonbills and herons flew in, pelicans had gathered in great numbers, emus wandered cautiously, and kangaroos sipped the iced coffee at the water's edge. Murray River Sunset Park was a popular haven. When our planned sandy beach opposite Lake Victoria Station showed up reed-free at 4.30pm, we pulled in just in time before the wind kicked up and clouds rolled in.

We set the tent among trees for wind protection and, with a hole in the sand on the beach, our fire burned safely. Dave finally got the energy to submit to his fishing passion and set a line with a lure to catch breakfast. Soup and dinner went down as usual and, while we sat around the fire watching Dave's kayak boots dry and waiting for a fish to bite, a green-eyed spectator had plans of its own. A wily fox crouched within 15 metres with a covert mission which would include either fish or dry bags full of provisions: or both. To its eternal disappointment we packed everything back into the kayaks after dinner.

We received phone reception briefly and headlining the news came reports of yesterday's storm. On May 8th *The Guardian* reported: 'A huge dust storm blanketed the northwest Victorian town of Mildura on Tuesday afternoon, turning daylight to midnight in a matter of minutes as the front blew in from the west,' adding it to be 'the worst storm in 40 years'. Forty river kilometres west, we sat in our kayaks upon the water experiencing the very same. As one fellow kayak traveller remarked, 'every paddler of the Murray has to experience one storm'. With expected rain overnight and tomorrow we hoped the 'one storm' was now in the back pocket.

By 8pm the wind had dropped. The river flowed quietly past. Nestling back in the soft beach sand, fire crackling, good company, the sky was clear all the way to the stars. I could hear something whispering. Maybe it was the fox.

'Are you watching? I see stars in the sky as well as stars in the river.'

Distance 727 – 688 39 kilometres
Moderate distance under nice conditions

Chapter 38

Lake Victoria Station to Customs House

Day 38

Thursday, May 9

Overcast with light breeze to storm to rain 16°C

Dave set the alarm on his phone for an early getaway ahead of the forecast poor weather. What Dave did not do was charge the battery. The kookaburras did not wake us either and must have known something was brewing, wasting no time in heading for the hills or wherever they go to avoid the elements. I accepted some of the blame with Dave in that the solar charger I carried was ineffective and provided little to no charge for my phone either. The poor performance of the solar panel and charger was frustrating also from the aspect I could not keep in touch with my children in England to allow them to share my journey.

We had packed the night before to fox-proof the site so with a quick breakfast and no coffee we paddled away at 8am. Dave had pulled in the fishing line before breakfast only to see it waving in the breeze. He blamed losing the lure to some giant lurking below the surface and its ability to wrap around snags to break the line. I blamed the fox.

The anticipated rain forecast for 7am to 7pm had not yet started. Cruising under an ominous sky facing only the lightest breeze conditions was eerily comfortable. This was typical of the last few days where predicted weather did not eventuate until around 11am. The scenery was exciting with high cliffs and low banks, more groynes to paddle around, shallow beds, through the bend of Devil's Elbow, and all the while enjoying the national park setting. The formerly *treacherous* Devil's Elbow proved a *piece of cake* Devil's Elbow. Since naming this bend the everchanging river had cut a new channel turning a 180 degree bend into a 130 degree bend although the shallow underwater beds around the bend still demanded respect from larger craft when passing through. After a joyful morning paddle we pulled into a small sandy beach opposite the old Lindsay Cliffs Station perched high above on the ... yes, Lindsay Cliffs.

A check of the *River Murray Charts* book indicated we had travelled 28 kilometres during the excited morning session. Over a protein bar and an egg we sat speculating what other unexpected joys awaited while paddling towards our destination of the old Customs House, a mere 23 kilometres downriver. Dave handled the longer than usual morning distance pain free and we celebrated him breaking through the pain barrier. A closer check of the chart book dampened the celebration. With no evidence to suggest the river had created a cutting we had paddled through without noticing. Reducing the length of the river by five kilometres, the old section was now inaccessible leaving a lagoon surrounding what is now known as Pollard's Island. There were no signs to suggest Mr and Mrs Pollard had the island on the market.

Once back in the water we travelled for six kilometres around snaggly, long bends passing more of those insidious date palms before being revisited by our old friends, the swirling currents and whirlpools. We then shot through a narrow waterway called Higgin's Cutting, another of the Murray's new pathways. As before, the old river was inaccessible leaving behind Reedy Island, also not on the market. The distance saved this time was three kilometres. The river then turned toward a north-westerly direction, heading for the borderline where New South Wales meets South Australia. Step right up! Step right up! The moment we turned, the skies darkened on the horizon and the show was about to begin.

The next 15 kilometres was a pure grind along the long reaches that gave breath to the ever-increasing winds. Waves rose up before us, splashing over the kayaks and into our faces as they grew higher and higher while getting closer and closer to each other. We hugged the banks as much as possible while negotiating the snags from fallen trees now dangerous both above and below the surface. Still only a line on the horizon the colour of the incoming front looked dark and sinister. We kept a vigilant eye on its progression. Having been through the dust storm of two days ago, did we learn nothing? The aim was to reach the border marker within a kilometre where we could take pictures for posterity while taking our afternoon break.

The front took us by complete surprise by the speed it came upon us and its ferocity. In mere seconds the wind blew up so strong that we were being forced back upriver out of our control. We were paddling close together and, with our paddles joining our crafts together for stability, we yelled above the noise of the storm to find a tactic for our survival. Close in my mind was a story told to us by an old-timer upriver. It concerned a couple of young lads kayaking along this very part of the river, a section normally easily navigated. In similar circumstances one of the lads became caught in strainers, overturned, was trapped underwater. Unable to clear himself, he could not be saved. Looking toward the metre-high bank, all I could see was strainer after strainer.

With our kayaks held together, the wind was forcing us to the bank. Unable to direct ourselves, we would soon be tangling with the strainers: a situation too dangerous in my eyes. Things were happening at break speed, and we could not agree on a plan. We separated and headed to the bank in whatever fashion possible. The wind pushed me directly to the bank and, with luck, approached into a gap between the strainers of two trees. Calling on my experience from Day 1, I leapt from the kayak into the water when I got within a metre of the bank. Bracing myself for the landing one hand took hold of the kayak but, instead of my feet landing in sand or mud on a shallow bit of beach, I completely submerged. Life jacket on, as is the law, I bobbed up and swam, guiding the kayak to the bank. Safely taking hold of a strainer and finding the riverbed on which to stand, I secured the kayak to the slippery tree roots with the marine cord that was still attached both front and rear. Turning to find Dave, he was nowhere in sight. When we parted, he had chosen to steer his kayak backwards up the river. I clamoured up the slippery bank and ran frantically in search.

I feared the worst and could neither see him or his kayak from my position on the bank. Across dense vegetation, I raced back upriver through scrub, leaping over fallen logs, in a mad charge along the bank. A hundred metres along, his kayak sat lodged in strainers at the bank. Dave was nowhere to be seen. As I got closer, I saw a rope tied to a tree root and as I raced even closer found him safely sitting against a tree on the bank. Oh, joy! The wind was howling, the rain raged down in sheets, we were both wet and freezing, and we were still here.

In the shelter of a large gum tree we sat talking over the ifs, buts, and maybes. Both of us were drenched and shaking with cold. Dave pulled some warm clothes and a groundsheet from his kayak to manage the situation as best we could. We agreed this was the spot for the afternoon break. Crackers with Vegemite and peanut butter—and he was welcome to as many as he wanted—was the best way to celebrate the escape from potential disaster. We agreed that this event be considered as a bump in the road, a mere distraction because to dwell on possibilities that never eventuated was unnecessary and unproductive. It reminded me again that this river can be a playground, filled with fun and adventure, but it claims lives and commands respect.

The wind subsided within half an hour and we took back to the water with our rain jackets secure and us freezing and shaking inside of them. We passed the New South Wales-South Australia border sign within one kilometre. If there was ever an anti-climactic designation of precinct, then this was it. A wooden sign, barely discoverable, with an arrow pointing in either direction of the river, it would be passed by without notice to all but a slow-moving kayak paddler. Considering the uninspiring river signage to date it should not have come as any surprise. Towns were not designated by signage along the river, bridges have names, but no visible indication is given from the river, and far less than half of the blue navigation signs remain in place.

Rain continued to tumble down from low, gloomy skies. The wind reduced to a breeze for a while but, as we came along the reach leading to what is now the Customs House General Store, it again intensified. The Victoria-South Australian border went by with its sign similarly forgettable. We had lost interest by then. But the Murray River was now the River Murray. The river that set the border between New South Wales and Victoria was now entirely enclosed by South Australia.

With a difficult day done, we were looking forward to set-tling in at the bar for a review of events. The sight of Customs House was as good as a rainbow any day of the week. Customs House was operational from 1884 to 1902 to collect excise from river craft transporting their wares into South Australia for sale. It ceased operation after the Federation of Australia united all states and custom duty between states no longer applied. Today, overlooking 500 year old gums, it operates as a tourist attraction, general store, and a houseboat marina.

The lockies upriver had spoken of a group of seven paddlers ahead of us and it was here we caught up with them. As we came to the bank, the sign inviting paddlers to alight was bent, broken, and camouflaged by reeds but, with Ron to the rescue, we were directed to a beach of sorts. The others in his group of seven occupied the entire other beach section where they had set up tents before the storm had hit. We had made good time despite the conditions and at 4.30pm, under the dark skies with rain still tumbling, we squelched our way up to the general store.

CLOSED

The attendant/owner had just left for Renmark and she would not be back for an hour and a half.

Lucky Lee and Lucky Dave!

Nothing to do but wait. The male owner/operator was no-where to be seen. One of the Robinvale friends kept a house-boat moored here and had offered the use of a hot shower; he could not have foreseen these conditions but this was a gift of major proportions. There were five houseboats moored off the bank and all I had to do was remember the name of Skeg's boat. But there was no one to tell it to anyway.

Shaking with cold, we set up the tent and changed into dry clothes. The shower was just a dream. In driving rain, on an open gravel park, it was nice to be dryish again, if not yet warm. Eventually the owner returned and reluctantly opened the store for us to get a beer, a bottle of wine and a packet of chicken chips. She pointed out Skeg's houseboat and confirmed his advice to her. A television in the sheltered entertaining area out from the store played the news as we all gathered around in the dark and cold waiting on the weather forecast. Phone reception was zero. The owner brought out some hot water for our instant soup before returning inside. Shortly after, the male owner wandered through, grumpily stating that he 'hates the cold'. He went inside the store, grabbed a beer, came back out, complained about the cold again, turned off the television, turned off the lights and went back inside without another word. We all stood dumbfounded.

As we all headed back to the tents we became aware that the male operator was informed of Dave and my arrival and that we might be in distress due to the cold. When the other kayakers suggested the combustion heater in the outside entertainment area could be lit, he merely replied, 'tell 'em to rug up'. Like the reviews from the Robinvale Caravan Park, bad news spreads quicker than a storm front. Why have a broken and bent sign half hanging from a post inviting paddlers to stay if you're not going to cater for them? The spirit of the Aussie bush and the camaraderie of the river had taken a hit. This was no Barham!

Still raining and a campfire impossible, Dave and I settled ourselves in the tent with our drinks, chips, crackers, and a couple of sachets of tuna. The kayaks were covered as best we could but were left to the elements. The night stayed cold and rainy, and we had a good laugh over events, expectations, and anything warm we could think of.

Distance 688 – 637 51 kilometres
Really tough day

Chapter 39

Customs House to Murtho Forest

Day 39

Friday, May 10

Overcast, breeze with rain 16°C

We woke to the less than inspiring temperature of 0°C. It was clear the pleasant days of Autumn were behind us. Everything we had left out was saturated. As the saying goes: We are in the water 8 hours a day, we drink it, we might as well be wearing it. The rain had stopped for the time being. Last night one of the kayak party had enquired with 'Old Grumpy' if coffee would be available to buy in the morning. The machine sat outside under the shelter and took coins, but it needs to be turned on.

'What time will you be open in the morning for us to get a coffee?' The request was polite.

'Early.'

'What time is that?' they politely asked again, to assist all nine of us organise our morning preparations.

'I'll be up early!'

He was not, and the hope for a coffee faded as quickly as Dave's wash just upriver from the Rufus.

We were cold, our hands were wet and cold, and the tent and fly were wet. The temperature topped it off and made packing up difficult. The other kayakers were hovering around, rubbing their hands together for warmth, and looking for a chat. They belonged to a group named, Just Paddlers, hailing from the New South Wales river city of Taree. In consideration of the weather forecast and following the stories of our misadventures of yesterday—which had grown out of proportion within their camp—they had mutually agreed to pull the pin on this next leg of their journey which would take them into the town of Renmark, some 70 kilometres downriver. They explained that each year they progressively paddle another section down the Murray. Due to the less than favourable conditions, next year's leg would begin here at Customs House. Mostly of retirement age, they paddle for fun, and right now it's not fun. So, why continue? Even though Dave and I cannot enjoy that luxury, I got it. Snug now in our kayaks with all our wet weather gear to protect us, the Taree paddlers stood in a line along the bank and sent us off with paddles waving in a 'paddler's salute'.

The swallows did not greet us this morning as we headed off. It was rain that swept in over the river. Fortunately, the breeze blew the rain into our faces to help us forget our freezing hands. 'Cold hands, warm heart'. That saying might be true but we needed a short time for the heart's radiator to fire up. When our jaws thawed conversation turned to laughter and the world turned back to its spicy, unpredictable, and colourful self. The banks, lined with lush trees, were at times two metres high and at other times descended gradually to meet the water on what might once have been a beach before its natural revegetation. Leaning into a bend, we listened for the sound of motorcycles: nothing. This Isle of Man, formed by the river once again cutting a more direct route, had no castles and no racetrack like its English counterpart.

Within a kilometre, the site proposed for the construction of the Chowilla Dam remained covered in trees. Controversial from the outset in the early 1960s, the dam to provide water for South Australia was agreed to by all states and associated bodies. The site was chosen because it is downriver of all the Murray's major tributaries. The reservoir would be 90 kilometres long and 32 kilometres wide and stretch all the way back to Wentworth in New South Wales. A strong environmental protection campaign halted its development in 1970 citing salinity concerns as well as protection for the natural forest. The Chowilla floodplain borders the Murray Sunset National park and is currently listed as 'of international importance' yet argument still rages over its benefit to the three states bordering the Murray and the prospect of turning South Australia into a 'garden state'.

The rain abated, the breeze did not. After 17 kilometres of cliffs and forest, long bends and reaches wandering along a narrow waterway, the weir of Lock 6 came into view. Without phone reception we could not draw attention from the lockmeister, so drawing the short straw, Dave ran the bank to his office. Dave refused to confirm or deny but the time spent, combined with his satisfied smirk, had coffee written all over it. Within 30 minutes we were on our way and when rounding a bend found a sandy beach for my first break of the day ... and Dave's second.

We set off in a shallow section of river where Saint Andrew's Crosses once again alerted larger river craft to observe the channels. The river stayed narrow, and we enjoyed a visual forest feast turning bend after bend in a return of the tight meanderings. Heading now in south-easterly direction the sheltered meanderings also provided relief from the prevailing breeze. The tops of the wooden groyne posts continued to appear with their safety beacon drawing us to the narrow channel rounding the bight of the bends. Just as we entered a long reach another weather front loomed ahead.

The front was obvious by the dark cloud line extending across the horizon over this flat country and even more obvious because it was making a beeline towards us. With yesterday firmly in the memory we took our second break in the shelter of two massive gums. The timing was perfect as the rain teemed down and the wind blew hard.

Bob Dylan wrote:

'And if I pass this way again, you can rest assured
I'll always do my best for her on that I'll give my word
In a world of steel-eyed death, and men who are fighting to be warm
Come in, she said
I'll give ya shelter from the storm.'

A hollow in one of Mother Nature's trees sheltered us from the storm as we sat facing upriver. From where we sat under the stormy sky, the haunting vision of a heavily wooded dead forest dominated the landscape before us. As far as the eye could see, the light-grey trunks of dead red gums stood side by side amongst their fallen comrades, their few remaining lifeless limbs reached toward the sky as though pleading for help. This devastation could not be from a change of season. These trees were two metres around the trunk and many hundreds of years old. This area has some of the oldest, naturally occurring river red gums forests along the Murray but they rely on regular floods for their survival. The current water management of the river has reduced the flood regularity with this area being just another consequence of 'management'. The rain stopped and the wind settled and within half an hour, with a belly full of biscuits, we ventured back out. Birds and animals had taken the day off. Wherever they were, we were not.

The final session for the day wound back and forth along many high red cliffs with vertical scarring etched by wind and rain. As we again bounced off another of the red cliffs a large sign on the edge of a cutting advertised the Woolshed Brewery at the old Wilkadene Station. The popular boutique brewery is within a short drive from Renmark, the closet town, as well as a short paddle for us. A magnet turned the noses of our kayaks but, with a few ums and aahs, we straightened up and pushed on. Having both been to this watering hole before, we would be setting camp there if we stopped. It was too early in the day and it would leave too far to paddle tomorrow to keep to schedule.

The wind was kind to us although the river threw up waves as we ground our way along the longer stretches. Working the leeward side of the river and keeping to the banks we were able to avoid anything too uncomfortable. Our wet weather gear had stayed on all day, for warmth as well as protection against the intermittent showers. When we passed the final cliffs for the day an eight kilometre reach rolled out before us. Not quite a reach, the bend was so long it gave the impression of being part of the reach. The wind subsided and the sun peeked through to suggest the promise of a nice sunset. The reach, being a reach, did not possess the bends that deliver sandy beaches, so onward we pushed, kilometre after kilometre, with one of us on each side of the river trying to pull a rabbit from our paddling caps to materialise a suitable campsite. On the edge of darkness, we compromised and pulled into the Murtho Forest Reserve in muddy gluck and dragged the kayaks ten metres along and up a small rise.

Setting up in the dark was not preferred but inevitable. With both of us now familiar with the morning and evening routines we were soon in our night gear under the stars. The tent site was upon a bed of leaves providing an extra-comfortable mattress for the night. The fire was good, the food was good, tomorrow we would head to Renmark for a luxurious stay in the caravan park. Oh ... and hot showers.

Distance 637 – 588 49 kilometres
Long, cold day

Chapter 40

Murtho Forest to Renmark

Day 40

Saturday, May 11

Cloudy and calm 16°C

The Kaa-kaa had a sleep-in, but we were ahead of the game.

'The Kaa-kaa?' said Dave.

'Never too late to learn a new language,' I said. 'It's in the Noongar Dictionary I was reading last night as you snored.'

'Too early, brother.'

And he turned back over with a faint 'kaa-kaa' to resume his 'sleep to wake' procedure.

I had been browsing online over the *Noongar Dictionary*, compiled by Rose Whitehurst, as I wound down in the tent last night. The Noongar translation was the first to pop up on the internet of the 120 languages that remain since British occupation. There is an eagerness and an urgency to preserve these languages, all that remains of the 250 thought to originally exist.

The internet also alerted me to strong winds forecast for today. Last evening's late push cut our remaining distance into Renmark to a mere 20 kilometres. Even so, we wanted to get away as soon as possible before the winds rose up in anger. Dave rose from the tent to see me covering the fireplace with sand. His words were unprofessional. After all, his mother and mine are the same!

'Coffee can wait,' I said. 'We'll be in Renmark in time for morning tea.'

The river was flat, calm, and shiny and in record time we ate, packed, and slid in. The slide was after dragging the kayaks back ten metres to the bank, through mud to our knees, with boots saturated, and plenty of laughs. Within a kilometre, the end of the everlasting Woolenook Bend turned away but not before exposing the remnants of the Woolenook Bend Internment Camp. It is now reduced to a couple of old sheds and rocks designating the pathways and worksites. It was originally established in 1942 to contain Japanese internees and prisoners of war who worked to provide timber to fuel the Renmark and Berri pumping stations. When the Japanese were relocated in 1945, Italian internees carried on the work until the end of the Second World War some months later; although some Italians were held until January 1946. The interning of Australian immigrants has become more controversial as the years have passed. My own grandfather was interned during the war in the country he chose to live and love, leaving his family to fend for themselves. This was despite his entry into Australia in 1899 and being Naturalised in 1915. Dave and I talked for while remembering the 'ship in a bottle' he constructed during his time in internment and which now holds a special place in our family's history.

A light breeze popped up every so often but along the broad meanderings it did not impose on our paddling. The river became wider contained by one-metre-high banks. Any time the banks looked like they would descend down to a beach, reeds had taken over. Fifty metre high red cliffs rose up on the southern side and it gave the impression the river bounced off of them before returning to be bounced off again. We were paddling with intent and the wind was holding off, so we entered a bank at Ninkle Nook Bend through the curtain of a weeping willow tree. We had no reason to stop so soon but the joy of landing on a place named Ninkle Nook Bend was too inviting.

River lesson #69: Ninkle Nook! Ninkle Nook! Ninkle Nook!

The final assault into the town of Renmark drew us along a nine kilometre reach directly south along a river so wide a golf ball could not be hit across it. Pelicans sat lazing in numbers facing the breeze and watching our progress, knowing they were safe from check-panted golfers lurking upon the bank. We pushed hard to beat any oncoming wind front but need not have bothered. The morning breeze remained the same and just strong enough to keep the perspiration from or brows. Renmark came upon us in quick time. Before long, the substantial Ral Ral Creek to our right came and went and the old magnet, the Renmark Hotel, drew us ever closer. The 320 kilometre journey from Mildura passing only one town, Wentworth, had been completed.

The town of Renmark opens along the river with a rotunda, rowing club, riverside bar, and expansive lawns. There was no sandy beach on the banks, but it took Dave and I no time to find a suitable place behind the Tourist Centre to alight. Dave's poly Banana did not mind crunching up the rocks to the concrete pathway and I nestled Precious into a clump of soft reeds nearby. We left them in trust as I had done all along the river. Dishevelled and smelly, we wandered up the grassy bank towards the hotel where we were to meet a friend for lunch, breakfast, snack—it did not matter which—having spent the last seven days in the bush we just wanted, no, needed treats.

It was 11.30am and our friend was yet to arrive but who should we see, but two separate friends wandering into the pub for a morning tipple. Is that a Saturday Renmark thing? Apparently it was, as it was for the legendary 'Breaker' Morant who lived in Paringa, the town across the river before he took a paddle steamer and train with his Renmark and Paringa mates, the 'Glory Boys', to enlist for active duty in the Boer War in 1899. He was known to have ridden his horse up the stairs and into the Renmark Hotel for a drink, some claiming he would jump the horse over the bar. The name given to the front bar until recently was Breakers Bar before renovations removed the honour. To pay homage, or not to pay homage? Either way, it was not for us, with the temples we call our bodies, unwilling to imbibe that early—it is a long day after having a beer for morning tea.

Our friend arrived shortly WERRNRER and we did our best to infuse the sweet aroma of seven collective weeks of camping into her car.

'You stink,' were the first words that came from her mouth.

The Bakery and coffee shop were happier to excuse our bush company and accept our travelling dollars; although the lamb's fry pie in mixed company tested the boundary of etiquette.

'You're not getting into my car after *that*,' came a more direct response.

But we did.

We shopped for provisions during the early afternoon and replaced the battery in my phone. With luck the solar charger will now keep up with charging our phones. I learned that a federal election had been declared since my journey began and would be held in a week. How relieving to have escaped all the palaver that goes on during the laborious campaigns. Renmark had a pre-election voting station in case we were somewhere more interesting on the special day. Dave informed me he had already voted.

A site to camp was offered by locals, Brad and Lorna Taylor, with running water and facilities. Problem was, none of us had a clue where. I phoned Brad to ask for directions and made the mistake of asking whether it had survived the '56 flood. There was no answer because of all the head shaking and, after five minutes, I hung up. The Riverbend Caravan Park near the Paringa bridge, however, had way too much going for it. At $135 for the last available two-bedroom cabin, I will remember the comfort way longer than the exorbitant price better known in the trade as highway robbery. We paddled the kayaks three kilometres down to the photographic little park and pulled them up onto the grassy bank for the night. Removing everything for drying and cleaning, the afternoon was taken up with maintenance.

Come evening, we headed to the Renmark Club, overlooking the river where we discovered an irresistible 'all you can eat' buffet on the menu. The buffet filled every possible need for me and Dave, and 80 per cent of the clientele. Brad and Lorna had offered to have us over for apple pie but overeating at the buffet was always possible, probable, and proven.

Was it the food? The drink? Was the bed too soft? Too hard? Was I worried by all the noise coming from a cabin across the way with the potential for one of the revellers to do damage to the kayaks? Either way, I slept poorly and rose at 5.30am to make notes on river conditions and distances between the towns in the days to follow. The chart book we'd come to rely on finished at Renmark. Winging it in the river above Yarrawonga, before the chart book began, was risky in comparison, but so natural. The Breaker wrote in a poem published in the Renmark Pioneer on June 14th, 1901: 'Our deeds of "derring do" I guess, in years to come we'll well recall'.

While drawing up the plans I had to consider our health. Dave has continued to rely on painkillers to help him cope with shoulder and back issues. The distances covered were less than expected but beneficial for his overall wellbeing. It was now touch and go as to whether he would finish the journey to the mouth with me or if he stopped because of his next work schedule. My hip pain remained, with the prospect of it continuing throughout the adventure a distinct probability. Being in otherwise good health, it was disappointing rather than debilitating. Painkillers were off the menu and it was only when bending over to the ground to prepare food at nights that the pain bit. Dave is careful not to get his waterproof paddling boots wet, I had not, thinking that my feet could dry overnight. I had taken to leaving the boots off during the middle sessions of the day to help them dry and warm. The continual dampness had often left my feet quite cold and, consequently, the pressure on them when paddling and steering, resulted in numbness to my toes. A mild swelling behind my right knee had developed and I could not identify what was causing the problem. Stretching helps a little but the continual inactivity of my legs, effectively immobile for six weeks, was a rather weird circumstance which could manifest other problems. Other than that, we had pains in the side of our faces from smiling too much as we enjoyed this amazing adventure. May *that* problem never be cured.

Distance 588 – 565 23 kilometres
Easy

Chapter 41

Renmark to Lyrup

Day 41

Sunday, May 12

Mother's Day

Overcast, calm with light breeze later 16°C

I hardly needed to wake because I hardly slept. Dave was having no such problems so, as siblings do, I woke him at first light so he would not miss the fresh new morning. Peering out of the front window of the cabin we turned to each other with the same questions. Who would have imagined the grass in a caravan park would need watering and who would have imagined sprinklers would come on at night to perform that task? The kayaks were left on the grass between the cabin and the river but only Dave had the foresight to turn his over. Precious, with the trolley and the solar panel loaded on top, sat upright and full of water. At least they had not been interfered with.

The busy morning went like: shopping centre for provisions, the Old Firehouse for a coffee and breakfast burger, hunt unsuccessfully for a Whisperlite stove repair kit, then on to Brad and Lorna's for the much-anticipated apple pie. Of course, it was only to catch up with them and hear about why we could not find the campsite on the river that they had offered. Dave brought up the subject of fishing and before we could blink, Lorna had him out in the yard filling up a container of worms guaranteed to catch half the supply of the Murray.

Back inside, over a cup of tea, Lorna chose not to speak of the '56 flood. No, but a story even more incredulous. She talked of THE pelican invasion. Lorna worked for the Renmark Pioneer newspaper forever, until her retirement into the rose business, and stories of the Riverland rarely got by her and Brad. Her lips tightened and she shook her head in reverence.

'It was one hot summer,' she began, still pursing her lips. 'There must have been hundreds, maybe a thousand pelicans.'

'It was in the mid '80s, Lorna,' Brad chimed in.

'Yes, the streets of Renmark were overrun,' she continued. 'There were so many, they were walking into the shops to cool down in the air-conditioning.'

Brad let go a chuckle. 'One even stole a lady's handbag and took off with it.'

'It's happened often over the years,' Lorna said, pursing her lips again. 'There's no warning.'

All this time I had been worried a long-toothed platypus taking off with the rations and now there was an even more sinister predator gathering daily in numbers around us. I will not look upon the squadrons of pelicans the same from now on.

We returned to the caravan park eager to continue our journey. While Dave finished packing, I called the lockmeister of Lock 5. It was 11.27am.

'G'day, mate,' I said. 'We're leaving from the Paringa bridge and we'll see you in five minutes.'

'Bad timing,' he replied. 'I knock off for lunch at 11.30.'

We had forgotten their hour and a half lunch break. To be fair, most of the lockies would need that hour and a half to maintain their impressive protection against the risk of gravitational degradation. Working on that same principal Dave and I headed to the bakery to fill *our* gravitational tanks. Passing the pre-electoral office the 'Closed for Mother's Day' sign gave notice as to who really wears the Prime Minister's pants.

At last, back in our comfortable seats, we slipped away at 1pm. The 24 hours of eating did not sit unrecognized as we paddled under the Paringa bridge with the weir in view. Within five minutes we were down three metres and being spat out of lock 5. The advantages the chart book, which had finished at Renmark, were immediately evident. The river's direction was confusing with a complex organization of back-waters all as wide as the river and all inviting us in. The first fork was solved by Google Maps and gradually the river-proper became more obvious. The river's width narrowed a little and we paddled under an overcast sky with nary a breeze, slipping into the zone and charging along. We passed the free-camping area of Plush's Bend, full of its happy free-loaders and headed through bends, turns, and reaches with many shallow areas that stretched seven-eighths of the way across the river. Nav-igation markers appeared in the water and on trees to help larger craft negotiate the difficult sections up and around this region that has, we were proudly informed, the fourth busiest lock on the Murray. Oh, yeh – that's what they all say!

The waters remained calm throughout the afternoon while we continued in quiet conversation until 4.30pm. One kilome-tre short and with the Lyrup ferry in sight, we slid onto a piece of carpet and into a most remarkable campsite. The site is a popular local spot with its tall, shady gums, manicured grass and even a designated fireplace ready to go. But not so popular that anyone was sharing it with us tonight. We were only in town one night, but it was so nice to get back to nature. Dave dropped in a fishing line and as quick as he could take his seat for soup, the bait was gone. Three baits later he gave up for the night. Early indications were that these worms may feed half the Murray rather than hook them. Lorna is a wily one and might be anticipating some nice well-fed fat fish coming her way upriver before long.

With a new phone battery and every device fully charged, I set to write up diaries and post our progression on social media for the many that had kept me company for the adventure to date. Even though the reception was good, the post would not upload and frustrated, I accepted this game is best left to the young. But only for tonight.

The night was clear and calm and as we sat by the fire enjoying a little evening wine, the lights of the ferry shone through the trees as it went on with its business. It may well be the fourth busiest ferry on the Murray.

Distance 565 – 537 28 kilometres
Easy and reasonable distance for a 1pm start

Chapter 42

Lyrup to Proud's Sandbar

Day 42

Monday, May 13

Sunny, light cloud with slight breeze 20°C

At 6am we rose with the full intention to wake the kookaburras. Not a sound from them—they were not laughing now! The inside of the tent was covered in condensation and the outside was covered in dew. The price had been paid for camping on grass. Dave struck up the remnants from last night's fire and as it warmed our hands we boiled the billy for a coffee. Every morning was cold now. This morning's sun, when it did arrive, was ineffective and did nothing to dry the tent. A quick shake to remove, or at least disperse the droplets was the best we could do before packing up. I was still on the usual six spoonfuls of muesli with four prunes for breakfast. I gave up trying to rationalise Dave's rationing.

The slide into the river from the grassy bank and over the carpet was luxurious. Through the tress we had observed light

from the Lyrup ferry going back and forth across the river all
night—well, it was moving every time one of us rose during the
night. The ferry operators work 12-hour shifts starting at midnight and midday before being relieved. A check with the ferry
operator disclosed a disappointed admission of this being the
seventh busiest ferry on the Murray. He was considering ways
to promote his ferry but, well, there was no rush. We came
upon the ferry and waited for the cables to be at their slack-
est, and therefore deepest, crossing as it pulled into the bank.
In near perfect conditions we glided along through sparsely
vegetated one metre high banks and without needing to use
the rudder for nine kilometres passed the manicured lawns
of the Berri Ski Club. Signs offered free camping with the
grounds offering shelters, amenities, tables, and bench seats. I
remembered John, the fisherman from upriver whose mother
had sent a photo of hippies on the stone wall at Martin's Bend.
I could see nothing remaining of the hippies or the stone wall.
There was something in 1989 about a wall coming down in
Berri, Bali, Berlin ... could be this one. Anyway, there were no
remains. Nor were there any remains of the sticky green weeds
that were reported to be growing like ... well, weeds. However,
by the dreary look on the puss of a couple of kangaroos lying
around with nothing to do and nowhere to go, there might
have been a secret stash nearby.

Two kilometres later the grand presentation of Berri opened
before us with its steep bridge in the background rising above
like a Riverland version of the Sydney Harbour Bridge. Dave
needed a sun protection cap, so we pulled in. His successful
catch from the Berri Sports Store was celebrated with a bacon
and egg sandwich and a coffee at a most pleasant café on
the waterfront. As always, interesting characters can be found
along the river and John, the bike rider from Loxton, was no
exception. Similarly aged, he takes life easy and his morning
rides to Berri or other Riverland towns form part of his mission

to meet as many people as possible to hear and share their unique stories. He will never run out of people, nor pleasant Riverland mornings to ride.

We left Berri within the hour and when our discussion turned to Lock 4 at Bookpurnong in nine kilometres. Lockmeister's lunchtime? With the only lock problem for lunch, that of the fourth busiest at Renmark, we thought it just a one-off. No! Long lunches are the answer to a healthy mind and body. Our paddle pace turned to 'very relaxing' while passing the many houseboats moored along this wide river. The flow slowed, the banks lowered, trees grew to the water's edge, and we glided into the bank to wait for the lock to re-open after lunch. Lying around on the lawns eating oranges in the sun while we waited was not our preferred pace option, it was choice number two, and unavoidable. But not quite unavoidable. The lockie informed us later of a long cut (slightly longer than a short cut) through an easily accessible anabranch just upriver where we could have avoided the weir altogether.

Forty-five minutes later we dropped three metres into a shallow groyne river once more. Initially, the barren white banks of four metres surrounded us with many sandy riverbeds covering up to three-quarters of the river. A paddle steamer approached as we came to a groyne and, rather than travel through the narrow channel against its wake, waited on the shallow bank. The wake was negligible and we shot past without delay. The river then narrowed, compelling us to navigate the outside bends like larger craft to avoid the wide-reaching sandy beds.

We entered the Murray River National Park with Katarapko Island on our right and the Gurra Gurra lake area to our left. During higher water the many entries and exits to anabranches on both sides might deceive a river traveller but at this time the river proper was obvious. The forest-like surrounds brought back memories of the beauty of the forests upriver with a kookaburra, as if by design, shooting across in front to complement the memory. Much of this area downriver from Renmark is a koala sanctuary where they are protected against those wishing to catch, pat, or eat them. Australians do not really eat them—firstly, it is illegal and secondly, most would opt for a lifetime diet of haggis in comparison. The river wound back and forth exposing long high beaches of orange sand on the inside bends angling up to three metres above the river. The small settlement of Bookpurnong—named in the 1860s as a portmanteau of Aboriginal words meaning wide open and swimming place —perfectly described the backdrop and it was only some months ago we had pulled in here while travelling upriver in a yacht. At that time we had refreshed ourselves with a swim and a couple of gins with tonic: not today. The passing of Bookpurnong signalled the end of the forest environment with the saltbush scrub now visible to the horizon. Animals had again taken the day off, apart from two kangaroos with their joeys drinking from the bank so close yet quite calm. As many kangaroos as Australia has, even over-populated in some regions, they remain dear to my heart and I never tire of their company.

The recommendation for today's gold star destination was Thiele's Sand bar but with the delay at Lock 4 it became evident we could not make it in daylight. Additionally, the expectation was that being so close to the next major town of Loxton, it would likely be occupied, if not crowded. And if so, it would require travel on past Loxton to find another suitable spot in the darkness. The decision became easy when within five kilometres we paddled around the mid-river Rilli Island and chanced across Proud's Sandbar just around the bend. Like last night, carpet adorned the bank leading to a manicured grass bank. Trees led well back from the river and with plenty of firewood on offer we were set for the night. Being set for the night in Dave's fire expectations did require more than one collection. Terry Pratchett said, 'Build a man a fire, and he'll be warm for the day. Set a man on fire, and he'll be warm for the rest of his life'. Dave subscribes to the 'Pratchett Principle'.

One-hundred metres up along the river, and still part of the campsite, name signs were nailed to trees stating 'Thiele Christmas', 'Singh Easter' and numerous others. This local custom secures bookings for families during the peak holidays. Other times, like tonight, the whole area was unoccupied. The Thiele name had reserved trees over an area of 30 metres. Clearly, their own sand bar downriver has become overrun during the busy times.

As we dined on the routine meal of couscous with vegies, Dave turned the fire up to eleven to counter the 1°C temperature. Cold but peaceful, we opened a packet of dried fruit from Renmark in pure extravagance and let our minds and conversation wander back in time. The red limestone cliffs we have bounced off since before Renmark are features of this Murray region known as The Gorge Country. A popular discussion in the front bars' around here talks of the changes that formed the River Murray basin as it's been pushed and shoved during the past 130 million years. But it was as recent as 30,000 years ago that the river in South Australia gouged its new path through the limestone to eventually unveil the spectacular cliffs we had passed over recent days. To think of this ancient river cutting its current path 30,000 years ago is remarkable but to consider the river is 130 million years old is truly mind-boggling. Our country's original inhabitants have been here for the past 60,000 years, living among the changes and sitting by their fires along the banks—just as were doing. Cheers!

Distance 537 – 498 39 kilometres
Easy day with wind at our backs

Chapter 43

Proud's Sandbar to Cobdogla

Day 43

Tuesday, May 14

Blue sky, no breeze 22°C

In freezing conditions, we looked from the tent to smoke on the water. Positivity can build Disneyland, but it could not change the fact that warm is nice and cold is miserable. There was no fire and no coffee and we packed quickly with freezing hands to get away by 7.45am in the light fog. The tent was still wet from yesterday and was now wetter. Is a tent once wet, just wet, or can it get wetter?

As we slipped into the water and took our first strokes we passed my guilty pleasure, my chocolate, a blue kilometre sign with the numbers 498 smirking right at us.

'Not gonna make it, Brother,' said Dave.

'I don't think we can get much further each day.' I replied.

'I could ring and see whether I can get a couple more days leave,' he said. 'It's all it would take.'

He was right, but our phones had no reception and the short notice would be problematic. The distance we were covering each day will leave Dave short of reaching the river's mouth. His goal to complete the South Australian leg of the Murray together was slim. We could paddle by night but Dave's injuries, being controlled by painkillers, was a further complication. For my part, being within 500 kilometres to the mouth and the end of the adventure was not reason for celebration. Progressing at around 50 kilometres a day, the completion of the odyssey in 10 or 11 days brought, rather than elation, a sickening feeling. I likened it to my time with my children, listening to people say, 'enjoy them now, for time will disappear very soon and they will be gone'. I did spend time, yet it also disappeared in a flash—a much too quick flash. Can I have some of *that* time back, can I have some of *this* time back? No, sir. Request denied.

We had been sliding along in our own thoughts through the Murray River National Park on one side, red cliffs on the other, in one of those moments where you wonder 'where the time went and how you got here'. Whistling kites sent their regards as we paddled past Loxton North and around Media Island that splits the river at the overgrown, over occupied, and overrated Thiele's Sand Bar. Encroaching sandy beds continued to force us wide and we took note of the many attractive camping areas over the nine kilometres in and beyond the small riverbank footprint harbour of Loxton. Apart from the empty houseboat moorings and the deserted historical village, Loxton came and went without a whimper. Shortly along we passed old Jack travelling upriver in the 'River Lady' houseboat I had cruised on with Brad and Lorna 12 months earlier. Small river! After 18 kilometres we paused for a protein break on what would be Forby's Island in higher water but, for now, a wide sandy beach.

The day's meanderings disappeared with the river turning north-westerly and going straight and wide. Long heavily wooded islands popped up mid-river providing the afternoon's entertainment. Any breeze that popped up favoured our backs. The birds and kangaroos came out visiting during the afternoon as did a cheeky native water rat swimming along with its head just above the water. At first it looked like the snake we had been longing to see until it smiled to show its gold tooth.

As we approached 1.30pm and our second break we entered Seven Mile Reach, a reach of around 12 kilometres which set a challenge for energy over distance. During this section, where we passed the settlement of New Residence, locale of Metho and Nicola our new friends from Robinvale (the twin town of Euston that had been decimated by hungry goats) we lamented the now lost hope of a hot shower and the grassy lawn campsite they had offered. Too early to call it a day it also removed all hope of Welsh-style scones. Despite one of us being on each side of the river to find a suitable spot to pull in, all possibilities were either too high or covered with reeds. The second session ended after a gruelling 20 kilometres.

With towns more regular and supply lines plentiful, our rations had now been boosted. Extra crackers with a combined application of peanut butter and Vegemite were declared totally acceptable. Apples were a regular treat as were hardboiled eggs. Meals had turned into quite culinary feasts with last night's meal of chicken Kung Pao one for the ages—as it turned out it was ages before we could find a supermarket stocking Lee Kum Kee's special sauce again. Salivating at the prospect, the Trident Tom Yum Goong was still going down a treat each evening and we had even spruced it up with sliced mushroom and spring onions.

The river continued down with long wide stretches as we passed the inside of Moorook Island, exposing the pretty settlement of Moorook with its inviting grassy bank and 189 residents. Within a kilometre we gazed open-mouthed upon the spectacular lagoons for which this area is famous. The banks were narrow and sparse giving us uninterrupted views across the lagoons, one of which alone covers 1905 hectares— an area that would accommodate 220 million pizzas and who knows how many Kung Paos. There was no breeze and with sunshine glistening on glassy water, the birds had gathered in abundance. Squadrons of pelicans were the dominant species, but spoonbills, egrets, parrots, swallows, ducks, and an endless array of birds swam on the placid waters or rested on the fallen trees and stumps laying in the water. And these trees were not all dead; gum stumps from trees drowned and given up years ago were sprouting new growth and the place vibrated with energy. We were tempted to venture into the living postcard but as like upriver, that was saved for another time. Our conversation shifted to Euston. In all the time on the river the only animal that was in abundance and out of sync with the land was the non-native goats. Even stock animals can only survive in numbers that can be supported by the land and prevailing conditions. Okay, there is the Darwinian argument regarding natural selection within species and a type of species self-regulation for survival in consideration of the prevailing environmental conditions. But goats bypassed those rules. They survive and even thrive on just fresh air and rocks. Of course, European carp are the other pest in proliferation along the river with their numbers accounting for 90 per cent of the fish mass in the Murray. Birds also fall within this self-regulatory state and there does not appear to be any which are in invasive abundance. The bag-lady of Renmark could proffer a case for the proliferation of pelicans, but they are far too cute for contemplation.

The difficult to pronounce town of Cobdogla, more easily referred to as Cobbie by the locals, was our favoured destination and as dusk rolled in, we came within sight. While the distance was in sight there was not a mooring opportunity in sight. It was odd considering the effort so many of the more recent towns upriver had made to proudly present themselves. Thick blue-green algae covered all the thin entrances that might have given a clue to a landing bank. By chance we pushed through a gap into Bruno Bay, a small cove set up with a wharf and the town's boat ramp. It was less than salubrious so we paddled back out and found the thinnest of landings 10 metres upriver next to the pumping station. We dragged the kayaks onto the bank as the sun was setting and set camp. Devoid of wood, there was no option for a fire and therefore no option for a cooked dinner. The caravan park towards town some 150 metres away was out of the question as a place to stay. In the darkness, we dressed up and headed into Cobbie for a night on the town. One of the 381 residents would be engaged in the supply of feasts.

As we got closer to the township the only lights visible were coming from the football ground where training for football and netball was underway. The available feast-making population was down to 310. The town has nice wide streets, clean and well laid out. By all appearances the stores had closed permanently shortly after its first resident was born. But there had to be a pub or something open—it's a town. Then, rounding a corner at the far end of town, lights. The Cobbie Club, 'Open 7 days', the sign stated. With a sigh of relief, a slap on the back and a high five, we entered through the front door. Hmmm, quiet tonight.

A smiling attendant greeted us as we interrupted her cleaning.

'Sorry, boys,' she said. 'We're open seven days but we close Tuesday nights 'coz it's a bit quiet.'

Now I have been optimistically defining myself as Lucky Lee, not always with the success that a 'lucky' person should expect, but this was too much.

To the rescue, as a good country host always is, she plied us with stout—one of which Dave took the opportunity to spill, as he has done at every bar so far—and heated a couple of frozen mini pizzas to help us along. It got us as far along as back to camp and, with a bit of scrap-wood we found along the way, we fired up to cook pasta. But not before we had to duck and dive to avoid the sparks flying out at us like a Tommy gun from a pine branch we had laid upon the fire.

There we sat on our tripod chairs, full bellies, modest fire glowing, five kilometres from the Sturt Highway, listening to the semi-trailers roll on by.

The pumping station was not pumping. Lucky Lee!

Distance 498 – 443 55 kilometres
Easy paddling but long day

Chapter 44

Cobdogla to Maize Island

Day 44

Wednesday, May 15

Blue sky, no breeze 24°C

We woke to the gentle tinkling of a piano thanks to the small birds in the tree above us. I waltzed around on our grassy knoll at the river's edge. Rather than live with a *can't unsee* image I excused Dave from the next number. The Be Good Tanyas sang in my head:

'I wake you up in the morning so early, just to tell you
I've got the wandering blues, I've got the wandering blues
The littlest birds sing the prettiest songs
The littlest birds sing the prettiest songs'

We ate and packed to the birdsong then carried our kayaks and gear to the boat ramp, a stone's throw away, at the ostentatiously named Bruno Bay. The wharf, boat ramp and conveniences have been set on a graded gravel ground over-looking the small cove choked by blue-green algae. A sign at the entrance to the boat ramp read, 'DUCK HUNTING SEASON TIMETABLE'.

Once through the algae congestion we slid out of the small entrance to a glassy river under a cloudless sky. The nature reserves, or more succinctly named 'game reserves', were picture-perfect and like yesterday laden with birdlife of all shapes and sizes. I yelled to the ducks as we passed to inform them of the impending doom, or boom, or whatever term they recognize. Either they did not speak English or my command of duck is wanting because they remained stationary as though made of rubber. Trying to picture the eruption of duck, dog, and hunter would spoil the scenic bliss so we spoke of pizzas, spilt stout, and tommy gun wood as we paddled on.

The river ran parallel to the Sturt Highway for three kilometres with the 1236 hectare Moorook Game Reserve opening in full view of both kayakers and motorists. Turning away and under the highway bridge we paddled past the cosy settlement of Kingston on Murray with its broad lawns sweeping down to the river; a far different picture than the dusty shantytown passed in the blink of an eye during the heat of summer. Lagoons continued left and right with the 1905 hectare Loch Luna, equal to all before in its scenic beauty, sadly also part of a native duck's nightmare. Despite the river being at such a low level and Lake Hume now expected to be as dry as a bone, the abundance of water suggested the area was in flood. We learned the reason within when the weir and Lock 3 appeared in the distance.

Many a person spoke of the beauty of the river between Mildura and Renmark as the most spectacular of the Lower Murray. It was, as was every part of the river to date, unique and breathtaking, yet my choice so far had been the section between Renmark (Lock 5) and Kingston on Murray (Lock 3) and even more specifically, between Bookpurnong (Lock 4) down to Kingston on Murray. My theory is that, when standing or sitting in larger crafts as they navigate Mildura to Renmark, they view the land and river from above the banks whereas the lower section toward Lock 3 requires more concentration for navigation to avoid running aground; the complexity not only being awkward but removing sightseeing opportunities. For the case of the kayak paddler, who paddles down in the river below the banks and through any depth without difficulty, the sheer beauty of the river itself is remarkable. So equal points to both sides.

Down another three and a half metres past the weir, the banks turned barren and white with no visible vegetation on the outlying land. The few spindly gums that tried to make a statement along the bank were either dead or resembled a wizened old man in the last throes of annoying his relatives. Within five kilometres it all changed. Overland Corner with its famous watering hole, the Overland Corner Hotel, offered food and refreshment. The pub, established in 1860, had been set high on the hill behind the flood plain but was too far to walk from the river for Dave and Lucky Lee. We would need to return for more refreshments by the time we had got back to the river. Turning the corner, it marked the emergence of some unique sandstone hills with their layered colours striking against the blue-sky backdrop. We stopped on the bend across the river to admire the hills, the pub in the distance, and our protein bars.

Paddling on, the conditions of sun and water remained perfect as we travelled the five straight kilometres along Wigley Reach, all the time admiring the sandstone hills to the right while heading straight for the massive 80-100 metre Telegraph Cliffs in the distance. We had now in entered gorge country. Travelling continuously along the whole river, I had been hit with surprise after surprise at the unexpected transitions of a river I thought I was familiar with. My occasional camp at specific locations or short, localised two to three-day journeys was akin to marvelling over a single float in a parade. As we approached, the Telegraph Cliffs loomed larger with their sheer drop to the water. Gazing upward, a few houses sat precariously at the edge.

'Wouldn't chase your hat if the wind catches it up there,' said Dave.

We edged closer to the bank but there were no hats, washing machines, or lounge suites.

The paradox of the excitement of travelling along these cliffs was the monotony of the endless reaches that run alongside them. After 18 long kilometres we finally found a suitable place to pull over for an afternoon break. The reaches we had endured all day travelled due west and I shuddered at the inevitability of the predominate westerly wind and the grind it would be on any given day. There had not been even a zephyr all day.

Devlin's Pound is a pumping station with grassy rolling banks that come down to the river—a virtual oasis in reverse. And certainly, an oasis in the metaphorical sense when it ended our long search for a break amongst the tall banks and reeds. We slid the kayaks up and unpacked all our gear before laying it out to dry in the sun. The tent had been wet for days. A swim and a wash were essential and, when finally paddling off, two workers emerged who may or may not have just arrived and may or may not have been forced to endure our presentation *au naturel* for the previous half an hour. Unluckily for them they were the only people we had seen on the river all day.

River lesson #7: Timing is everything.

The long slow grind and the efforts of the past few days finally laid bare on Dave's shoulders. Painkillers to relieve the pain in his back, neck and shoulders had become less and less effective. The fine balance between driving to reach the mouth and paddling comfortably to enjoy the journey was tipping against him. Strong will kept him going, but every session above 15 kilometres brought trouble. The problem we faced was finding places to rest at convenient distances. He was pushing on so as not to delay my progress in case it spoiled my journey. I tried to maintain a pace that would see him to the end before he had to go back to work. Neither of us were cognisant of the other's expectations and the needlessness of our mutual consideration.

The river was entering middle age. It still had some kick from time to time but for the most part it was going to fiftieth birthday parties: remembering the past, hoping for a catalyst to spark up the party but ultimately going home before midnight. With the state the river had now become we managed good distance during the day despite the slow flow offered. The continual series of weirs had slowed the flow a bit more with each successive passing and now we were enduring sections of what can only be described as 'dead water'. One moment paddling was easy, gliding along normally, when without warning we were being retarded as though dragging a bucket behind us. We struggled to maintain any respectable pace. To find an answer we tried shifting to the outside bends, the inside bends and into the middle of the river, all without success. We even tried separating to opposite sides of the river when this phenomenon hit, again, without success. Then, as suddenly as dead water occurred, paddling would return to normal. This could happen over any distance from 500 metres to three or four kilometres.

Combining the dead water and the banks lined with cliffs or reeds the final session became a slog. Finding a campsite proved elusive and as with previous evenings we travelled on separate sides of the river in the hope one of us would get lucky. Maize Island was just around the bend and then just around the bend. A clear spot opened along the three-metre banks and, like a rat up a drainpipe, we were in. On checking the map, we were on Maize Island but still three and a half kilometres from the site I remembered back from my time camping as a young man.

This campsite was an unexpected treasure. Back from the bank was another of the local destination camping areas with dirt tracks leading left and right through the thick scrub from our site. Tonight, we were alone. With flat, clear ground and plenty of wood, we settled in for a night by one of Dave's *les spectacles somptueux* fires while the moon provided a light show on the stone cliffs opposite.

Later, as I laid in the comfort of my sleeping bag, Dave asleep —imitating a chainsaw—I contemplated my platypus quest, lamenting its lack of success. My hopes of a sighting from here were nigh impossible. But what did it all mean? Surely my journey had not been wasted. Michelangelo said, 'There is no greater harm than time wasted'. I have a portrait of the odyssey in my head with so many colours, shapes, and textures—I have left space for a platypus. And yet, with 394 kilometres to go, that space is filling rapidly. Dave farted, and I turned over hoping for sleep to come.

Distance 443 – 394 49 kilometres
A real slog in easy conditions

Chapter 45

Maize Island to Hogwash Bend

Day 45

Thursday, May 16

Blue sky, little to no breeze 24°C

A fire was burning bright before our alarm went off 6.15am in the usual form of kookaburras in the wilderness. The kookaburra alarm had become so natural I vowed to work out a way to have it installed permanently on my phone.

The saying goes 'it is darkest before the dawn', but I declare it is coldest before the dawn. Whether that is true or not is irrelevant; once said and repeated it eventually becomes folklore. I still believe in Father Christmas and I still keep getting presents. The morning was cold and as for the 'darkest', it was a moot point because the stars were still out to decorate the night sky. We warmed our hands by the fire waiting for the billy to boil. Warm water in our muesli was a little luxury which we washed down with coffee. As usual, we used the leftover water to wash up last night and the morning dishes. Good for dishes. Good for cold hands.

There was no way to dry the tent so it was packed wet again. The dew point must be reducing because we were witnessing more condensation inside each day to the stage we got wet just getting out. With the yaks loaded, Dave sat in his Banana and slid down the twiggy bed of a dry creek entrance into the river while I carried Precious to the riverbank and soaked my neoprene boots while entering in knee-deep water. We were underway in another breathless river day.

We glided past a couple off mid-river islands as we rounded Maize Island, a popular camping spot for the people of the neighbouring town of Waikerie. Old campsites looked familiar but were overgrown with reeds and no longer discernible. Meanwhile, a persistent buzz invaded the serenity.

'Dave, can you tell whether they're planes or gliders?'

'What?'

'Dave, they must be planes because there's too many of them now.'

'What?'

'I'd hate to be living up there on the cliff.'

'What?'

The number of planes circling above from the Waikerie airport increased to the point of distraction. I pitied the poor residents in the houses on the nearby cliffs that sit under the flight path. While paddling along Hart Reach into Waikerie a rare break in the overhead noise brought the sound of crashing water to our ears. Angling closer to the cliff face, the sight and sound of a permanent waterfall cascading into the river from 30 metres above was our first surprise. Having always entered the town in the past by road, which does not offer a view of the river, the second surprise was the 40 metre cliffs the town is built upon. On the other side of the river, low lying scrub lined the one and a half metre banks—no surprise.

The odyssey to date had brought to light the many complications in naming a bridge. Waikerie avoided the problem altogether by not having a bridge at all, instead remaining reliant on its ferry to go across the river to a road that goes to nowhere in particular. With planes distracting us and the ferry aiming to sink us, we shot past the steel cables and, though we had only travelled 12 kilometres for the morning, the expansive lawns of the Waikerie riverfront called us in. We needed provisions, including water, as well as the mandatory coffee and egg 'n bacon toastie. Egg 'n bacon toasties had never tasted as good as on this trip.

Waikerie township has enjoyed some major changes in recent years and is quite the sparkling, modern country town. People were happy and friendly which was always a good sign of not just prosperity but also community spirit. Checking into the local post office for electoral pre-voting I was advised to return to the Riverland's only pre-voting station—upriver, at Renmark. After a little too much relaxing we trundled on down the lawns to the bank where our kayaks glistened in the sunshine, waiting safely for us.

We paddled past the small settlement of Ramco within eight kilometres, another of the camping spots of my youth, and this time at one of the old campsites, the swing-rope we had secured to the branch of a gum tree some 40 years ago dangled still. The push to Lock 2 continued for 13 kilometres along Woodcutter Reach and Penns Reach through lowlands, floodplains, and tall cliffs. The river was now content to roll straight and the joy of us meandering, once again, through a narrow river was disappearing with every kilometre. The weather pattern, at least, was holding to the predictions made when this adventure was planned, and I was thankful to be travelling along the reaches in calm conditions. High banks, with reeds covering any potential shallow beaches on the inside bends, continued for kilometre after kilometre and, without the chance for a well-overdue break, we came upon Lock 2, 21 kilometres from Waikerie. Dave was hurting, and silent: stoic.

Down another three metres to the other side of the weir, the banks became high again and it took some time before we settled on a small beach for our afternoon break. The crackers, vegemite and peanut butter went a good way to settling any discomfort and when the hard-boiled eggs came out all talk turned to tonight's landing site. The talk revolved around 'the sooner the better'.

Along cliffs, cliff after cliff, conditions remained sunny and calm through the last 14 kilometres of the day with the final, long bend stretching on for 12 kilometres. In what was becoming the new normal, the closer we got to our destination beach the more difficult it was to find a suitable landing. With each of us on different sides of the river, we paddled on, hopeful for any small opening. With dusk coming upon us we found a clearing. Three weeks ago I would not have even considered it but now it was a blessing.

It was coming on 5pm and the day was turning to dusk. The daytime hours were fading day by day. I had gone from the warmth of Autumn to being within a month of the shortest day of the year. Not only were the daylight hours for paddling restricting the potential daily distance but more often we were having to set camp in the shadow of darkness. The bonus of the cooler weather was that we had avoided mosquitoes along the journey, apart from a couple of days where one or two buzzed us. Similarly, flies had left us alone as did snakes that had clearly gone into hibernation for the approaching winter. I was happy with no snakes, but I would have liked to have seen one just for the rush. For all I knew there could have been one camping in my kayak. I had not conducted a morning check since...who knows?

Like so many of the camping spots along the river in South Australia and Victoria, dirt roads led in and away along the river to other sites. And, like most of late, we were not within coo-ee of another camper. I needed to be wearing an Akubra hat when even thinking of a coo-ee. The well-known Australian bush call of coo-ee, dates to the earliest times of western settlement as an adaption of the Aboriginal Dharug mob's long-distance call of 'guu-wii', meaning 'come here'.

'Coo-ee,' I called to the wind.

From around the back of a tree came Dave's face. 'What?'

Works, every time.

It had been a long, arduous paddle at times, with little help from the river as it was pulling us ever so slowly towards the mouth. Paddling more often now went from gliding to areas of 'dead water'. A blue sign, my early but no longer guilty pleasure, stood opposite us displaying the unwanted news that there were only 348 kilometres from the end. This equated to seven days. It was all ending so soon, too soon. The well-used quote attributed to Ralph Waldo Emerson in 1844 of 'It's not the destination, it's the journey' could never have more meaning as I sat on the bank under the sunset with the fire crackling at my back. The quote had grown by repetition from the original prose 'To finish the moment, to find the journey's end in every step of the road, to live the greatest number of good hours, is wisdom'. With respect, I amended it slightly 'to find the complete satisfaction in every paddle on the river'. With only 348,000 paddle strokes to go, I have time for wisdom but none to waste.

Distance 694 – 348 46 kilometres

Easy, beautiful day

Chapter 46

Hogwash Bend to Brenda Park

Day 46

Friday, May 17

Blue sky, no wind 23°C

We woke early with the condensation in the tent performing like a dripping tap. There was no need to wake so early with today's goal to reach Morgan an easy 36 kilometres away. The stars were heading off leaving a bright blue sky. We sat close to the fire. There was no rush. There is no stopping a moving train and our usual morning routine kicked in. Packing a wet tent was also now part of the usual morning routine and the tent fly now resembled more condensation than fly. At 8.30 am, through the scratchy reeds, we slid into the river with our paddles creating the only sound and the only ripple on the water.

Within two kilometres while swinging around Hogwash Bend we came across the beach where we had hoped to land last night. It had changed since the 2016/17 floods—changed to reeds and no beach. Heaven knows what the '56 floods did out here and there was no old bushman to poke his shaking head around a tree to tell us. The chance find of last night's campsite had proven fortunate and we soon discovered there were no other suitable landing places for kilometres to come. On the far end of Hogwash Bend the very inviting Caudo Winery sat, splendidly landscaped to attract the passing tourist. A visit to the winery with its modern eatery was highly recommended but, at 8am, any temptation was in the negative. No doubt it would have been closed anyway. Lucky Lee!

The landing rights on properties for overnight camping had been on my mind before the trip and with natural scrub sites now disappearing my research could be worthwhile. It led me, though, into more rabbit holes than the sheared rabbits of Punyelroo could occupy. History recalls after having saved the free world from Napoleon's forces, Colonel William Light sailed for Adelaide in the mid-1830s to design the new city. Having completed the plans in only eight weeks he ventured north to the Barossa Valley region where he discovered wine. None of this is particularly important to my journey apart from the fact that Bill, under instructions from The Colonial Commissioners, was also to provide a roadway one and half chains wide along all coastlines and 66 feet wide on each side of navigable rivers. The Department of Lands has endeavoured to maintain this parcel for the people, and it is along this riverside corridor we have camped since entering South Australia. But times have changed and as we now work our way along the river, the land in question is being made available by the relevant authorities for private ownership on a freehold or lease basis. Signs stating private property, keep off, etc., are now common with some enforceable and some erected erroneously, either deliberately or out of ignorance. When contacted, local councils along the river were unwilling, or unable, to provide any indication of private ownership rights for the nightly campsite pull-ins.

Furthermore, they explained, as ownership rights can change at any time, the maintenance of any records proves problematic. The advice given recommended the use of common sense and respect when camping overnight with most owners unlikely to take offence if approached with a friendly smile and a bottle of wine as Bill did when visiting the Barossa.

'How far is the Barossa from here,' asked Dave.

'One hundred kilometres,' I said. 'What's on your mind.'

'Can we reach it by kayak?'

'No.' I said. 'What's on your mind.'

'I drank the last of the cask last night.'

I think he had missed the point but travelling on the river develops alternative perspectives.

Breathing in the fresh country air, we posited, is the secret to a long and happy life so we took full advantage of the benefits in perfect paddling conditions during the 17 kilometres to Cadell. The entry to the township was not inviting so after scooting past the ferry we aimed for a manicured grassy landing at the next bend. It had shelters and a clubhouse, tinnies were moored at the edge of a low bank, and men lounged around in hope with fishing lines dangling in the river. On this day of our mutual leisure I called to Dave that the gods were smiling upon us with Lucky Lee finally finding a river café that was open. He continued to paddle as I pulled towards the bank with hearty greetings to the fishermen. A gentleman with an obvious level of authority came to greet me as I paddled in.

'G'day, mate,' I said with the taste of coffee already in my mouth. 'Permission to come ashore.'

'No,' he said. 'Not unless you're wearing one of these blue T-shirts.'

Yes, they *were* all wearing the same dark blue T-shirts. The gentleman of authority pre-empted my 'But...buts...'

'And,' he said with a smirk. 'I don't have one your size.'

Aah, hah! I had arrived at the euphemistically named Cadell Correctional Services Training Centre: Cadell Prison for short. A short chat with the guard revealed the prisoner's sentences ranged here from two to ten years and, as always, there were good days and bad days for prisoners and guards alike. This being a low-security prison has had its share of prisoners 'wandering off', only to be returned with the gift of a longer 'holiday'. I bid him adieu and paddled to meet Dave who had found a sandy beach just around the bend, directly opposite and out of view of the prison authorities. We were now flies on the wall. This fly saw nothing yet I did get a snapshot of what I hope never to see at close range again.

Back in the saddle the river remained wide, calm, and straight, with lines of gums along the banks not quite thick enough to disguise the barren land behind them. High cliffs watched over us on the southern side for the remaining ten kilometres into Morgan. We cruised past a couple of old settlements and at 2pm we rounded North West Bend to see the historic Morgan Pumping Station, in operation since 1940 sending the Murray's water to towns across South Australia: the driest state in the driest continent. Within minutes we were pulling up to the grassy banks of Morgan. Dave went for pain medication while I patted the imaginary solitary horse. A short snack later we were heading back to the kayaks when a middle-aged woman, lazing on the lawn with her elderly mother, garbled something out of her mouthful of food.

'Bin out for a paddle?' she said, refilling the empty space in her mouth.

'Perfect day for it.' I replied, overlooking her obvious question.

'You should think of doing the Murray Marathon someday,' She continued, with just a hint of sarcasm to suggest she perceived our capabilities would not extend beyond a 'fun' paddle around the holiday shacks.

Oh, how we limit others with our own imagination. The (Massive) Murray Marathon is an annual kayaking race travelling 400 kilometres over five days. Challenging, no doubt, but no greater than our odyssey.

'One day,' I replied, and Dave and I exchanged a nod.

We slipped back into the river, dodged the ferry, and continued five kilometres past the many holiday shacks downriver until we reached the holiday settlement of Brenda Park. We unloaded our gear on the grounds of our brother, Paul and Mousha's holiday shack spending the afternoon drying the tent, washing clothes, washing the yaks, and washing ourselves; all the while promising our bodies an afternoon kip. We had no sooner completed the chores when sitting under the massive gum trees watching the river gently flow past, the sound of a car horn signalled the end of any plans for that quick snooze. Brother's, David and Geoff Inglis, had arrived to drop off their kayaks for tomorrow's casual joint paddle. An inspection of the kayaks suggested the paddle tomorrow might not be a casual as anticipated.

Dave and I were dropped off at one of the two pubs in the one-horse town while our friends went to drop-off vehicles for the anticipated landing in Blanchetown tomorrow. The pub we settled in was pumping, with cheap drinks to celebrate the birthday of the publican—Lucky Lee, they call me! With drink in hand, we watched from the veranda as the third brother, Steve, rolled in with another friend, Malcolm Cheffirs. They had come from Mal's shack directly across the river, via the ferry, where we would stay overnight.

One can never underestimate the company of good friends and after a journey of 46 days it was good catching up. In the friendly and entertaining atmosphere of the local patrons we dined, drank, laughed, and ate birthday cake. With an unnecessary nightcap back at Mal's, we all retired in good spirits, ready for an early start in the morning for what promised to be an easy paddle over a moderate distance.

Distance 348 – 312 36 kilometres
Very easy day

Chapter 47

Brenda Park to Blanchetown

Day 47

Saturday, May 18

Blue sky, calm to light breeze 23°C

I roused the group of lazy good-for-nothings at 7am. All the plans of bravado and early starts had sunk to the bottom of last night's beer glasses. Slowly, ever so slowly, with yawning and scratching they rose with the urgency of a Martin's Bend kangaroo. That was, until the smell of coffee raised them out of last night's dreams of delusion. Kayakers of the highest order!

Mal, a perfect host, fired up the BBQ and before long the smell of bacon and eggs drew everyone to the riverfront where the murky plans of today's paddle resurfaced into reality. While this process took place I gazed upriver to the township and across to the Morgan Ferry Hospital where all ferries get sent for an annual check-up and a bit of TLC. The river was as charming as it had been for all 46 days of the journey.

It was election day so after breakfast we all packed into the one remaining car that had not been left downriver and headed across the ferry to the local football club for our right to make a difference. As election day was declared after I began and, with the serenity infused from life on the river, news in general had not been my focus. Not having to listen to the political bunkum, as my father would call it, had made it the best election ever. And, in the true apathetic ethos of the Australian people, I weighed up the pros and cons, the unlikelihood of any promise coming to fruition, which leader sported the best nickname (as is the latest media standard of social relevance), and when, at 8.30am sharp the doors opened, I voted accordingly.

Let the fun begin. Once at Paul and Mousha's we all packed and by 9.30am the three brothers had left with varying degrees of professionalism and good fortune. With a wave farewell to Mal, unable to join us due to a suspect shoulder, Dave and I followed shortly after. David, in a flat-top fishing kayak, had led the way but to witness Steve and Geoff's attempts to maintain some level of balance as they entered their rudder-less canoes from a pontoon took the cake. We were soon all together. David pushed ahead relentlessly, Geoff settled into a rhythm and Steve, traversing back and forth across the river as though holding the tail of a Barmah Forest brumby, covered twice the distance as any of us. The harder he tried to steer his canoe the less responsive it became, which is not exactly accurate. It responded as it should to the shifting balance and stroke of Steve. It was just that each shift and stroke was the technical opposite of what he wanted to achieve. At this rate, the chance of reaching Blanchetown by the time the lock closed at 4.30pm was in doubt. In our favour was the five kilometres saved by starting at Brenda Park and the determination for which our guest paddlers are known.

The morning conditions were perfect with swallows darting all over the river, calm flat water, and healthy banks supporting massive gum trees holding against lagoons and backwaters. The distraction of the landscape held mouth-open wonder for us all. I was conscious not to burn the guys with too much too soon so when a suitable bank came into view at the 14 kilometre mark, the morning session was reigned in before any physical damage curbed enthusiasm. The exits from the canoes were as hilarious as the entries and the cooling swim was confirmed as refreshing. Then, like a Michelin Star restaurant, food suddenly appeared from everywhere. Nuts, fruit, cakes, fruitcakes, lollies, scroggin; their boats must have been full to the brim. And sharing is caring, so it was nice to enjoy all the treats just to help them reduce boat weight. Break-time over, I cracked the whip to the sound of complaints about this being a day of leisure and pleasure. Welcome to a normal day of paddling on the river, boys!

The river from Morgan turns south through South Australia until it reaches its conclusion at Goolwa. Long reaches prevail with very few snags and fallen trees—all removed before the new regulations. Any inclement weather from the south would make the last 300 kilometre arduous, to say the least. There were no such problems on this day, with a nice 23°C accompanied by the occasional waft of a breeze to keep everyone comfortable. We passed many small settlements and, with Steve making full use of the wide river, he visited each one to the left and right. Meanwhile, David had slowed and, under sufferance having damaged his back from his early enthusiasm, pushed on resolutely. Geoff maintained his composure, yet the smallest of wry grievances could be heard: if anyone would listen! Dave and I paddled along at a casual pace, enjoying the company.

During the second session we all settled into a groove which ever so slightly disguised the distance travelled. Because of cliffs on one side and reeds on the other, the lack of a suitable pull-in opportunity meant our guests were forced to work beyond reasonable expectations. I paddled alongside Geoff while our general group formation resembled a search party.

'Must be getting close to a rest time,' Geoff pleaded.

'Just around the bend there'll be a nice beach,' I promised.

There was no beach around the bend.

'Nothing here,' he said.

'Don't worry, there'll be one just around the corner up there.'

There was not.

'How much bloody further,' he said with more intent. The smile on my face gave it away.

When we finally slid into a less than ideal spot after 20 kilometres, the initial enthusiasm of the group had started to wane. There was a bit of method to the madness, though. Firstly, it was beneficial to keep the kilometres passing while conversation and eagerness were maintained; secondly, it meant only a five kilometre easy paddle to our destination of Blanchetown; and, thirdly, with only five kilometres to go, we could force the pace to the lock if necessary. Masses of food came out once again with the boys eagerly offering their treats, surreptitiously attempting to reduce their boat weight.

Fired up now for the charge to Blanchetown, we headed off together still discussing the implications of missing the shut-off time. Three mid-river islands covered in reeds were the only obstructions and with the breeze just enough to keep the sweat from the brow all enthusiasm had returned. As one, we entered Lock 1 at 4.15pm with 15 minutes to spare. It was all jokes now as the boys celebrated the conclusion of a hard day's work. The lockmeister must have thought we had accomplished a 100 kilometre day. Once through this final lock of the river, we came out from under the two bridges of Blanchetown to the familiar voice of long-time friend, Peter Wareing, calling from half a kilometre downstream. The rickety wooden wharf that supported him was barely holding together since the last flood. Oh, joy! Happiness and relief broke out when Peter offered to drive them to their car instead of having to paddle the final two kilometres to retrieve it.

'Would you like a beer, boys,' offered Peter. 'There's a hot shower if you want to freshen up.'

Now ordinarily, any offer of beer would represent cause for celebration. But the boys were at the edge and no amount of enticement could raise their interest. They politely refused. With few words David, Steve and Geoff packed their canoes on the roof racks and dragged their sorry, tired, and cold bodies into the car. Driving back to Adelaide in comfort, they took with them the knowledge and, sometime later, the satisfaction, of what a day on the river entailed.

Dave and I retreated to Peter's river home for a hot shower and a night of extreme hospitality with his brother Anthony and joint river shack owner Wayne. They laid on food and drinks and gave up their beds for our comfort on the pretence that they usually sleep on the couch. The attribute of generosity had been on my mind for many days, weeks in fact, mulling over how it could be considered a virtue. Because, I reasoned, people can give under obligation or self-interest, and either begrudgingly or with indifference. Surely that is not true generosity, nor truly virtuous. I concluded graciousness to be the key. When generosity is extended graciously then it is true generosity. And here it was in spades.

The barbeque dinner was designed for carnivores, for which we were thankful, but the salad proved the most interesting. I was given the job of preparing the salad, or more succinctly, the tomato. Yes, the tomato. The salad consisted of one tomato shared between five guys. At the risk of being gender generalising, this may provide the best indication that no female partners were present on this night. I sliced the tomato, took out the buttered white bread and, as with all five of us, slapped on a bit of sauce and enjoyed every morsel. This funny and enter-taining night went on until 1am. We should have by rights be exhausted and need sleep. Yet quite the reverse, all this exer-cise had built both fitness and strength. Not necessarily to party, but if the kayak skirt fits ...

I opened a text message from a family member of one of our paddling crew. It read: By all reports, the day represented a gruelling relentless slog into a strong headwind. David drove home to the sound of stereo snoring.

Distance 312 – 273 39 kilometres
Very easy day

Chapter 48

Blanchetown to Kroehns Landing

Day 48

Sunday, May 19

Blue sky, no wind, then rain 22°C

After only six hours of sleep I woke, naked, in a strange room, with a lolly snake on the pillow next to me. I had woken under each of these conditions before but not all at the same time. When the house finally came to life, I declined the offer of bacon and eggs on behalf of both Dave and me, much to the former's disappointment. Firstly, because I was still full of meat from last night's meal, and secondly, we had a substantial and unavoidable distance to travel. Architect Ludwig Mies van der Rohe reputedly popularised a phrase in 1947 when he was late for an appointment, most likely as an answer to his greedy little grandson, Dirk, who was requesting a third helping of bratwurst. And now, 'time was of the essence' for us. He also coined the phrase 'less is more' for which a starving Dave had little appreciation.

Peter is a thinking man, especially when it comes to matters of physical exertion. With his help we hoisted the loaded kayaks onto the back of his 4WD ute and drove them down to the water's edge. The other housemates had risen by this stage and agreeing with the idiom of 'less is more' watched from a safe distance. With fond farewells we were pushed into the river, and I suspect they were all back in bed before we reached the first bend.

Rain had been forecast for 4.30pm but for now the skies were blue and conditions could not have been better. We paddled down past the old part of Blanchetown through what would be from here to the mouth traditional Ngarrindjeri country. The town, established in 1841and the first on the Murray in South Australia, was originally called Moorundie before it was relocated to its present position above the floodplain. It was named after the original clan as well as being descriptive of the area as 'sandy'. Land and towns from here down respect many of the traditional names. A study of the various dialects from the 18 district clans has grown from 1750 in 1843 to a Ngarrindjeri dictionary comprising 3700 items. Not unlike the French language, the nuances of the words and phrases cannot be given justice in the English language. Blanchetown, named after Blanche, the wife of the South Australian governor, Sir Richard Graves MacDonnell, was as far away from a nuance as the morning's bacon and eggs.

As we turned the bend the old shacks disappeared. The banks were now lined with the follies of the set requiring fancy new two-storey holiday homes that they visit four weekends a year. What would they think of my now-dry one-room tent? The occupancy of houses is such a strange modern phenomenon. The trend, driven mainly by the lure of increased social status, is to acquire a house so large where rooms are plentiful and go mostly unused. The acquisition of a holiday home is similar, with it no longer acceptable to own a 'shack' but now a two-storey mansion. And yet, when going on vacation, most choose to stay in a caravan or single hotel room, returning to tell stories of their amazing holiday. I have lived for the past seven weeks like the original inhabitants of this land, under a single shelter, and while I will enjoy the comforts of returning to my modest house, it strikes me that this simplicity had brought an equal level of happiness, if not in some ways, more. Henry David Thoreau in *Walden* goes one step further, suggesting our toil to acquire extravagant houses that 'own us' is unnecessary, irresponsible, and unproductive on both personal and social levels. At a time when the social fabric needs rejuvenation, the man from 1854 struck me as more relevant than ever. A short distance along we passed the original settlement of Moorundie where little other than a couple of building foundations signify the importance of the heritage listed site.

'Less is more,' I said, a little louder than I wished.

'Don't you start bringing up breakfast again,' said Dave.

The river narrowed a little while the sheer cliffs, high and mighty, alternating between left and right and sometimes both, confirmed our continued presence in the gorge country. When the cliffs from went wide of the river, reed-covered banks of two metres kept us enclosed. Reaching out to the cliffs, inlets to lagoons and waterways to the left and right were continuously visible and inviting. The absence of any wildlife on the river or beyond sent in a foreboding air. The river proper was obvious enough and being enveloped by cliffs there was no chance of taking a wrong turn. With long, long reaches, turn was not a word we were using—the rudders on the kayaks were superfluous to needs. Any wind from the south though would be brutal. After 20 kilometres a small window of opportunity in the form of a dry creek bed offered me and my semi-starved brother a slide-in to take a welcome protein break. The land was barren apart from the thin line of gums lining the banks.

The thickening clouds looked ominous, suggesting the expected front was coming in sooner than expected. Despite the heat of the day, we donned the wet weather gear and headed back in. Having woken a little dusty from our long night of revelry, the simulation of a sauna while paddling was a great way to overcome any emotional tiredness. The banks laid low giving the impression we were travelling along a canal. The water resembled unsettled oil. Still the wildlife remained in hiding. The rain began as a light patter and with no wind to speak of, the heat our bodies were generating was more of an inconvenience than the dampness. After only 10 kilometres we took a second break on another barren bank before the full force of the weather set in.

The break was short with Dave and I wanting to push through the front and set camp earlier than later. As the front advanced, a light northerly wind pushed us down past the ferry at Swan Reach, then on to Punyelroo, and Nildottie. The first two looked like interesting places of old-world character and the third yet to achieve either characteristic. The cliffs folded to the right in the shape of a big bend that went on for such a distance they needed to be divided into the names of Big Bend East and Big Bend West. We paddled on, circling around the bend for hours, weather patterns coming and going, children growing into adults then grandparents, flared pants and mullets returning to fashion then going, then returning again. It went on so long we began to leave markers on the cliff-side in case we had entered a mid-river time warp. Sheep and cows began to look familiar, and we started assigning them names. It was probable they were assigning their children *our* names.

As darkness approached, to signal either the night or world's end, we spat out from the cliffs and looked desperately for a campsite. Anything that looked reasonable had private property or no entry signs which we were reluctant to ignore, even though South Australian law suggests we have a right to enter.

Rain tumbled heavier, making it all the more gloomy before we came across Kroehns Landing, a choice site in fine weather, but not tonight. Its modest grass area lay soaked with pools of water. Cold and wet and with no better option, we dragged the kayaks 30 metres from the concrete boat ramp and up two metres onto a bank next to a rickety, corrugated iron pumping station. Two spindly trees served as a bare shelter for the tent and our gear. Rain continued to fall while we set the tent and changed into our dry night clothing. Stretching from the tent towards the cliff, a jigsaw of roads ran around 30 shacks that sat on what is best described as a flood plain. No lights were on tonight. The gloomy day had turned to night.

A hot meal appeared out of the question, but the rain abated giving us just enough time to scratch around for some semi-dry wood and kindling to start a fire. In the middle of the dirt road, surrounded by puddles, we managed to cook a quick dinner. With that over, I hit the sack while Dave stayed up to dry his boots and gloves. Before my head hit the pillow, Dave was in the tent with rain coming down hard. Everything had been a rush since landing, but we considered everything critical was sheltered from the rain and so slept soundly while the heavens unloaded.

Distance 273 – 219 54 kilometres
Hard day

Chapter 49

Kroehns Landing to Younghusband

Day 49

Monday, May 20

Sunny to overcast and windy 19°C

What we considered was a reasonably tidy collection of our gear last night looked more like a dog's breakfast. I, for one, was so cold and worn-out when we pulled out of the water last night that my attention to detail lacked discipline. Whatever I thought was covered was not. Dave spent more time covering his gear but it was not much drier. The rain had smashed down during the night but at least we had slept dry. Now, cold and in wet clothes, neither of us could explain why we had left our paddling clothes out to air. We chewed our muesli and, with no chance for a fire, coffee was scratched off the menu. The sun shone brightly but not enough to warm the earth or the humans. We got our gear together and dragged the kayaks back down to the boat ramp. Sliding in around 7.45am we chatted away vigorously, having a laugh at what we had got ourselves into. At some stage yesterday, we passed the mark of having travelled 2000 kilometres: two million paddle strokes. It was probably around Punyelroo where the rabbit shearing sheds are supposed to exist. We had travelled a wearing 54 kilometres and with rain tumbling it had all gone by unnoticed.

'Damn! Dave, all that rain yesterday. Did you look out for those shearing sheds for the rabbits?'

'Forget about it, brother.'

The sun was out, there was no wind, the river was calm, we were cold, and paddling in wet clothes. The conversation for distraction continued. Distance versus time it has become less likely that Dave's quest to complete the South Australian leg of the Murray would eventuate.

The terrain was same, same, same, with cliffs on one side and thick impenetrable reeds on the other. Someone is going to discover a use for these reeds and, when they have disappeared, we will lament their loss to the scenery. Not today. A light north-easterly breeze came within the hour, helping us down towards the sleepy settlement of Walker Flat. In a short 11 kilometres the Walker Flat ferry, snoozing motionless at the bank, came into sight. We spied the grass landing and the quaint little general store that must be overstocked with coffee and Anzac biscuits. The distance covered was short of the usual morning push and the stop was unwarranted, but we were still feeling a bit precious after last night and agreed, with some feeble excuse, to opt for a bit of TLC.

We took a seat by the window overlooking the river: it was always about the river. The store attendant engaged in conversation with a local person as we waited for our treats and we caught up on all the latest gossip. So and so's wife...blah, blah; so and so got caught...blah blah; oh, and so and so has been...blah blah! The news we wanted eventually came, albeit with a bit of encouragement from us. The weather will be overcast but fine for the next few days. The news that was not so nice was that a major storm front would sweep in on Thursday afternoon: in four days. Immediately our travel plan became important. Dave's work commitments, combined with his injuries and pain were working against him. Time and distance were also barely achievable by me. If I could manage 50 kilometres a day, then paddle the final stretch across the notorious Lake Alexandrina by night, there was a chance to finish before the weather front arrived. If not, the winds would render the lake crossing too dangerous and I would have to sit out the time at Wellington, the last town in the river proper, to wait for conditions to change. The decision was clear-cut. To Dave's absolute credit he dismissed all personal concerns in favour of my cause, as he had done since he joined me. We finished the coffee and Anzac biscuits: all of them.

Back in the saddle, the river and landscape remained the same during the second session with cliffs bordering the river and reeds occupying the other side. It was *deja vu* with these endless cliffs taking us in ever-increasing circles. Small settlements lined the banks when the cliffs took a break on both the left and right side. Reaches now replaced meanderings as we headed south to the mouth and without any leeward respite, paddling comfort was now at the mercy of the winds. But for now, a westerly wind blew up just as we tracked along the only westerly direction of the river for the next 100 kilometres. My prediction of light northerly winds over late Autumn was now to be tested. We passed the ferry at Purnong and having completed a 20 kilometre grind from Walker Flat we climbed two metres onto a scrappy landing for the second break. The land back from the river was barren apart from small sections of native vegetation. Lagoons ran parallel to the river left and right but like yesterday, all wildlife had chosen the comfort of cover. We were all alone on our journey.

Again and again, the same countryside and river conditions continued as we endured our westerly charge through another

20 kilometres, past Bowhill, past Teal Flat, past shacks along any floodplain that offered river access and that might survive the next flood: a '56 flood aside. Two metre banks blocked with reeds offered no obvious campsite, but it was time to stop.

The smallest of gaps, likely chopped away for the ladder of a houseboat, appeared in the fading light—it was only 4.45pm. Springy, slippery tree roots ran along the bank which we were able to climb upon to see if camping was possible. Yes, was the short answer but we were between the bank and Lake Carlet on a 20 metre strip of thick scrub, three metres high. Small pathways led randomly in various directions. We guessed they were from animals but from the height of the tunnels we did not wish to meet them during an early morning comfort break. Getting the kayaks up two metres to the top of the bank took some effort with one of us, me, in the water, due to a short straw. The muddy bank worked in our favour as we slid The Banana and Precious up without a scratch. The nightly dried mango reward tasted particularly good as we sat in admiration of the achievement.

A small clearing where the paths converged was the only possible tent and fire site. Tent erection had become a joint exercise of late followed by a joint run-around for dry wood. Fuel was damp and scarce but typical of the skills of the fire-meister, Dave created bread and fish from wet scraps. Using only damp wood he worked the fire like a Grand Master to keep it attentive to our cooking and heating needs. With patience, we souped and couscous-ed our way through a most pleasant evening, adding a wee glass of our delicious cask red to help the lies sound more plausible.

Distance 219 – 169 50 kilometres
Nice conditions that became tougher through the day

Chapter 50

Younghusband to Mypolonga Flat

Day 50

Tuesday, May 21

Cloudy, calm conditions 21°C

It was cold when we woke: really cold. Dew had covered every-thing yet, somehow, coals were still glowing in the fire—the fire that had required so much effort to keep burning last night. We charged that fire up and enjoyed a rare morning coffee. Coffee bags used to be quite strong and flavoursome. Maybe my taste buds had changed on the river, but the coffee was weak and pretty much tasteless. We persevered because of the ritual and, at best, still enjoyed the satisfaction of a hot drink. Two out of two people at this campsite agreed. We got away dry at the normal time with a cheeky little entry into the kayaks via the slippery, strainer roots at the bank.

The sky had patches of blue as we paddled down the strait with the omnipotent ones again providing us with a river of perfect glass. A myriad of shacks and settlements and even a

Younghusband went by in a morning surrounded by, just for a change, cliffs and reeds. Small birds squeezed out the faintest of sounds from the low-lying scrub but there was no room amongst the shacks for kangaroos, wombats, pigs, or platypuses. We warmed up quickly with the enthusiastic morning paddling. The morning session is our best with Dave's painkillers working well in his rested body. Apart from my residual hip pain, a swelling behind my right knee, and numb toes, I coasted along in perfect health. Twenty kilometres down we landed in Mannum without having needed to put on the blinker.

People at the Mannum landing could have witnessed a disaster at a point so close to the end. An impossible possibility, another 'white sails in the sunset' moment, the ferry at Mannum is two ferries moving in conjunction and, naturally, in opposite directions. Dave was onto it, but I must have become mesmerised by the smells of baking bread, or coffee, or both, for as I waited for one ferry to reach its shore I inadvertently wandered into the path of the other. The cables of number two were tightening under me. What a galah! No wonder ferry operators, ferriers, ferrymeisters, or whatever nomenclature they prefer, dislike houseboats and kayaks. We are a nuisance. All danger was averted. It was not exactly at race speed for ferry or kayak but it was quicker than Shizo Kanakuri's 1912 Olympic marathon time of 54 years, 8 months, 6 days, 5 hours, and 32 minutes. In both of our cases there were mitigating circumstances. He had the distinction, though, of having married during that time and had since sported six children and ten grandchildren.

We pulled up to the grass landing in Mannum with the aim to replenish our fresh water supplies. Mannum has become one funky town. My memory of it being a dusty old country backwater was removed forever. Reflecting on my near disaster, I remembered a disaster of another time. The '56 flood! Here in

Mannum it created a more humorous circumstance: in retro-
spect, of course. With flood levels so high (recorded at over 12
metres or 40 feet in old speak) the bar of the local pub was
completely underwater. With typical country ingenuity, they
merely moved the bar facilities upstairs to the second floor.
Patrons with a thirst would tie their rowboats to the balcony
balustrade, step inside and carry on as usual.

Somehow, we ended up at the bakery. The sound of text
messages loading signalled a return of phone reception. A
message, and now phone capability, brought us together with
a fellow adventurer living in Mannum. So many offers to catch
up with people along the way had gone begging, with invites
only discovered the odd occasion phone reception kicked in
some days later. Karen Parry, at short notice, strolled into the
bakery within five minutes to discuss her future river journey
and chat about our experiences. A nice chat, yes, and with no
offence, we were soon on the march. With mutual understanding, we waved our riverbank farewells and paddled away with
the expectation all our paths will cross again. This experience
is typical of the way of the river. I understand there is no word
for goodbye from our indigenous Australians, but one of see-
ya-later. I find that much more agreeable.

Our friends, the cliffs, were reduced to rolling hills out of
Mannum and, as though framing a painting, were lined with
the mandatory reed banks. Settlement after settlement occupied every bank and anywhere it was possible to put a dwelling,
one had been erected. After enjoying forests and wilderness
for so long upriver I expected Murray, and certainly me, felt
somewhat violated. Reality is, though, people love the river for
all different reasons. The banks now are evidence of the small
price to pay for occupying every possible space along the river,
removing all the natural wildlife environment, replacing ugly
gumtrees that drop branches with trendy palms, and everybody can have their very own piece of paradise.

The paddle through and past Caloote took eight kilometres to do a 180 degree bend before heading down a wide river past any number of popular river tourist destinations. Within a short distance the river travelled at the closest point to South Australia's capital of Adelaide, and Mount Barker, one of South Australia's fastest growing towns. Added to this was our advance towards the river town of Murray Bridge, South Australia's fifth largest town by population. Houseboats and riverboats out on day trips began to increase in numbers. The empty river we had travelled for the most of May remained tucked away upstream.

Calculating all the compounding settlements consuming the banks to come, we chose not to get too close to Murray Bridge in case we lost all opportunity for a campsite and fire. We searched for the blue distance signs for guidance. There were houses on one side and reeds and scrub on the other and it soon became obvious there was no tree nor place for them to be posted anyway. Houseboats and riverboats now lined the banks and the search for a suitable campsite was problematic. The distance up from Goolwa, a river port housing river craft in the thousands, added one more excuse for 'bank' robbery. A mere 124 kilometres from here, it is a popular run, with all craft requiring an overnight mooring. Added to all these impediments, the houses along here have had some serious money spent, not only on the residence but on the landscaping, and there were no invitation signs posted for Lee and Dave. We would have settled for a small gravel road.

As the sky grew dim, the searched continued desperately for a campsite. We settled on a small gravel road that either began or ended at the bank and went towards a farmhouse some 400-500 metres inland. The bank's retaining wall was reinforced with rocks. A threadbare carpet stretched over the rocks sat conveniently to provide the barest level of access. Behind the camping spot a walking track ran parallel along the river with an electric fence to protect the safety of the only wood that we could gather for a fire. Danger aside, I called upon my vast experience of commando practice. Truth is, I have had no commando practice, but I had seen movies. And where was Dave to be found when needed? Dave was not to be found. At all risk to personal safety the commando crawls and rolls allowed me to slip under the fence and collect plenty of wood for Dave to light a fire.

This was Dave's last night. Tomorrow we would head into Murray Bridge where he will leave this journey, to be continued by himself at some time later. With none of our 'Grange' cask wine left we celebrated with a third food course of fried potato chips. The high level of satisfying indulgence in this fried delicacy should not be underestimated. Salt takes them to a higher level again. Once the fingers had been licked, we got down to the business of studying the official Bureau of Meteorology weather charts, going over and over the probability of fine weather for the final day and night of my journey across the notorious Lake Alexandrina. A high-pressure system was forecast to settle over the lake during Thursday night allowing the perfect opportunity to cross entirely free of wind and, therefore, waves. I contacted fellow adventurer and experienced journeyman of Lake Alexandrina, Brad Butler, who, despite the late notice, happily offered to join and guide me across under the moonlight—the same moonlight that seven short weeks ago had cows and horses nudging me through the tent. The crossing would be tomorrow night with the end so close. It was lovely that Dave was as excited as me to see the goal so near and within reach: it is brotherly.

We were cold, breathing out fog smoke, and every time we stepped away from the fire we were covered in dew in a flash. The night was perfectly calm and the stars burned bright as we crawled into the wet tent, zipping our doorways, before slipping fully clothed into the minus temperature sleeping bags.

Our beanies were on for extra warmth. As my head rested on the pillow a level of satisfaction that words cannot convey washed over me.

Distance 169 – 124 45 kilometres
Easy day

Chapter 51

Mypolonga Flat to Wellington

Day 51

Wednesday, May 22

Fine and sunny, no breeze 21°C

I needed sleep but it would not come. According to reports sleeping in the foetal position can tell a lot about a person. You are likely to be shy and sensitive, possibly conscientious, or even a go-getter with a tough exterior and a gentle soul. Some suggest it's the best way to fool a bear if you happen to be around when it gets hungry in the middle of the night. There had been no bears on this trip to date and, although 'sleeping foetal' might dissuade a hungry bag-snatching pelican, my excuse for sleeping that way was that it was just so bitterly cold. When the alarm went off at 5.45am I was almost thankful. Almost! Dave and I mutually agreed there was no time for coffee and got underway at 7.10am in cold, dewy, and foggy conditions. The sun was resisting its rise.

Paddling in fog entered my list of things I did not want to do again. We were unable to see beyond 30 metres with no idea where we were and no idea where anybody else was, either. Snags were not so much the issue because the banks had been clear for some days, but a rogue houseboat moored on the bank was more probable than possible. Gradually, peering into the fog it lightened, and we began to make out the banks. Paddling became more comfortable. Comfortable in mind but not in body. It was so cold with both hands and feet refusing to accede to the rule of increased blood flow when exercising. Visibility improved by degrees, but it was over an hour before we could make out what the shapes were that we were carefully avoiding. By good fortune there was no other craft on the water. That is to say; none that we saw.

As the sun began to burn through the fog, we rounded the bend to see the city of Murray Bridge. Originally named and still called Pomberuk by the indigenous Ngarrindjeri people, the city has undergone three colonial name changes. Known formerly as Edwards Crossing after George Edwards bought adjoining land it later became Mobilong until a road bridge was built across the river. Rather than the city of Murray Bridge being rather audacious in assuming its name above all other potential towns with bridges the town was named after the bridge itself. Built in 1879, it was the first road bridge over the River Murray.

We passed under what is now two bridges, watching cars pace slowly over one bridge, built slightly wider than Tooleybuc Bridge over Murray River. A horn in the distance signalled the other bridge would soon be serving its function as the rail link between Adelaide and Melbourne. A kilometre further down the grassed park of the Murray Bridge Rowing Club offered a welcoming beach landing. We commemorated our travels together with a celebratory piece of dried mango each.

Dave's daughter, Soraya, met us at the bank without treats but we were friendly anyway. After unpacking all unnecessary weight, I loaded further necessary weight with an EPIRB, flares and other assorted safety paraphernalia in a bag which weighed the same as what I had taken out. It was an emotional moment when leaving Dave and The Banana behind after having shared the whole of the South Australian leg with him. But there were no tears. I now had bigger fish to fry, and I pulled away at 10am knowing the last 112 kilometres promised me everything and owed me nothing.

River lesson #56: There are not enough Dave's on the river.

The river was laid flat and smooth and the wind non-existent. The width from bank to bank was as wide as any part of the river and did nothing to assist the flow. My travelling pace went down and the supposed 'lighter kayak' had no effect. The reach through to Tailem Bend was a laborious 15 kilometres with the water tower of the town visible for nearly two and a half hours before reaching it. I drew on one of the many things I learnt in the early days of paddling practice. I could not go any faster or reach landmarks quicker than under a standard rate of paddling. All day the river had been 'dead water'. I told myself patience was the key when you do not have a motor. I was still telling myself patience was the key when halfway down to Tailem, spiders the size of a thumbnail appeared in great numbers either flying through the air or on top of the water. These were not the regular water skeeters but actual spiders. I was not fussed until noticing they were running across the water in search of...the kayak! With their sticky little feet, they started to appear on the deck. I had no choice but to flick them off the deck. I had no choice but pick them out of the cockpit with my fingers to throw them back in the water. Yew! Where was a long-toothed platypus when you need it? The attack continued for six kilometres. As quickly as they came, they disappeared.

The answer to yesterday's question of how the blue kilometre signs could be posted without trees appeared in the form of a marker buoy bobbing in the river just inside the bank. The number on the sign: 100

Having travelled 22 kilometres from Murray Bridge, I arrived at the Tailem Bend wharf at 2pm and tied up. It was hardly necessary. With zero flow, the tied kayak did not move one inch. The cliff to the town needed an effort to climb the 30 metres and, having been to Tailem Bend many times, I remained at the wharf in the company of any spiders I had yet to remove. During this last day of crackers for late lunch, I splurged and had eight with the standard Vegemite and peanut butter—but not together on the same cracker.

I waved away the second last ferry on the Murray and paddled down through banks of reeds, low lying scrub, the ever-abundant lignum, and willows, in what was just two long bends for another 12 kilometres to Wellington. Apart from the spiders, there was little in the way of wildlife today with only the odd pelican, the usual darter, a few ibises, and the whistling kites interested in completing the odyssey with me. The old river had become wide and lazy while making its way to the end. It appeared to have given up, now resigned to seeing its time out. With no flow, its banks had given out to wetlands and marinas, both occupied and deserted. Considering only four percent of all the water gathered in the Murray-Darling basin makes it this far, it is little wonder the river has lost interest.

At 4.30pm, the sight of the Wellington ferry signalled that the day's final resting place was nearby. Seeking advice from a local homeowner as to the best place to set the tent, he kindly offered his front lawn. Hoping to avoid sprinklers and to get closer to the meeting place with Brad I respectfully declined and slipped on down to the pub to a berth at the old, rickety wooden wharf.

The hotel manager kindly agreed for me to set up the tent on the terraced lawn at the riverfront for no charge. It was out of view of the patrons and in the shelter of a willow tree. I erected the poor wet thing vowing to give it a good dry out in a day's time. The pub is old and in original condition, with loads of character. An outdoor decking takes full advantage of the river views and across to the new marina in a backwater the river is too lazy to fight over. Dinner was served at exactly 6.30pm and, with the need for some sleep after today's hard slog, I was in the tent, now wetter than wet from the new dew. I needed as much snooze time as possible before the allotted time of midnight when Brad and I would tackle the lake crossing.

The weather forecast had held true and if the storm front did not come early, conditions for the crossing would be perfect. With a full stomach, wanting and waiting for sleep, the excitement of the final charge had me racing. My mind was in a mouse wheel. One day remaining. Shhh, sleep time now!

Distance 124 – 76 48 kilometres
Slog but perfect conditions

Chapter 52

Wellington to the Murray Mouth

Day 52

Thursday, May 23

Fine, foggy to blue sky to wind 19°C

An alarm went off and I sat bolt upright, shaking my head to disperse the dreams that had not yet left my head. I found the culprit, turned off the offensive noise, and switched on the tent light. I prefer kookaburras to wake me these days. It was 11pm. My attention turned to the job at hand. THE LAKE! Based on the temperature of previous mornings I dressed in Dave's thermal top as well as two paddling tops: extra layers but not so much as to be uncomfortable. Beanie and scarf were essential. Next, everything inside the tent was stuffed into its regular drybag—those same drybags I had been carrying since Lake Hume. I got lost in a minute of deep thought when I came from the tent.

Lake Hume, Lake Mulwala and now Lake Alexandrina: engineered, counterfeit lakes. All these lakes have taken lives. This

330 ~ LEE SALVEMINI

lake is the largest and I am going to be paddling through the middle of it. The facts all rushed in at once. With old river dogs at the second storey of the Mannum pub reporting sightings of sharks, whales and even tall ships in the river, the authorities accepted it was time to act. Barrages were built in 1939 to prevent salt water from the mouth intruding up the river. They are now strung between the many islands that run parallel to the sand dunes on the oceanfront. The lake engulfs the river which once wound its way to Goolwa before heading westward, parallel to the ocean to find its mouth; a mouth which has moved back and forth up to eight kilometres during the past 3,000 years. Between the dunes and the islands, the stretch of saltwater which is under tidal influence is known as the Coorong, running from Goolwa and following the coast southeast for 200 kilometres. Back on the other side, the lake is 26 kilometres long and up to 20 kilometres wide, seething unpredictably, restlessly, ominously, between the mainland and the barraged islands. Lake Alexandrina is not for the faint-hearted and is known best for its infamy. I was still standing at the opening of my tent. I stuffed the poor wet thing into its bag expecting it would be the last time it would be used on this journey. Three hours sleep should be enough. After 51 days of paddling, I was as strong as a Barmah brumby.

At 11.45 Brad and I met on the old wooden wharf. He had stayed with his wife at the hotel in preparation. As anticipated, the night was perfectly calm but the one thing that neither of us anticipated was the likelihood of fog. It was so thick that the first I knew of Brad being there was when I bumped into him. With the slap of hands, we paddled away at midnight. I stayed close, very close. Any distance between us beyond 15 metres and I would have lost Brad. We attempted to keep one bank in sight for navigation. I was so thankful for his familiarity with this section of the river and lake: my trust in him was unequivocal. Our first destination was to reach Pomanda Point where the river ends and the lake begins. The final charge to the end was here.

As we paddled down the final straight reach of the river, snags and posts appeared, not totally unexpected, yet surprising when popping up out of the fog without notice. The river was so full of these obstructions and they materialised time and again both left and right. Without a view across from bank to bank it was difficult to assess if they were in the middle of the river or at the banks. Navigation was proving problematic and I might as well have been wearing a blindfold. Yet, with the same enthusiasm of the first paddling session of each day we were powering along the 13 kilometre section. Brad stopped to check his GPS tracker.

'I think we've been going around in circles,' he said.

I laughed at his joke.

'We've been lost out here for an hour,' he said with no hint of humour.

The snags and posts had looked identical because they were identical. Brad was my navigator, and my progress was entirely in his control. To think that I would have tackled this alone if he were unable to join me was now incomprehensible. People had warned me against attempting the crossing at night. They had warned against crossing by day. But even they had not ventured to the absurdity of paddling in fog. My faith in Brad did not waiver for a moment.

'We've got two choices,' he said. 'We can stop here and go back. Or, if you're in for the challenge we can go on. It's your decision.'

'Let's go on,' I said without a moment's hesitation.

'Good.'

With stronger attention to the GPS directions we made it to the end of the river. After rounding the two kilometre spit which had separated the river from the lake we stopped for a break and snack on a small wind-swept beach. We had travelled

18 kilometres—an extra five—and the clock had struck 3am. Fog remained thick, so thick my perception of the lake before us extended no further than a circle with a 15 metre radius. During this early stage Brad's pace had been to the edge of my capability although my efforts were hampered by the weight of my kayak compared to his empty kayak.

We headed into the abyss to paddle 26 kilometres directly across the middle of the lake to Point Sturt. The night sky opened every so often in patches enabling us to navigate by the stars as we forged ahead. A compass on the decks of our kayaks allowed us to continue straight and true during the long periods of fog and darkness. The lake was without flow and Precious dragged heavy. Dragging it through the dead water, I found myself boat lengths behind Brad as he set the pace. I could not afford to lose him and I was working hard. While he was good company and extremely considerate, I could recognise the times when he zoned into the paddling groove and powered along as I had done unconsciously at times with Dave. The wind was negligible, as forecast, and the water 'soup' as Brad described it. I rated it oily but unsettled.

The concentration required to paddle in the dark and fog, together with the unsettled turbulence of the water brought me to the edge of my limits around the halfway mark across the lake. The lake is shallow, with an average depth of under three metres. That is shallow enough to generate treacherous waves when the wind whips up but not shallow enough that I could get out and stand up for a break. With the crossing 26 kilometres long and the lake up to 20 kilometres wide, I was not heading left or right for a break. The pace had been relentless. I should have been strong, but the drudgery of yesterday's paddle and the lack of sleep had overtaken me. I became unsteady, hallucinations clouded my vision, and my head jolted awake with every splash of water. Still, I kept paddling. In a moment of clarity, a thought rocked me conscious: I vowed in the first week to check the cockpit every morning for snakes that might seek refuge in the warmth. Not once had I checked since that moment. It was either the prospect of a snake or my conversation delving into the realms of the hallucinations, or a combination of both, but Brad must have sensed my discomfort. We stopped for a moment's rest and after a couple of pieces of dried mango my second wind kicked in. With the mind refocused, I was confident of being in the cockpit alone. The time was 5.15am.

Under clear conditions the navigational light on Pomanda Point would fade when reaching the halfway mark of the lake and the navigational light at Point Sturt would come into view. The stars suggested we were travelling a steady course; the GPS tracker confirmed our successful navigation, but the lights were impossible to make out in the fog. A faint glow of yellow lights left and right also confirmed we were in the middle of the lake. When the northerly breeze popped up, I was all ears and eyes as small inconsistent waves rolled in against the side of the kayak. The efforts to match Brad's pace worked in my favour when trying to maintain balance with the slap of the paddle blade on each side correcting any overbalancing. Brad, the perfect guide, was mostly close and in continual conversation. Still, there was an eerie silence that enveloped us as we paddled through the cloistered bubble of soup above and below. The silence was broken as a huff, puff and splutter rose up through the soup behind us. On the last stretch, a platypus was calling after having followed me for over 2,000 kilometres.

'Looks like a seal is coming along for the ride,' said Brad.

'Oh,' I replied.

A seal. It followed for a short while but lolling around is a seal's game and swimming at our pace is not. Authorities have declared we must not approach a seal within a 30 metre radius—this seal obviously did not get the memo. These New

Zealand Long-nosed Fur Seals have been attempting to re-take the lake and Coorong after commercial hunting during the 1800s all but wiped them out. They can survive and feed in fresh and saltwater, but their diet of fish is at odds with the local fisher folk. One suggestion to solve to the problem involved bombing them? Why not put them in stocks and throw fruit at them, read them stories from The Advertiser or make them watch Channel 7 News: all equally cruel and barbaric.

The bright lights of Narrung and other southern settlements to the Coorong side of the lake shone through dimly as we continued in a south-westerly direction looking for the lighthouse signal at Point Sturt. It remained hidden. My eyes were playing tricks and what I determined was the cliffs off Point Sturt was a mirage which tormented me kilometre after kilometre. At around 7am we reached the other side. I was taking Brad's word for it—the numerous red beacons were directing us to the channel but still there was no land apart from the mirages. I was happy to be able to find a landing beach and take a break but Brad had other ideas. We pushed on around Rat Island, Goose, Goat, Snake, and various other islands where creatures have assumed control, towards Clayton Bay. Around the back of Rat Island the water was shallow, too shallow for the kayaks, and with posts and fences appearing in the water for our amusement we pushed on around.

The fog lifted gradually around 8.15am and with only five kilometres to complete our crossing, we aimed for the opening of Clayton Bay. We slid into a small inlet by the Clayton Bay Park at 9am having completed nine hours of paddling and achieving what we had set out to do. I was exhausted, relieved, and happy. Brad looked like he was just warming up. My intention to attempt the crossing if Brad had not been able to join me was absurd and I shuddered at the naivety. People die on Lake Alexandrina and, even knowing this, I had not appreciated the enormity of the undertaking.

I dragged myself across the park and into the café to join Brad for a coffee and check over the path of our journey on the GPS tracker. Most of our travelled direction was spot on but the section of the river where we got lost resembled a spider web with turns of 90 and 120 degrees. Maybe we were better off with blindfolds. No attempt to explain how the fog could have distorted our sense of direction was plausible. I blamed him and he blamed me, but we agreed it was best kept between us. But my mind was fuzzy and maybe we did not agree to that.

I sat gob-smacked as Brad informed me he had no time for breakfast and was leaving to go to work. I stayed on at the café to regenerate my energy in preparation for the final assault. The forecast for increasing westerly winds around 4pm allowed time to catch my breath and relax. Another coffee, two bacon and egg sandwiches, and a bowl of hot chips later, my wits had returned. The fog had lifted, the sun was shining, a gentle breeze wafted along, and I stripped down to the regular paddle attire for the final leg of the odyssey.

It was now 11am and Clayton Bay disappeared behind me as Precious set its new course heading west toward Goolwa. This region is known as Goolwa Lakes, or Lower Lakes and through here I was following the direction of the river's original path. The path was not obvious but during the 2010 drought pictures show it trickling along a narrow bed so low people could walk across it. The barrages now were holding the water to a level where the river is 600 metres wide. The cliffs have gone, the hills sit a long back in the distance and the terrain from the river is flat with only a small rise as it heads back inland. The vegetation is windswept and swampy with no shortage of reeds. Sun glistened on the surface of the water. There were so many reasons to be happy.

Singing along while paddling between Hindmarsh Island and the mainland, swans began to appear on both sides in great numbers. It was if they had organised a congratulatory parade. I called greetings as I had done whenever seeing them since my chance connection in the early part of the journey. It was a fitting end. Then, while I continued along, they paddled out to greet me before flying back away as I reached them. Was I really seeing this? The tough John 'The Duke' Wayne persona that I had been cultivating since the beginning of the odyssey was again under scrutiny. Something special was happening that I could not explain. That emotional discharge when long quests have reached their conclusion is not new to me and, with my end in sight, this proved to be the time when my emotions got the better of me. Tears fell from my eyes. Those beautiful black swans of the Murray will always hold a special place in my heart. After two kilometres this parade concluded just as the north-westerly front blew in ahead of schedule.

Two waterways that empty into the Goolwa lakes were now between me and Goolwa. The wide-open space where the mouth of the Finnis River emptied was where the north-westerly first hit me. What was a pleasant, final singing rhyming paddle took a major turn for the worst as if all hell had broken loose. Tackling waves whipped up by the strong winds, I headed to the northern bank for shelter. The experience of 52 days paddling told me the river was not finished with me just yet. The wind grew stronger while paddling past the mouth of the Finnis and then smashed me again as I paddled past the mouth of Currency Creek, the second waterway. Hugging the leeward northern bank at every opportunity brought relief all the way into Goolwa. I passed the wharfs of the many old and restored wooden riverboats before cruising under the Hindmarsh Island bridge and past the Goolwa wharf. With the time at 1.15pm, only 11 kilometres flowed between me and the culmination of a 33 year old pipe dream.

Frank Tuckwell, Kaylene Maalste, and Kathy Sutton, all from the Goolwa National Trust met me at the Goolwa wharf for congratulations, photographs and to conduct an interview to assess my eligibility to enter the register of successful river travellers known as The Inland Rivers National Marathon Register. In the shelter of the historical buildings overlooking the wharf, the sun was shining, giving no indication of the water conditions only one kilometre away.

'Congratulations,' said Kathy. 'What a pleasant way to end the trip.'

Apart from my brother, I had spoken very little to anyone over the past 52 days. My brain was not engaged for conversation and the mouth did not function sufficiently well to fluently formulate the words I needed to speak. More like a wild bushman, clothes hanging off me, unable to communicate, I was undoubtedly a sight to avoid. To their credit, they did not run. With patience, photographs were taken, and the interview concluded to validate my experience.

While resting in readiness for the last short paddle, I made calls to organise a lift home for me and my Precious. I was so near home I could smell my winter jonquils blooming their winter show. All local friends were either unavailable or had gone north for the winter. All local pubs would also likely be closed for renovations. An option was to paddle from the mouth back to Goolwa, chancing the lock at the Goolwa weir would still be open. From there, arrange a taxi home to get my car while leaving my kayak on the bank until I returned. I jokingly considered pushing out into the surf from the mouth and paddle the ten kilometres west in the waves and wind until I could safely land on the beach within walking distance of home. The crashing surf in the distance meant choosing this option would be 'romancing with myself' as my father would say. With so many obstacles overcome during the last 52 days, this snag in the water was the least of my worries. As if on cue, Matty Eldred, a local paddler from Strathalbyn, appeared at the wharf to meet me and pass on congratulations. On hearing my plight, he kindly offered to collect my car from home and

wait in the carpark at Sugar's beach on Hindmarsh Island, directly across from the mouth—a mouth that is surrounded by
working dredges removing 2,000 square metres of sand a day
at an annual cost of $6 million just to keep it open. A mouth
that I was waiting to see. A wind at my back would blow me all
the way to the journey's end. The carrot was before me and it
would soon be caught and eaten. But, as with every good tale,
there was one more sting left.

River lesson #100: The end is never the end.

The name of Goolwa means elbow in the local Ngarrindjeri
language and, true to that description I headed back in an
easterly direction around the other side of Hindmarsh Island
to go through the final lock and on to the mouth. The distance
from the wharf to the Goolwa barrage and lock is only four
kilometres, yet the waters themselves conspired to challenge
me one last time. The lock is in the middle of the barrage as
opposed to the far left or right of the upriver lock and weir
arrangements. The wind was blowing waves at a 45 degree
angle to the lock opening. The wind and waves intensified as
I paddled across, with waves breaking over the back and side
of me while I attempted to surf the awkward direction down
and across them. Fabs was here to the end. I had forgotten
to cover the logo on the front of the kayak. He could hear
the surf in the distance and was now revelling in the rising
crescendo of wind and water. Having now paddled for around
15 hours since midnight, I was not so much fatigued, as jaded,
and the wind and waves being thrown at me were not my ideal
way to complete the last hour. I laughed. After all this time, I
might yet end in the drink at the end of this journey, as I had
begun. Tossed, turned but not tumbled, I waited in turbulent
water at the lock opening, clinging to a wooden pylon as the
lockmeister ambled along the barrage path to the lock for my
transition through to calmer waters on the other side—most
probably, hopefully!

'Runnin' a bit late,' said the lockmeister.

My mouth was working better, and I nearly released a comment about his potential time over a 100 metre dash but thought better of it.

'Little bit rough out there,' I advised.

'Well, she's gonna be smooth travlin' down the other side.'

His words were music to my ears.

Once out of the lock into the seawater of the Coorong, the waters smoothed. I breathed in the salty air for the first time in such a long time and the smell of sea and sand excited my nose and brain. The mixture of the fresh and saltwater produced a tea colour for the first 500 metres before the deep blue colour of seawater brought contrast to the river that had undergone changes from clear to murky, iced coffee and tea along its path. With sand hills separating the sea crashing only 100 metres off to the right and the low-lying scrub of Hindmarsh Island to the left, the last seven kilometres toward the mouth were comparatively serene. The sea's tidal influence directly affects the Coorong and now, at low tide, the rocky banks and beach on either side were exposed. Sticking within the channel markers, I paddled on.

By 4.30pm the barges that dredge to keep the mouth clear came into sight and my goal, though crowded with machinery, was a beautiful sight. After travelling nearly 2300 kilometres of bends and reaches, forest and desert, sun and storm, under 26 bridges, past 12 ferries, through 14 locks, around two weirs, over three lakes, past too many towns and settlements to count, and zero platypuses, the river had finally run out. The sea swell sent waves into the mouth washing out any enticement of paddling into the sea for posterity. The mouth was 30 metres wide and, as I got closer, the wind coming through the opening forced me back to a beach off to the side. A swim, surely? Well, the temperature, combined with the wind, made conditions quite uncomfortable so, with a nod of esteem to river and sea, I stood at the point from where I could paddle no more and munched down two pieces of dried mango and one extra in celebration.

True to his word, Matty was waiting directly across the Coorong channel with my car which, when loaded with the kayak and the gear I had carried for 52 days, took us home. Fifteen minutes later I sat with a satisfied smile on my face, a cider in my hand and released a heavy sigh allowing for a plethora of memories to fill the empty space left from having no river under, over or around me.

Lucky Lee!

Distance 76 – 0 85 kilometres (with added distance for getting lost)

Mostly hard

Chapter 53

Afterword

The next day and beyond

A satisfying contentment swept over me after scratching the itch of a 30 year fascination. It was not the achievement of the completion that took precedence in my thoughts but the memories of the journey. There was so much generosity and happiness along the river. It truly is a place for people to gather for adventures of many kinds, some of which we share, and others that are just not our bag. The big old river endures and will be here far beyond any of us. It must be used for pleasure, farming and for consumption and for this reason, we are not just obligated but compelled to assume a level of responsibility for its management and wellbeing.

Despite the search, I did not see a platypus. I have a bookmark once owned by my late father presenting two quotes from *The Bible*. The first states 'Seek and you shall find'. What that does not specify is what you will find. The second quote provided greater insight: 'Knock and the door shall be opened for you.' The platypus I sought was not a distraction but a call to observe; to observe and acknowledge pathways more prolific than the labyrinth of roots extending down from a gum tree on the river's bank. The local First Nations people call it Mi-Wi and, for my opportunity to engage with nature and the wildlife in mutual communication and consideration, I will hold memories deep within me. To think Mother Nature opened her door to this willing advocate even for just a peep, was a gift.

That alleged seal on the last night kept playing on my mind. I have always been running, charging, looking for a new adventure, looking for new heights. Maybe I needed to sit awhile, soft hands, wait for things to come to me. But I had been sitting, sitting for 52 days and yet still I was one paddle stroke ahead of my platypus. Brad said it was a seal. Neither of us saw it. I think it more likely it was a long-toothed platypus still after my rations. Maybe that is what life is about—always be one stroke ahead of the platypus.

Feeling strong and fit, one month later, Dave finished his journey to the mouth over two days. Under perfect conditions during the day, I chaperoned him across the lake in a motorboat. It looked so crazy to see in daylight what I had paddled over in fog and darkness. Crazy: not a single corella picked up on my speech lessons. If you ever hear one call it out, though, you will know where it began.

Inevitably, some niggles will take time to repair. A swelling behind my right knee that I carried for the last three weeks and that made walking difficult, subsided after approximately three weeks. My knees reflect the lack of walking over the couple of months in the kayak and even months later, they are still weak despite a combination of rest and rehabilitation. The hip injury sustained on Day 1 continues with a deep pain remaining, despite the thoughtful consideration of qualified professionals. The three middle toes on each foot remain numb although I am sure circulation is okay. I am hungry all day, every day. Paddling strength—yes, I'm still loving paddling

—has remained even with a lower workload of small journeys once a week. The tripod stool lasted the trip and is still holding up with intermittent use.

I met with Frank Tuckwell at Goolwa the following week to collect my Certificate of Completion. In payment of the suggested donation of $5, he received ten 50 cent pieces which were somewhat matte-finished from laying in dirt but well-travelled with plenty of stories to tell.

Lee
La Misma Nada

Appendix A

Kayak and related equipment

Kayak: Seabird Expedition XP 507 – Carbon hull and fibre-glass deck

Length: 507cm (16'8")

Weight: 23kg

Load capacity: 145kg

Aqua-Bound Sting Ray Carbon paddle

Sea to Summit paddle leash

Sea to Summit Flexi-fit neoprene kayak skirt

Railblaza C-Tug Kayak Trolley and ties

Lambswool seat pad

Voltaic 6-watt solar panel – ineffective despite full sun most days

Voltaic V15 USB Battery pack

Nanuck waterproof case for USB battery

Comments

All items met or exceeded expectations apart from the solar panel which did not charge the USB battery or mobile phone sufficiently from day to day. This was despite full sun for most of the days. As this potentiated a safety risk, I cannot recommend this product.

Appendix B

Paddling attire

Rash vest – long and short
Board shorts x 2
Sea to Summit Ultra Flex neoprene paddling booties
SEAK short finger paddling gloves
Adapt-a-Cap Ultimate Hat – with UPF50+ fabric
Polaroid sunglasses
Rain jacket
Ultra Pinnacle L50 personal flotation device (PFD) with a rear pouch for a water bladder
Camelbak two-litre water bladder with drinking tube
Dri-Dock waterproof phone pouch – ineffective, splitting at the zip locks seals.
Camera

Comments

All items met or exceeded expectations apart from the Dri-Dock waterproof phone pouch. It was replaced twice and, in all three cases, split around the zip locks after a modest amount of use. Additionally, the clear case was not suitable for taking photos as recommended.

I did not take a GPS but I know other paddlers have found one useful, if not essential.

Appendix C

Personal attire

  Rain Jacket
  Jumper (sweater)
  Beanie
  T-shirt
  Light weight camping trousers
  Thermal underwear
  Socks
  Shimano Evair enclosed sandals
  Underwear
  Toiletries
  Mobile phone

Comments

All items were of use except for socks which I did not need because of the generally fine weather. More substantial foot-wear is advisable during cooler travelling times. All the above items were in single quantity.

Appendix D

Cooking and Food equipment

Billy
Non-stick lightweight frying pan
Plate, bowl, and cup
Knife, fork, and spoon
Plastic wine glass
Sharp knife
Wooden spoon
Tongs
Non-stick spatula
Cutting board
Collapsible waterproof containers for foodstuffs
Lighter, matches and flint
Whisperlite fuel stove
Sponge and scourer
Tea-towel

Comments

All the items were used every day and night.

Appendix E

Food

    Breakfast: Muesli, prunes, coffee
    Morning break: Musashi Growling Dog bar
    Afternoon break: Vita-Weat crackers, peanut butter, Vegemite
    Dinner: Dried Philippine mango
    Trident, Tom Yum Goong instant soup
    Rice, pasta, couscous
    Tuna (sachets)
    Onions, carrots, potatoes
    Capsicum, broccoli
    Condiments: Garlic, cumin, chilli, salt, pepper
    Snacks: Apple, hard-boiled eggs
    Drinks: Water and wine
    Daily supplements: Magnesium tablets, BCAA's

Comments

Foods were chosen for strength and endurance with the necessary amounts of protein, carbohydrate, and fibre. Additionally, all these foods can be quickly prepared with the modest cooking equipment being carried. The weight capacity of the kayak restricted excess treats but with two or more kayaks travelling together the options for variation increases.

Appendix F

Night and Sleep Essentials

Tent
Sleeping bag with dry bag
Inflatable mattress
Inflatable Pillow (optional)
Ground-sheet – also to erect for cover from weather
Head torch and/or lantern, spare batteries
Garden shovel
Toilet paper
Three-legged collapsible chair

Comments

All items were used nightly/daily although when the inflatable pillow sprung a leak my dry bag stuffed with clothes proved more comfortable.

Appendix G

Travel Essentials

Chart book

Compass

First-Aid kit with Emergency 'Space' blanket

Insect repellent

Sunblock

Dry bags for food and clothes

5 Minute Araldite for kayak repair

Small toolkit with nuts, bolts and wire for kayak repair, aluminium snap hook carabiners

Leatherman and/or Pocket knife

Twine (baling twine is fabulous and unbreakable), nylon rope, zip ties, Velcro straps

Duct tape

Flares, EPIRB for safety

Comments

Fortunately, I needed to use very little of these but the comfort of having them stashed at the back in the kayak in a dry bag that I did not need to open was worth it.

Acknowledgements

I wish to thank the following people for their contribution to the journey of paddling or the writing of this story: David Salvemini, Jim and Linda Ainsworth, Peter Phillips, David Inglis, Stephen Inglis, Geoffrey Inglis, Malcolm Cheffirs, the Robinvale family members, Brad and Lorna Taylor, Peter Wareing, Anthony Wareing, Wayne Meeker, Soraya and Elise Salvemini, Alicia Salvemini, Bobby Salvemini, George Hilton, Brad Butler, Matthew Eldred, Chris Ford-Davies, John Scardigno, Daryl Warren, Donna Mulvenna, Julian Moore, George Cooper, Jen Watts, the many people who stopped for a chat and offered a cuppa along the way, and the friendly Lockmeisters along the river. Nothing would have stopped me, but everyone here made it easier and more enjoyable.

The Platypus

Ornithorhynchus anatinus, or platypus as it prefers to be known amongst friends, is an Australian native mammal of somewhat dubious origin belonging to the Monotreme family; a small family consisting only of the species platypus and another Australian native—the echidna. Monotremes are different to other mammals in that their young are born in eggs but as with other mammals, suckle their mother's milk. In stating they are of dubious origin let me explain and allow you to decide.

The Australian countryside varies from forest to stark desert with a human footprint permanently living on approximately 5% of the total landmass. That leaves a whole lot of land where the native creatures get up to who knows what during the day and, even more intriguing, under the blanket of stars at night. Enter the platypus who lives within the waterways occupying both land and water along the eastern side of Australia from northern Queensland to Tasmania. Classified by George Shaw in 1799 accompanied by a pelt received in London, it was initially considered a hoax (Shaw, George; Nodder, Frederick Polydore (1799). "The Duck-Billed Platypus, Platypus anatinus". The Naturalist's Miscellany. 10 (CXVIII): 385–386. doi:10.5962/p.304567 – via Biodiversity Heritage Library.)

The platypus is approximately 20 inches and has the body of a mole with front and rear legs that stick out sideways ending with clawed, webbed paws. To the front, a duck bill has been attached to the head while a flat beach bat style tail brings up the rear. Its brown fur glistens in the daylight and becomes fluorescent when swimming under the water. The ears are hidden like that of a frog and the eyes have double cones like that of a fish. The Aboriginal creation story of Tharalkoo, the rebellious duck, swimming into dangerous territory only to be ravished by a sly water rat is a more plausible explanation for its bodily eccentricities. Either way, weighing in at a mere 2.5 kilograms one might think it a cute toy to hold and cuddle. But wait!

On the rear legs of the male a sharp claw resembling the dew claw of a dog protrudes menacingly for protection. These dew claws excrete a toxic venom and while not life threatening to humans, you will be doing little else than laying prostrate calling pathetically for help. Not so lucky if you are a dog—no because dogs can not call for help but because the venom is toxic enough to kill the animal. These days this lovely creature, like other native species in Australia, is a protected animal no longer stalked for its fur.

And what of the less cuddly long-toothed platypus with its multitude of long sharp gnashing teeth spreading fear akin to the threat imposed by a great white shark as it singles out its unlucky dinner. Picture the primeval animal roaming the land with its 5-6 foot body seeking out kangaroo, crocodile, and giant koala. While this description might benefit from slight exaggeration, the point is that there is evidence of an ancient platypus dating back somewhere between 5 million and 250 million years. And, if there is so much conjecture to the timing of the beast then it is quite conceivable a specimen still roams the land in search of mischief, a mate, or my picnic basket.

On a more serious note, the modern-day platypus while not under threat of extinction is listed as vulnerable due to the loss of the pristine habitat necessary for its continued survival. Polluted waterways including fishing lines and yabby traps contribute to the problems as well as their exposure during low water to the ravages of non-native foxes, dogs, and feral cats. The population of platypuses once native to South Australia is no longer seen in that region of Australia: the obstructed flow of waterways due to the construction of weirs being but one of the contributing factors.

Lee Salvemini is an adventurer having completed challenges that include trekking The Himalayas, The Kokoda Track, the world heritage South Coast Walk of southern Tasmania, and a six-day triathlon over 560 kilometres. Following a business career over 30 years he pursued another passion attaining writing degrees as a mature age student at Flinders University in Adelaide and at University of Texas in Austin, Texas. A free thinker, optimist, and fun seeker his writings invite readers along an unforgettable journey.